CALIFORNIA SLAVIC STUDIES

CALIFORNIA SLAVIC STUDIES
Volume VIII

EDITORS

NICHOLAS V. RIASANOVSKY

GLEB STRUVE

THOMAS EEKMAN

UNIVERSITY OF CALIFORNIA PRESS
BERKELEY · LOS ANGELES · LONDON

CALIFORNIA SLAVIC STUDIES
Volume 8

University of California Press
Berkeley and Los Angeles, California
University of California Press, Ltd.
London, England

ISBN: 0-520-09519-7
LIBRARY OF CONGRESS CATALOG CARD NUMBER: 61-1041
© 1975 BY THE REGENTS OF THE UNIVERSITY OF CALIFORNIA

LONDON, BECCLES AND COLCHESTER

CONTENTS

Paris 1848: A Russian Ideological Spectrum 1
    EDWARD A. COLE

Russian Ministers and the Jewish Question, 1881–1917 . . . 15
    HANS ROGGER

The Apparent and the Real in Gogol's "Nevskij Prospekt" . . 77
    OLGA RAEVSKY HUGHES

The Narrator and the Hero in Chekhov's Prose 93
    THOMAS EEKMAN

Osip Mandelstam and Auguste Barbier: Some Notes on Mandelstam's
    Versions of *Iambes* 131
    GLEB STRUVE

PARIS 1848: A RUSSIAN IDEOLOGICAL SPECTRUM

BY

EDWARD A. COLE

1

THE PARISIAN REVOLUTION of 1848 touched off major social, democratic, and nationalist upheavals in all the principal Central and Eastern European states with the sole exception of the Russian Empire, a fact that points out Russian uniqueness, not only in the economic and political spheres, but also in the realm of intellectual activity. For the Revolution of 1848 was led by intellectuals of all social classes and philosophical schools who nearly achieved their greatest success in the Austrian Empire, a land possessed of an autocratic regime which in many ways surpassed the Russian state in its reactionary aspirations. Yet with the exception of the rather abstract activities of the Petrashevtsy, there was no revolutionary response on the part of the Russian intellectuals to the wave of revolution that began in Paris.

It is inconceivable, however, that the Parisian revolution could have had a negligible impact upon the educated gentry of the Russian Empire. France, and in particular the French capital, had become symbolic in the intellectual rivalry of the age. This symbolic value accrued from the Enlightenment, the Great Revolution, and the Napoleonic Wars; Westernizers looked to Paris for inspiration, Slavophiles selected it as the antithesis to Kiev and Moscow, and those concerned with naked power never forgot that France, centered upon Paris, had very nearly dominated all of Europe.

The barrier to evaluating the impact of 1848 upon the Russian intellectuals is, of course, the firm and inflexible policy of suppression and control which was instituted by Nicholas I following the first news of revolution. For more than seven years Russian intellectuals were subjected to extreme demands for conformity, even highly patriotic utterances being regarded with suspicion by the omnipresent police. Those techniques of prudence and discretion which were necessitated by this irresistible policy have also worked to the disadvantage of later historical investigations.

Historians and biographers, however, have done an amazing job of circumventing the barrier erected by Nicholas, and with regard to the long-term effects of 1848 their efforts have frequently been enlightening. Of particular interest is the interpretation of Isaiah Berlin, who contends that the lack of revolutionary inspiration, disillusionment with the West, and the political repression brought on by 1848 produced in Russia a dedicated, native radical movement which later received Marxism and overthrew the state.¹ The immediate effect of the Parisian revolution has not received such satisfying treatment, however. Soviet scholars, intent upon fixing Russia's position in the revolutionary scheme of things, have done important work, but have concentrated on class structure, liberation movements, and the cholera.² The intellectual reaction remains incompletely described.

Fortunately, it is possible to go beyond the border of the empire to sample Russian intellectual responses; there were many Russian travelers who were in Paris in 1848, or were drawn there by events. Some of these, in particular Andrey Karamzin, Paul Annenkov, and Alexander Herzen, wrote letters and accounts of their experiences and observations which have survived the ravages of time. From these sources a partial evaluation can be made, and a few tentative conclusions reached, bearing in mind that these individuals had in common only their gentry background, their interest in the West, and their Russian nationalism, variously interpreted.

2

The Parisian revolution erupted with startling suddenness when, on February 22, 1848, popular pressures forced Louis Philippe, the "bourgeois king," to dispense with Guizot and to appoint the conservative Thiers as his chief minister. A chance volley into a crowd of demonstrators then brought public emotions to the boiling point, and within a day the king had abdicated and fled, and a republic had been proclaimed. Opposition journalists patched together a provisional government including the poet-parliamentarian Lamartine, moderate socialists like Louis Blanc and Ledru-Rollin, and several radical followers of the socialist Blanqui. The usual freedoms were proclaimed and a half-hearted beginning was made toward the major question of social reform with the opening of "national workshops" for the unemployed. There was surprisingly little bloodshed, and except for one or two false notes, such as Lamartine's defense of the tricolor against the red socialist banner, the initial revolution was unexciting, yet inspiring.

From the standpoint of social familiarity with the French political establishment, Andrey Nikolaevich Karamzin was perhaps the most qualified observer of the trio selected for this study. The oldest son of the famous writer and historian, Andrey Karamzin was born in 1814, received an excellent education

---

[1] Sir Isaiah Berlin, "Russia and 1848," *Slavonic and East European Review* 26 (1948): 341–360.

[2] See in particular: M. Akhun, "1848 god v Rossii," *Istoričeskij Žurnal* 1938: 65–72; A. I. Molok, *Revoljucija 1848 goda i naša sovremennost'*, lectures (Moscow: Akademija Nauk, 1953); A. S. Nifontov, *Rossija v 1848 godu* (Moscow: Akademija, 1953); A. S. Potemkin and A. l. Molok, *Revoljucii 1848–1849* (Moscow: Akademija Nauk, 1952).

at home, and attended the German-language University of Dorpat. In 1840 he married the beautiful and inspiring Avrora Demidova, the widow of one of the wealthiest men in Russia, and herself a distant relative of Louis Bonaparte. Karamzin was wounded while on active service with the army in the Caucasus, and was placed in a St. Petersburg gendarme unit. On a leave of absence he traveled through Europe, arriving in Paris in 1847. There he was received by the king, for whom he had little regard, and with his wife and young stepson began a lively social life in the Parisian fashion.[3] His long letters from Paris were modeled somewhat on his father's famous *Letters of a Russian Traveler*, and were addressed to his mother, the patroness of St. Petersburg's most conservative *salon*.[4]

A man so well acquainted with the ruling establishment of France was not likely to be too surprised when revolution broke out. Karamzin, borrowing the motif from Alexis de Tocqueville's famous speech in the Chamber of Deputies, had already informed his mother of the growing tension: "In Paris they have begun to dance; I have found that this has been a bad sign ever since the dance on the volcano in 1830."[5]

When it appeared that the revolution might break out at the site of the opposition banquet in the twelfth district, Karamzin and several friends made ready to engage a room from which they might observe everything, yet remain neutral in case of bloodshed. He confessed to an interest worthy of a well-bred Russian:

> As regards curiosity, I am curious about the exact course of events; they interest me as though they were actually happening to me or to my fatherland ... Can we remain indifferent in view of a struggle in which are concentrated and exhausted all the intellectual forces, all the passions of the select people of this country, of our neighbors? And this only because they dispute about their own affairs and not ours?[6]

---

[3] See the introduction to Karamzin's letters in E. V. Petukhov, "Pis'ma A. N. Karamzina 1847–1848gg." *Istoričeskij sbornik* 3 (1934), 263–312. These letters, originally composed in French, are also available in separate publication: *Pis'ma A. N. Karamzina, 1847–1848. Materialy po istorii Francuzskoj revoljucii 1848 g. Po dokumentam Krymskogo centralnogo arkhivnogo upravlenija* (Akademija Nauk S.S.S.R., Leningrad-Moscow, 1935.) Also of interest are travel letters of 1836–1837 and 1844: "Pis'ma A. N. Karamzina k E. A. Karamzinoj," in *Starina i Novizna* 16 (1914):232–322 (with portrait); 18 (1914):15–26; and 20 (1916):57–170.

[4] Karamzina's *salon* was primarily literary, and in the thirties most of Russia's leading writers had gathered there to discuss their works. See the descriptions by A. I. Koshelev, V. A. Sollogub, and A. F. Tyutcheva in N. L. Brodskij, ed., *Literaturnye salony i kružki, pervaja polovina XIX veka*, (Moscow: Akademija Nauk, 1930), pp. 213–220.

[5] A. Karamzin to Ekaterina Andreevna Karamzina, 12 February 1848, *Istoričeskij sbornik* 3:275. De Tocqueville's volcanic metaphor was in common use after his speech in January 1848. See: P. Robertson, *Revolutions of 1848* (New York: Harper, 1960), pp. 13–14.

[6] A. Karamzin to E. Karamzina, 12 February 1848, p. 276.

When the "volcano" erupted, Karamzin took to the streets to do some excellent factual reporting. The craven behavior of the troops did not surprise him, as he had questioned their reliability from the first, and therefore it was merely slightly remarkable that "only twelve hours were necessary to topple a crown which . . . was strengthened and prepared for victory on the day of danger."[7]

Paul Annenkov's reaction to the February uprising was quite different. A Russian intellectual of moderate Westernizing leanings, whose comfortable flat on the Rue Caumartin was a meeting place for Russian visitors and radical French journalists, Annenkov was caught off guard, and given a fright from which he did not recover until he left Paris. Annenkov was the offspring of a Simbirsk gentry family, and his income came from landholdings in that area. His two brothers had followed careers more in keeping with their birth, Theodore serving as a municipal governor, and Ivan as a wing-adjutant in the army, soon to be promoted high into the ranks of the St. Petersburg gendarmes.[8] Paul knew almost everyone worth knowing in Europe, even exchanging observations with Karl Marx on occasion. But for all his excellent contacts, he had not sensed the increasing tension. When the crowd forced the abdication of the king, Annenkov wrote to his brothers of the "terrible consequences" of this act, of the invasion of the Tuileries, and the formation of a new government "hastily and amid horrendous noise." He was relieved to report that Lamartine had joined "out of a desire to save his country from final destruction."[9] Annenkov did not rest easy until he could report that order was reestablished, and that pilferers were being shot without mercy.[10]

Alexander Herzen, whose comments about 1848 were to become famous in the annals of Russian radicalism, was in Italy at the time of Louis Philippe's abdication. Herzen was then a relatively minor figure, at odds with his moderate Westernizer friends in Moscow, and still outside radical circles in Europe. The legitimized son of a wealthy and tyrannical aristocrat, Herzen had run the gamut of fashionable philosophic studies, and had already arrived

---

[7] A. Karamzin to E. Karamzina, 25 February 1848, p. 282. For the description of events, see: A. Karamzin and Avrora Karamzina to E. Karamzina, 22 February 1848, pp. 278–282.

[8] See the preface by N. Piksanov in Pavel Annenkov, *Literaturnye vospominanija* (Leningrad: Akademija Nauk, 1928), pp. v–xii.

[9] P. Annenkov to his brothers, 27 February 1848, in: "Gorestnaja profanacija," *Istoričeskij sbornik* 4 (1935):245.

[10] Annenkov to his brothers, p. 246. Annenkov's news must have been alarming but his comments appropriate to the servants of Nicholas. However, in the same letter, he asks them to give his regards to Belinsky. See also: "Fevral' i Mart v Pariže 1849," in *Vospominanija i kritičeskie očerki* (St. Petersburg: Stasjulevič, 1877), p. 252.

at a position of total opposition to autocracy, disillusionment with the West, a penchant for anarchy and direct action.[11]

When Herzen first received news of the revolution, he became terribly excited, and wrote of the "strong pulse of history" and the "grandeur of events."[12] But unlike other interested Russians, notably Bakunin and Turgenev, he did not rush immediately to Paris. Perhaps he was unimpressed by the Parisian revolution, as he indicated in a letter to Annenkov, or perhaps he was distracted by the events in Italy and the rapid spread of revolution eastward through Europe.[13] At any rate, after the lapse of a month and a half he left Rome for France, celebrating his departure with gloomy paragraphs on the odor of Europe's decaying past and the unfortunate strength of approaching reaction.[14]

3

To categorize Herzen, Annenkov, and Karamzin as conservative or liberal is difficult because all three were remarkably complex and sensitive. The task is further complicated by the failure of the Russians to understand the radicals of Paris, and by their fondness for political terms more applicable to the Great Revolution five decades earlier than to 1848. Nevertheless, an investigation of their conservative and liberal attitudes toward social and political change reveals interesting contrasts.

Of the three under examination, only Karamzin seemed to have any practical grasp of the details of French politics, a grasp that gave his opinions clarity and force. He regarded the revolution as the unfortunate consequence of the ruling establishment's insensibility, the expected product of royal and military cowardice. With obvious implications for his own Russian class, Karamzin blamed the "select people" for a failure to strengthen their position in the face of mounting danger:

To me that which made the danger still more appreciable was the complete indifference on the part of all who possessed power, the majority of whom I saw daily; this majority not only disclaimed the danger, but was convinced that the fears and misgivings of "clairvoyants" were unimaginable.... It is highly likely that Louis Philippe might have been saved, barring the events of the Wednesday evening, but after that famous shooting the monarchy was lost and a republic inevitably proclaimed; and not because the republicans

---

[11] The conventional analysis of Herzen's ideas has attributed them to the shock of 1848. See the account of W. C. Barghoorn, "The Russian Radicals and the West European Revolution of 1848," *Review of Politics* 2 (1949): 338–354. The continuity of Herzen's ideas has, however, emerged from the excellent study by Martin Malia, *Alexander Herzen and the Birth of Russian Socialism*, 1812–1855 (Cambridge: Harvard University Press, 1961), esp. pp. 311–333.

[12] Aleksandr Gercen, *Pis'ma iz Francii i Italii*, Letter 8, in *Sobranie sočinenij* (Moscow: Akademija Nauk, 1955), 5:123.

[13] A. Herzen to P. Annenkov, 5–6 March 1848, *Sobranie sočinenij*, 25:65ff.

[14] Gercen, *Pis'ma iz Francii i Italii*, p. 131.

were stronger, and even less because they were more organized or because they went to their goal in close order with courageous and decisive men at their head.... The army went over and the National Guard stood aside from higher affairs. Only women conducted themselves splendidly! The Queen tried to convince the King to appear before the people and to face death at his post. The Countess of Orleans fought to the end ... [15]

Denying the radicals and republicans a positive role in the revolution, Karamzin initially discounted any possibility of social or political change in favor of equality, of "communism, the criminal and thoughtless dream of an insignificant minority." Although the disintegration of social values was a distinct danger, Karamzin cheerfully noted that "it is possible to live in spite of this terrible word 'republic.'"[16]

The revolution produced in Annenkov a quandary best described as "intellectual schizophrenia." From his *Literary Reminiscences* one gains the impression that he was intimately acquainted with all the radical journalists of France, and, moreover, sympathized with their views.[17] But from the letters written from Paris an entirely different picture emerges, a picture of a frightened Annenkov whose sympathies lay with the middle classes, the defenders of order and property. Annenkov was no hypocrite, and there is no reason to suspect that he was dishonest in his *Reminiscences*; as a man familiar with the intellectual currents of Europe, he could not help but admire the ideas and the motives of the European social critics. But as a Russian gentleman and a moderate Westernizer, he admired the bourgeoisie and valued the progress this class had made in Europe.

Annenkov's conclusions were that the people had simply punched such a hole in the body politic that the "so-called republicans" were able to get in. The republicans then held on to power by anticipating the extreme demands of the mob: free speech, free press, freedom of assembly, the right to bear arms, universal suffrage, and so forth. This, to the gentleman scholar from Simbirsk, was very ominous. If affairs continued in such a manner, the worker would be made part owner of his product and the farmer would seize his leaseholds. Industrialists and landlords could not be expected to accept such developments without a fight, and Annenkov feared a violent struggle when the National Assembly met in May.[18]

In March Annenkov confessed that he was amazed at "the unprecedented spectacle of a government without defense, without troops, without any means of resistance to an armed populace." He began to make plans to leave

---

[15] A. Karamzin to E. Karamzina, 28 February 1848, pp. 286–287.
[16] A. Karamzin to E. Karamzina, 1 March 1848, p. 288.
[17] See in particular the sections for 1848 in P. V. Annenkov, *Literaturnye vospominanija* ("Zamečatel'noe desjatiletie"), V. P. Dorofeev, ed. (Moscow: Akademija Nauk, 1960), and in P. V. Annenkov, *Annenkov i ego druz'ja* (St. Petersburg: Suvorin, 1892).
[18] Annenkov to his brothers, 9 March 1848, p. 248.

Paris for a more healthy clime, but was prevented from doing so by the spread of revolution through Europe. "In Paris," he told his brothers, "we live as if within a fiery circle, surrounded on all sides by riots."[19]

Life became more tolerable for Annenkov in April, when it became obvious that "the better part of the people" had no intention of allowing sudden change to take place. He was able to assure his brothers that Paris was not in the advanced stages of anarchic collapse, a conclusion they had evidently drawn from his earlier letters or from reports current in St. Petersburg. At the merest hint of a radical plot, *le rappel* was beaten and guards patrolled the city. But according to Annenkov, even the guards represented "the great strength and the great absurdity" of the revolution, since all the officers were elected.[20] As far as the National Assembly was concerned, the situation had improved vastly: "it is now known that the majority will consist of sensible and prudent people. Thus you see—the devil, as in the proverb, is not as terrible as he is painted. . . ."[21]

Herzen, in contrast to Karamzin and Annenkov, committed himself wholeheartedly to the revolution. Once in Paris his earlier pessimism seemed to vanish, and he began a description of "the new world" for his friends in Russia. He took great delight in the activities of the revolutionary workers and their police under the leadership of Caussidière. There was something "harsh and exciting in the air," journals had appeared everywhere, and the people expected great changes.[22]

4

The security and stability of the Russian Empire in the midst of general revolutionary turmoil produced a contrast that escaped none of the Russians then in Paris. Andrey Karamzin, as might be expected, pictured the relationship in the most dramatic fashion possible. From the very first he was anxious about the opinions of St. Petersburg society, especially those of the emperor; his interest became even more intense when he began to suspect that the censorship was reading his letters.[23] And as revolution marched eastward, approaching the imperial borders, Karamzin became extremely excited, as it seemed a great future was opening up for Russia:

---

[19] *Ibid.* Annenkov's attitude shows up in his selection of anecdotes for his brothers' amusement. An industrialist, Jean Leroy, has become "Jean Lepeuple." Workers have demanded the same pay for half the work, so that bootmakers now turn out only one boot per pair. *Ibid.*, p. 249.
[20] Annenkov to his brothers, the end of April 1848, p. 252.
[21] *Ibid.*
[22] Gercen, "Pis'ma iz Francii i Italii," Letter 9, pp. 134–136.
[23] A. Karamzin to E. Karamzina, 6 March 1848, p. 290.

All these shocks and disorders in Europe only widen and pave the road pointed out by Providence, along which our dear fatherland is to travel. Austria and Prussia, going down the revolutionary path, shatter as they rattle the fatal chain which binds them to us politically. Now Russia, free from similar movements, will begin to possess its natural position of a patient observer in Europe.... Russia will concentrate her attention, her sympathies and her forces in order to create around herself that Slavic world in which, in her primitive state, she found the answers to the questions which Europe has vainly sought for many centuries in blood and destruction! The recent events in Austria give a great political, and, simultaneously, an urgent importance to Slavic ideas.... Austria will not live long, and the Slavic elements which constitute her majority will necessarily become isolated from the German element; this formation of the Slavic element into a political unit will either be *for* us or *against* us—a choice must be made between one or the other. May God enlighten those who lead us![24]

Although Karamzin had concluded that the forces of change were not likely to achieve substantial success in France, he imagined that the forces that were operating in the Hapsburg lands were more powerful, and would triumph. Therefore he did not think that Russia could intervene to save the old order in Europe.[25] Nevertheless, the situation was dangerous. What if Polish regiments under Polish officers appeared along Russia's western frontier? What if Berlin were to become hostile toward St. Petersburg? What would be the effect of a free press in Lwów and Poznán? Karamzin could imagine a united Europe sweeping into Russia as in the days of his father:

I believe that we will not lose courage, we will be one heart, one soul, and a million hands! ... At the Europeans' arrival we will give them a cry: "There is room for you among familiar coffins in the fields of Russia!" If I were single, I would depart with this letter—all Russians should be at their posts ... now the affair approaches us, and in front of foreigners I feel like a worthy successor to the Russians of 1612 and 1812.[26]

In spite of an extension of his leave of absence for which he had exerted much energy, Karamzin passionately desired to return to his post. Most certainly he was not fleeing Paris like those "cowards" he so consistently scorned; when a letter arrived telling him of Tyutchev's agitation over the revolution in Paris, Karamzin wrote that he and Avrora had nearly died laughing at "Tyutchev's foolish fears." "I recognize in him one of the alarmists and cowards whose verbiage I listen to here in all the houses of legitimists..."[27] Of Grech's "Correspondence from Paris" in the *Severnaja Pčela*, Karamzin remarked: "it made all of us blush with its tone of the public-house and the antechamber."[28]

Urged on by an inspiring copy of a patriotic manifesto drawn up by his club

---

[24] A. Karamzin to E. Karamzina, 21 March 1848, pp. 298–299.
[25] *Ibid.*
[26] A. Karamzin to E. Karamzina, 23 March 1848, pp. 300–301. The quotation is from Pushkin's 1831 poem "K klevetnikam Rossii."
[27] A. Karamzin to his brother Alexander and his sister Sophia, 27 March 1848, p. 302.
[28] A. Karamzin to E. Karamzina, 5 April 1848, pp. 306–307.

in St. Petersburg, and cheered by a letter from the poet Vasily Zhukovsky, Karamzin took leave of Paris. He was headed for his post, certain that Russia would soon play a great role as the protector of the Slav against the German. His final statements revealed that he was psychologically prepared for his next tour of duty under Nicholas:

> In the moment of danger there can be in Russia only one feeling, one way of looking at things.... The more I observe events the more I find that Russia undoubtedly will triumph, remaining patient in her might, leaving Germany to stew as much as she likes in her own revolutionary juice.... [29]

Paul Annenkov was not given to such patriotic outbursts. As a moderate Westernizer whose views, if they resembled any others, resembled those of Korsh or Granovsky, Annenkov was inclined to think that "the West" had a role to play in Russia, not vice versa. The shock of revolution made him pause, but did not push him to any reversal of his previous position. Nevertheless, his eye was always searching for the cracks in the Western façade and his ear was tuned for the false note.[30] It is significant that he told his brothers that his Russian patriotism, which was "inferior to none," and his "isolated life as the cool observer of everything," served to keep him from becoming involved in the life of revolutionary Paris.[31]

Herzen had already formulated his concept of Russia's role in Europe, and it took only the stimulation of events on May 15, 1848, to bring forth a clear expression of his beliefs. On that day, the workers and radicals, sensing their impending neglect at the hands of the royalist- and moderate-dominated assembly, stormed the public buildings of Paris. Their defeat marked the end of the revolution. Herzen was naturally extremely upset at this outcome, and from his pen came a violent diatribe against the West. Europe was in decay, and the liberals and progressives were part of the process of decomposition. The principal enemy everywhere was authority, whether it be represented by a tsar or a greengrocer sitting in a constituent assembly. Once authority could be laid low, there would be "the freedom of mankind, of the commune, of departure from submission to a *strong* government."[32] Herzen's later essays, in particular his famous letter to Jules Michelet, make it clear that it was an idealized Russian freedom that he had in mind for the world.[33]

---

[29] *Ibid.*, p. 307. Andrey Karamzin remained true to his convictions; when the Crimean War broke out, he rushed away from the comfortable life of the Demidov villa to lead troops in battle. In May 1854 he died in a minor skirmish with a Turkish unit.

[30] See, for example, his observations on the ironic aspects of the February Revolution: Annenkov, "Fevral' i Mart," (n. 10, above), pp. 297–306.

[31] Annenkov to his brothers, the end of April 1848, p. 252.

[32] Gercen, *Pis'ma iz Francii i Italii*, Letter 9, p. 138.

[33] Alexander Herzen, "The Russian People and Socialism," in *Selected Philosophical Works of Alexander Herzen* (Moscow: Foreign Languages Publishing House, 1946).

5

The events in May which spurred Herzen to such bitterness marked the beginning of a period of reaction during which the socialists were arrested or set aside while the middle classes led the rest of France away from social reform. This reaction was climaxed in June 1848 when the "national workshops" were closed. With this, the working classes threw up the barricades again and began a bitter struggle. Finally, General Cavaignac, with artillery and regular troops, all but destroyed the working quarters of the city, effectively ending the revolt and paving the way for the ascendancy of Louis Bonaparte. This grisly slaughter, dignified by the name "June Days," was a disillusioning experience for the Russians in France. Annenkov and Herzen accompanied each other on a rash adventure into the thick of the fighting, barely escaping execution at the hands of the guards. Their factual accounts of the Reaction are nearly identical, which makes their differing viewpoints all the more striking.

Annenkov, "the cool observer of everything," informed his brothers that the "monstrous slaughter" which he had been compelled to witness had no equal in history for ferocity and disgusting barbarism. But despite his ruthlessness, Cavaignac was a savior:

The measures adopted by him [Cavaignac] were so decisive and energetic that the rioters, accustomed as they were to the feeble methods of the previous government, were struck dumb with amazement.
... A terrible—and one must truthfully say—a beneficial Terror spread over the city. The "February slaughter," compared to that which has now taken place, was a child's prank. Blood flowed in rivers among examples of unheard-of barbarities and atrocities committed by National Guards and rioters upon their prisoners.[34]

Paris was almost unrecognizable after the appalling carnage. Houses had been shelled apart, sand soaked up blood, and cavalry was bivouacked along the famous streets. All this, according to Annenkov, had been "an unbelievably useful lesson to the rioters, who thought that nobody could control them."[35]

Life in Paris had become loathsome to Annenkov, who made plans to return to Russia as soon as possible. "You see," he wrote to his brothers, "I can not and do not desire to remain here any longer, and only a malicious fate holds me in this unhappy land, steeped in blood and violence."[36]

---

[34] Annenkov to his brothers, 4 July 1848, p. 255.
[35] *Ibid.*, p. 256.
[36] *Ibid.* This sorrowful tone continued in his last letter before leaving Paris, in which he described the martyrdom of the "bourgeois saints," General Bréa, and the Archbishop of Paris. It must be recognized that for Annenkov to leave Europe was a decisive step, for he was in many ways more at home in the West than in his native land. Annenkov to his brothers, 14 July 1848, p. 257.

Herzen, like Annenkov, remembered that the worst aspect of the June Days was having to listen while outside in the streets artillery pounded the barricades, and prisoners were led off to be shot against a wall.[37] The experience heightened his bitterness, and dispelled his last illusions of Paris:

> Paris! How long this name has been a lodestar to people! Who did not love and worship it? But its time has passed. Let it leave the stage.... Paris shot people without trial.... What will be the outcome of this bloodshed?—who knows? But whatever it is, it is enough that in this fury of madness, of revenge, of conflict and retribution, the world which stands in the way of the new man, preventing him from living and establishing the future, this world will fall. And this is splendid! So—long live chaos and destruction!
> *Vive la mort!*
> And let the future come![38]

Herzen began a long commentary on the June Days which went on, in articles and letters, for over three years. In August 1848 he discovered the same "broad nature" in the defeated French proletariat that he loved in the oppressed Russians.[39] The Parisian situation was so odious that he was ready to use Nicholas as an instrument of destruction: "*The man without land, without capital,*—he will save France, or ... may God grant that the Russians take Paris—it is time to finish this stupid Europe, it is time to clear a space in it for the new world."[40]

With Annenkov's departure at the end of the summer, Herzen was left as the sole influential Russian voice from Paris. He was well aware of Annenkov's completely different conclusions, and several times he warned Botkin and Granovsky about "our friend Paul."[41] However, Herzen inevitably had the last word, as he remained for the dismal last act of the Second Republic. He felt that the "abusive" Russian autocracy was doomed to perish before the old Europe expired. The new Russia would rise to build socialism for the world.[42]

6

The emotional impact of the Revolution of 1848 was far greater than its impression on political and social systems. It was as though all the dreams of civilized man had achieved concrete form, only to be smashed by an interior

---

[37] Herzen to Astrakova, 30 June 1848, *Sobranie sočinenij*, 23:79, and A. Gercen, "Posle grozy," *S togo berega*, in *Sobranie sočinenij*, 6:41–43.
[38] Gercen, *ibid.*, p. 48.
[39] Herzen to his Moscow friends 2–8 August 1848, pp. 79–80.
[40] *Ibid.*, p. 81.
[41] *Ibid.*
[42] Herzen to his Moscow friends, 6 September 1848, p. 95; and Herzen to his Moscow friends, 5 November 1848, pp. 110–112.

barbarism of unexpected ferocity, and the resulting pattern of enthusiasm, exhaustion, and depression was the basis for the intellectual response. The degrees of enthusiasm and depression were not only determined by the philosophic and intellectual systems which individuals had accepted prior to the cataclysmic events on the streets of Paris, but also rested on the varying views of human nature held by the observers. In the case of Herzen, Karamzin, and Annenkov, we are presented with a particularly neat package, if a spectrum is constructed with the enthusiastic extremes tending toward brotherhood and anarchy on the optimistic side, elitism and authoritarianism on the pessimistic side. In this conceptualization Herzen belongs on the optimistic extremity, Annenkov in the conservative range of the vacillating middle, and Karamzin on the pessimistic extreme. Herzen and Karamzin were both raised to high levels of enthusiasm and inspiration; Herzen was thrown rather suddenly into melancholy depression, from which he rescued himself with his theoretical belief in the mission of Russian radicalism. It is unfortunate that we do not have similar evidence for Karamzin's reaction when the Slavic world of his dreams failed to materialize. Annenkov was never aroused to enthusiasm, and from beginning to end was dismayed by the breakdown of Western civilization.

The pattern is obvious in the attitudes that these three adopted toward the revolution. It must be noted, however, that these attitudes were in part conditioned by the fact that, by 1848, revolution had become a political phenomenon in Europe which, if not common, was not new and startling. All three gentlemen had an idea of what to expect: Herzen welcomed revolution as an attack on authority, Annenkov expected another Terror and had visions of a Great Terror sweeping Europe, and Karamzin zealously anticipated a fundamental political reorganization of the Continent. The enthusiasts, Herzen and Karamzin, had clear ideas of the kind of new world which they hoped would emerge from the turmoil, and Karamzin envisioned a method of controlling the process of change, using it to the advantage of Russia and "the Slavs." Annenkov, who for years had deplored the class divisions within Europe, did not expect great results, and prudently attached his sympathies to the champions of order and stability, the only moral choice he could have made. As for the immediate revolutionary process, Herzen, believing in the "broad nature" of the people, advocated the end "of submission to a *strong* government" as passionately as Karamzin censored the "select people" for losing their grip on the mob. Annenkov only wished that "the rioters" would learn to control themselves, leaving the practical goal of reestablishing stability to responsible people.

Although the positions of this diverse trio with respect to the Revolution of 1848 are interesting in themselves, it is only their relevance to the Russian situation which is of importance. Here the emotional force of the revolution produced an identical reaction: disillusionment with the West. In this they were not different from other educated Europeans, many of whom lived out the rest of their years in disillusionment with their own civilization, or chose to migrate to America. The Russians, however, possessed a distinct advantage over their Western counterparts in that they had come to view Russia as an alternative to the West, a fresh and vital alternative to the rest of Europe. Herzen concluded that the task of creating socialism had been "willed to the Slavs," Karamzin pictured Russia as the proud superior of Europe, destined to leadership because of its Slavic heritage. Annenkov sadly fled "the unhappy land" of France and took refuge in the Russia of Nicholas I. Throughout the next difficult seven years, each remained true to his convictions, Herzen becoming an isolated voice of Russian radicalism, Karamzin dying in the Crimean war in defense of his fatherland, and Annenkov persisting in moderate constructive criticism.

Only Soviet scholars have been able to find a serious revolutionary movement in Russia in 1848, and they have had to employ the broadest definition of the term "revolutionary." While the examples of Herzen, Karamzin, and Annenkov cannot tell the whole story, they left the most complete accounts of a direct encounter with the Parisian revolution, and each of these accounts reached a sizable portion of educated society. Under the influence of strong emotional stimulation, the only significant reaction on the part of these three was an intensified rejection of the West. If there was anything more, it was a heightened desire to make Russia more creative and dynamic than the official regime allowed it to become.

RUSSIAN MINISTERS AND THE JEWISH QUESTION
1881-1917*

BY

HANS ROGGER

THE ASSASSINATION of Alexander II, the pogroms following it, and the Provisional Rules of May 3, 1882, marked a sharp turn for the worse in Imperial Russia's treatment of the Jews. The government's harshly discriminatory and restrictive measures—when not ascribed simply to anti-Semitism, to Russification, or the determination to expel the Jews—have most often been viewed as deliberately designed to deflect onto the Jews the mass grievances and political protests threatening the regime.[1] These assumptions are of such long standing, they have become so central to all interpretations of Jewish policy in prerevolutionary Russia, that they bear reexamination not only because they have been held so long and repeated so often, but more importantly, because they are derived from an incomplete study of the evidence.

There is a vast literature which has described and, less often, sought to analyze the Jewish policy of tsarist Russia. Yet there has been no systematic examination or even survey of the stated motives of Russian policy makers, few attempts to relate their explicit reasons to their concrete measures, no sustained effort to determine their conceptions and images of the Jewish problem and how they viewed it and assessed their own, that is, the state's problem in reference to it.

The present investigation, with its focus on the ministerial bureaucracy, cannot hope to impose final order, coherence, and meaning on a refractory reality or to replace existing interpretations. Its purpose, rather, is to test and to refine these by taking the indispensable first step of asking what the men who formulated and enacted the regime's Jewish policy actually said and did about the question that occupied so large a place in their minds and deliberations. Our study may help us to see why anti-Jewish measures were carried to

---

* I wish to express my gratitude to the following for their support of work of which the present study is a partial result: Center for Slavic and East European Studies (Berkeley), Committee on International and Comparative Studies (UCLA), and the American Philosophical Society.

[1] I have attempted a brief survey of the most widely accepted theories on the nature of Imperial Russia's treatment of the Jews in "The Jewish Policy of Late Tsarism: A Reappraisal," *The Wiener Library Bulletin* [Institute of Contemporary History, London], 25, nos. 1 and 2 (1971): 52–51. For examples of the view that the tsars and their officials were engaged in a conscious and consistent effort to clear Russia of Jews, see n. 121 below. The standard treatment of the period is S. M. Dubnov, *Evrei v Rossii i zapadnoj Evrope v èpokhu antisemitskoj reakcii* (Moscow-Petrograd, 1923), books 1 and 2.

[15]

such extraordinary lengths by traditional, cautious bureaucrats not normally given to extreme visions or dogmas, men who did not usually pay heed to public opinion or the cry of the streets and who could occasionally see the harm they were causing.

For a full answer to this question or a collective biography of our subjects we would have to know more than we do of their life histories. An inquiry into context and circumstances, into the universe of discourse in which policy was shaped, may, however, enable us to discern patterns as well as sources of conduct and guiding assumptions. Such an inquiry can account for changes of course and differences of view in the top levels of government, enhance understanding of its operations, and begin the work of uncovering the relationship among policy, prejudice, and public pressures.

1

In discussing the politics of an autocracy, it is necessary to begin with the autocrat.[2] Alexander III and Nicholas II were confirmed anti-Semites who freely vented their dislike of Jews before members of their official and private families. Their strong feelings could not, therefore, be a secret or fail to set the tone for the behavior of their subordinates. Both rulers intervened at decisive points to veto proposals for the expansion of Jewish rights submitted by their advisers; both viewed with sympathy the suggestions made to them for limiting Jewish rights; neither, however, initiated anti-Jewish legislation or prescribed its specific direction and content.

On only one other point is it possible to be quite certain. Alexander and his son looked upon pogroms as understandable outbursts of popular wrath against the Jews—in the case of Nicholas because of Jewish prominence in the ranks of the opposition, in that of his father because the Jews were exploiters against whom popular resentment had easily been stirred into violence. Such dangerous

---

[2] On Alexander III: G. B. Sliozberg, *Dela minuvšikh dnej* (Paris, 1933), 1:115-118; A. Poljakov, "Car'-mirotvorec; iz rezoljucij Aleksandra III," *Golos Minuvšego*, no. 1-3 (1918):219-299; P. A. Zajončkovskij, "Aleksandr III i ego bližajšee okruženie," *Voprosy Istorii*, no. 8 (1966):132; A. A. Polovcev, *Dnevnik* (Moscow, 1966), 2:276, 390, 429; S. Dubnov, "*Furor judophobicus* v poslednie gody carstvovanija Aleksandra III," *Evrejskaja Starina*, 10 (1918):28; A. S. Suvorin, *Das Geheimtagebuch*, trans. and ed., O. Buck and K. Kersten (Berlin, 1925), pp. 117-118; *Istoričeskij obzor dejatel'nosti Komiteta ministrov, 1881-1894* (St. Petersburg, 1902), 4:183, 184, 436. On Nicholas II: Ernst Seraphim, *Russische Portraets* (Zuerich-Wien, 1943), pp. 97-98, 121, 257; Dubnov, *Novejšaja istorija evrejskogo naroda*, 3rd ed. (Berlin, 1923), 3:345; Sliozberg, *Dela*, 3:93; Alexandre Spiridovich, *Les dernières années de la cour de Tsarskoïe-Selo*, trans. M. Jeanson (Paris, 1928), 2:447, 472-476; Alexander Gerassimoff [Gerasimov], *Der Kampf gegen die erste russische Revolution*, trans. E. Thalmann (Frauenfeld und Leipzig, 1934), p. 146; A. N. Kuropatkin, "*Dnevnik*," *Krasnyj Arkhiv*, 2 (1922):43; Salo Baron, *The Russian Jew under Tsars and Soviets* (New York, 1964), pp. 74-75; *The Secret Letters of Tsar Nicholas* (Edinburgh, 1938), pp. 191-192.

challenges to public order and authority had to be and were stopped, if neither permanently nor always quickly. The pogroms of 1881 and 1882, moreover, convinced Alexander that some solution to the Jewish question must be found.

Beyond that, the available materials cannot account for the origin, character, and persistence in the two Romanovs of a sentiment which, if we exclude its legislative reflection, is recorded in only a few brief expressions of theirs. They did not take part in the major governmental debates of the Jewish question and gave no instructions how it was to be dealt with. By their marginal notations—no more, as a rule, than a "Yes" or an "Attend to this!"—they began the process by which subordinates' reports of Jewish transgressions were transformed into official acts; but to discover the justifications, arguments, and rationales offered for actions taken in their names, we have to turn elsewhere.

Alexander accepted the judgment of his first Minister of the Interior that the simple Christian people of Russia, meaning primarily the peasants, needed protection from the economical domination of the Jews. For Count N. P. Ignatyev, more than for any minister of the old regime, anti-Semitism was a key ingredient of a comprehensive world view and program. His program embraced three other elements: a populist form of Slavophilism (muzhikophilism, his detractors called it); an aggressive Panslavism, which Ignatyev had tried to further as head of the Foreign Ministry's Asiatic Department and Ambassador at Constantinople, only to see his dreams of glory blocked by Bismarck and Disraeli at the Congress of Berlin; and the certainty that the healthy part of the nation, organized in her traditional estates, could buttress the throne if assembled, consulted, and aided by it.

The supposed admiration of the healthy elements of the nation for Ignatyev, his "possession of Russian instincts and a Russian soul," caused Konstantin Pobedonostsev, Director of the Holy Synod and former tutor to the tsar, to recommend him for the most important office of state. It was a surprising recommendation from a man who distrusted Ignatyev and all enthusiasms and, as the candidate lacked extensive administrative or military experience, an unusual "ideological" appointment. It testified to the uncertainty and fear that still pervaded the heights of power in the wake of the assassination of Alexander II.[3]

---

[3] P. A. Zajončkovskij, *Krizis samoderžavija na rubeže 1870–1880 godov* (Moscow, 1964), ch. 5; H. Rogger, "Reflections on Russian Conservatism," *Jahrbuecher fuer Geschichte Osteuropas*, N. F., 14, no. 2 (June 1966):206–207; Stephen Lukashevich, *Ivan Aksakov* (Cambridge, Mass., 1965), pp. 153–157; Hans Heilbronner, "The Administrations of Loris-Melikov and Ignatiev," unpubl. doctoral dissertation, University of Michigan (1954); R. F. Byrnes, *Pobedonostsev* (Bloomington: Indiana University Press, 1968), pp. 118–119, 151, 162–163.

For Ignatyev that event strengthened a long-held view of Russia's predicament, and he communicated it to the new sovereign within days of his accession. In a memorandum of March 12, 1881, he wrote:

> In Petersburg there exists a powerful group of Poles and Yids [*pol'sko-zhidovskaja gruppa*] which holds in its hands direct control of banks, the stock exchange, the bar, a great part of the press, and other areas of public life. Through many legal and illegal ways it exerts an enormous influence over the bureaucracy and the general course of affairs. Parts of this group are implicated in the growing plunder of the exchequer and in seditious activity... Preaching the blind imitation of Europe, while cleverly pretending neutrality, these people gladly point to extreme instances of peculation and rebellion to recommend their remedy: the granting of the most extensive rights to Poles and Jews, and representative institutions after the Western model. Every honest voice heard in the Russian land is... silenced by the shouts of Poles and Jews who insist that one must listen only to the "intelligent" class and that Russian demands must be rejected as backward and unenlightened.[4]

When the so-called Loris-Melikov Constitution, a very modest proposal for advisory bodies (some of them to contain elected public representatives), was rejected by the tsar in late April and its author resigned, Ignatyev replaced him on May 5. The first wave of pogroms was already receding and on May 6 Ignatyev made public a circular calling on all governors to do everything in their power to prevent and stop the anti-Jewish excesses. Rioters taking the law into their own hands were merely carrying out the schemes of the revolutionaries. An instruction of May 23 stressed again that the repetition of anti-Jewish disorders could not be tolerated and must be averted by timely and appropriate measures of the local authorities.[5]

Even before he became convinced that the disturbances were not connected with the revolutionary movement, Ignatyev was able to identify their chief source without difficulty: the Jews—their tribal separatism, their religious fanaticism, and above all, the economic harm they were doing. It was against the latter, he told Alexander, that the rioters were protesting, against the policy of the past twenty years in which the expansion of Jewish rights had led to the concentration in their hands of trades and crafts in the affected regions and to their acquisition, through rent or purchase, of much landed property. Their activities did not benefit the state and were particularly damaging to the poorest classes of the population. Having put down the violence of the latter, the government must no less energetically remove its cause: the abnormal relationship between the native population and the Jews. To that end, Ignatyev in August 1881 called into being commissions of inquiry

---

[4] Zajončkovskij, *Krizis*, p. 338; cf. p. 380.
[5] *Ibid.*, pp. 385, 389; Heilbronner, "The Administrations of Loris-Melikov and Ignatiev," p. 478; Michael Davitt, *Within the Pale* (Philadelphia, 1903), p. 185; Rogger, *Wiener Library Bulletin*, p. 51, n. 11.

in each of the provinces of the Pale of Jewish Settlement. Chaired by the provincial governors, the commissions were to determine what aspects of Jewish economic activity were most injurious, what practical difficulties stood in the way of enforcing legislation (on Jewish land purchase and leasing, the sale of liquor, and money lending), and what legislative changes were required to prevent circumventions of the law.[6]

Even before answers could be received to the questions he had posed, Ignatyev received imperial assent in October to the setting up of still another in a long line of "Jewish committees." Its stated aim revealed his larger conceptions and purposes: "to discuss the Jewish question in its entirety," that is, to lay the groundwork for its overall solution. The fourteen points which the chairman, Assistant Minister of the Interior Gotovtsev, placed before the committee for its guidance, add up to the most far-reaching program of its kind ever to originate in official circles and to reach the state of serious discussion.

To begin with, and "until the final settlement of the Jewish question," all removals from the Pale of Settlement to the interior provinces were to be stopped; Jews would be expelled from rural districts at the request of village communes; Jewish mechanics and artisans residing outside the Pale but no longer plying their trades had to return to it. Jews were not allowed to sell liquor in the countryside, wholesale or retail, and only the latter trade was to be allowed in the towns. They should sell only the products of their own labor to the peasants; local authorities everywhere would be encouraged to see to it that food products bought by Jews locally were not resold locally at marked-up prices. Rural and urban communities should have the right to expel Jewish moneylenders by majority vote; suits by Jews against peasants for nonpayment of debt could be suspended or stopped under certain conditions. Jews were to be prohibited from doing business on Sundays and Christian holidays and from representing non-Jews before justices of the peace and peasant courts—unless they were licensed attorneys. Their membership in organs of elected self-government (town dumas and zemstvos) as well as their presence in primary and secondary schools was to be limited to certain percentages. Purchasing or leasing land was to be entirely prohibited and the

---

[6] The fullest account of Ignatyev's views and plans on the Jewish question is by Julij Gessen, "Graf N. P. Ignat'ev i 'Vremennye pravila' o evrejakh 3 maja 1882 goda," *Pravo*, nos. 30 and 31 (1908):1631–1637 and 1678–1687. On what follows, see also his *Zakon i žizn'* (St. Petersburg, 1911), pp. 153–161, and his *Istorija evrejskogo naroda v Rossii* (Leningrad, 1925–1927), 2:215–227; Zajončkovskij, *Krizis*, pp. 413–419; V. M. Khižnjakov, *Vospominanija zemskogo dejatelja* (Petrograd, 1916), pp. 109–114; Julius Eckhardt, *Russische Wandlungen* (Leipzig, 1882), pp. 389–390; *Evrejskaja Énciklopedija* (St. Petersburg, n.d.), 1:130; 5:815–822; 9:690–691; E. A. Peretc, *Dnevnik, 1880–1883* (Moscow-Leningrad, 1927), pp. 130–133.

Society for the Spread of Education Among Jews, "a branch of the *Alliance Israélite Universelle*," was to be closed down.

The committee regarded its proposals as necessary to prevent future disorders and to restore the situation that had prevailed before the liberalizing measures of the previous reign had disturbed the natural relationship between the native population and the Jews. By introducing principles shown by experience to be in conflict with the national spirit and with older laws that had regarded the Jews as *inorodcy*, the misguided policy of giving them the same rights as full-fledged citizens had infinitely complicated the Jewish problem. For the sake of the people's welfare and in order to make the Jews into useful subjects, it was time to turn back from the wrong course entered upon in 1856. Some of the suggested measures, bearing on Jewish residence and activities among the peasantry, required speedy enactment, so that, as one member of the committee put it, the rural population would know that the government cared about them and was protecting them from Jewish exploitation.

At the beginning of March 1882, Ignatyev transmitted to the Committee of Ministers six of the fourteen points which he wished urgently to have adopted as temporary administrative regulations, even before the remainder could be reviewed and existing laws revised through normal legislative procedures in the Council of State. The first two of these points abrogated the right of residence and the building or purchase of homes outside of cities and towns in the Pale of Settlement. Points three and four prohibited the ownership, administration, or exploitation of lands in any form in rural districts of the Pale, as well as the sale of liquor in its villages. The last two points restricted Jewish craftsmen and mechanics to the towns of the interior provinces, and forbade Jewish commerce on Sundays and Christian holy days, "in order not to offend the religious feelings of the Russians." This curious mixture of prejudice, paternalism, and primitive anticapitalism did not address itself to the most pressing and basic problems of the Russian countryside or to the security interests of the state, for most pogroms had occurred in cities and small towns. Ignatyev's colleagues did not fail to point out and to oppose what some of them considered his reckless populism.

Every member of the Committee of Ministers took exception to the Ignatyev proposals. Some objected on formal grounds: such far-reaching decisions should not be taken hastily by a purely administrative body. One minister advanced humanitarian considerations on behalf of tens or hundreds of thousands of human beings—"even if they were Jews"—who would suddenly be expelled from their homes. Others warned of disturbances to which such a vast disruption of an entire social and economic fabric could lead, disturbances as severe as those that were to be prevented. The sharpest and most sustained critique of Ignatyev's proposals came from the Minister of Finance, N. Kh. Bunge, who was seconded by the chairman of the Committee of Ministers, M. Kh. Reutern, a former Minister of Finance, and by D. M. Solsky, the State Comptroller. Bunge took issue with the view that the government's past conduct had been the result of weakness or lack of principle. It had been dictated by the national interest and by the significant role the Jews played in trade and industry.

These men were obviously troubled by the threat pogroms and *ad hoc* measures posed to economic stability and property, to hopes for industrial development and foreign investment. Bunge mentioned the Rothschilds' unwillingness to continue buying Russian bonds, and the decline this had caused in their value and in that of the Russian ruble. If, he warned, the extreme measures proposed by Ignatyev were approved, the Jews would have no choice but to emigrate, with unthinkable damage to the country's economic life. Adverting to the pogroms, Solsky exclaimed:

Everyone must be defended from illegal attacks. Today they are harassing and robbing the Jews. Tomorrow it will be the so-called kulaks who, morally speaking, are also Jews, except that they are of the Orthodox religion. Then it may be the turn of merchants and landowners. In a word, if the authorities stand by passively, we can expect the development of the most terrible socialism.[7]

Ignatyev's six points, already scaled down from the fourteen his assistant Gotovtsev had developed, were not adopted. Yet he did not come away empty handed. His ministerial colleagues agreed, "in the interests of the local population," to forbid the future settlement of Jews in the rural districts of the Pale as well as their purchase or rental of land there. The Committee of Ministers also imposed minor restrictions on Jewish taverns and trade. All these measures were to be strictly provisional, to remain in force only until existing laws and regulations could be examined by a new committee and the State Council. The Emperor did not, in this instance, override the advice of his ministers. He approved these Provisional Rules (which became known as the May Laws) and also appointed a High Commission for the Study of Existing Laws on the Jews. The ministers' final recommendation to the tsar, that his government make entirely clear to its provincial agents that they would have to answer for any breaches of law and order, was also carried out—by Ignatyev's successor, Count Dmitry Tolstoy, a no-nonsense kind of administrator who said that his entire program could be summed up in one word: order. Although he had no liking for Jews, Tolstoy took little interest or initiative in Jewish

---

[7] *Ibid.*, p. 133. Peretz's account of the meeting is based on what he was told by one or more participants. On Reutern, see *Evr. Ènciklopedija*, 13:363–364 and Gessen, *Zakon i žizn'*, pp. 124–125, 127–133, 150.

matters and, on occasion, tried to relieve the hardships his predecessor had caused.⁸

Ignatyev was dismissed in May 1882 when Pobedonostsev and the Emperor learned that he had taken up the idea of the Slavophiles to summon a *zemskij sobor*, an assembly of the land, of over two thousand delegates—landowners, merchants, clergy, and some one thousand peasants—to demonstrate the nation's unity, its loyalty to the throne, and the superiority of Russia's political system over all others. Even so purely theatrical a summoning of the people into the political arena frightened Alexander and Pobedonostsev who also denounced Ignatyev for letting demagogues stir up the mob against the Jews. Ignatyev disappeared from view and played no further part in public life. But the legacy of his brief tenure of office survived until 1917 in the Provisional Rules, and even more in the underlying premises of his program. These premises his ministerial critics had either left unchallenged or failed to refute, and they continued to loom large in the bureaucratic mind.

Indeed, in the very act of pointedly reminding the Interior Minister and his subordinates of their duty to prevent violence to the persons and property of all citizens, and implying that they had not done enough to repress it, the Committee of Ministers partially accepted Ignatyev's definition of the root cause of the violence. The official résumé of the committee's deliberations concluded that there was adequate explanation for the ill will that native Christians, peasants and townsmen alike, bore the Jews. It was extensive indebtedness and economic dependence, which were the consequences of a very low level of literacy and education and of the special traits of the Jewish people (*plemja*), especially its resourcefulness and cleverness in business. Given that combination of factors, and physical proximity, it would take but little effort to stir resentment into riot.⁹ Thus were set some of the basic terms in which governmental debates of the Jewish question would henceforth be conducted and by which policy would be guided.

It was to the High or Pahlen Commission¹⁰ that the task of examining the

---

⁸ On Tolstoy, see n. 37 below.

⁹ Cited by Gessen in *Pravo*, no. 31 (1908): 1682. Cf. *Istoričeskij obzor dejatel'nosti Komiteta ministrov*, 4:183.

¹⁰ The full, official title of the Pahlen Commission was: *Vysšaja kommissija dlja peresmotra dejstvujuščikh o evrejakh v Imperii zakonov*. L. S. Makov, its first chairman and a former Minister of the Interior, was replaced, after his death in April 1883, by Count Pahlen. The commission's members and consultants, including several Jewish "experts," are listed in *Evr. Enciklopedija*, 5:862–863. Zajončkovskij, in *Rossijskoje samoderžavie v konce XIX stoletija* (Moscow, 1970), p. 16, reports his failure to find the materials of the commission (or of its successor, chaired by Pleve) in the archives. A printed summary of its findings and recommendations, intended only for official use, was all that was available to me at the time of writing. A copy, inscribed in an unknown Russian hand, "To his Excellency, K. P. Pobedonostsev," is in the Bodleian Library of Oxford University: *Obščaja*

whole range of issues raised by Ignatyev was next entrusted. Named after its second chairman, Count Kh. I. Pahlen, Minister of Justice (from 1867 to 1878) and member of the State Council, the commission included representatives of all the major government departments. In five years (1883 to 1888) of sifting materials and discussing the conclusions to be drawn from them, the members of the commission did not shy away from questioning the presuppositions they knew to be held and respected in high places. But in laying bare and disposing of some grounds for past laws and discriminations, they unwittingly gave new weight to others.

Best remembered of the commission's work is its majority's endorsement of Jewish emancipation and the removal of all discriminatory legislation. It is also well known that its recommendations were not approved by the Emperor, that the commission was dissolved, and that Vyacheslav Pleve, then Assistant Minister of Interior, was named to head its successor. The Pahlen Commission's labors, it is believed, had no further influence or importance. But this is true in only one respect. A look at the volume summarizing the commission's findings suggests that they may have helped to perpetuate the conviction of senior bureaucrats that the Jewish problem was an especially troublesome and stubborn one.

In lifting sole blame from the shoulders of the Jews, the commission found that the problem they posed was very real and so complicated that its solution had to be approached most carefully and deliberately. And it was just this frightening complexity that was invoked for thirty more years on behalf of caution, gradualness, or inaction. The commission's majority had not, of course, intended to supply pretexts or arguments for postponing measures beneficial to the Jews; in fact, it had asked that the easing of their disabilities begin at once with the repeal of the rules governing residence in the villages of the Pale. It did, however, cite as one reason for going slow what Ignatyev had called the abnormality of the relationship between Russians and Jews, and the tensions between them that would be exacerbated by precipitate action. Whatever historical causes there might be for the peculiarities of the Jews—and the contradictory and inconsistent treatment they had received at the hands of the government was surely one of them—there were also innate Jewish vices that were harmful and nourished the hostility of their neighbors, especially among the lower classes.

Not all Jewish moral and civic shortcomings could be removed; not all of them could or should become objects of state intervention. Nor did the

---

zapiska vysšej kommissii dlja peresmotra dejstvujuščikh o evrejakh v Imperii zakonov (1883–1888). Its recommendations and conclusions, contained on pages 252 to 295, were signed by eight and opposed by five of fourteen members. Gessen, apparently, had access to the commission's journals. See *Evr. Ènciklopedija*, 1:832.

commission think that complete assimilation was a realizable goal. It had never yet been achieved anywhere and would not be in future, "because of the too sharply pronounced characteristics of the semitic race" and the depth of religious sentiment among the Christian masses. But government and society had to battle against the separatism and self-willed isolation of the Jews; their striving to gain economic power over the people in whose midst they lived; their tendency to evade public duties; and their avoidance of physical labor. To expect complete reformation on the last score would be excessively optimistic, although Jews should not be denied the opportunity to take up agricultural work; they were already showing improvement in fulfilling state obligations and would undoubtedly continue to do so. "As far as the first two evils are concerned, they constitute entirely real accusations against the Jews, and the laws must work gradually to weaken them—all the more so since it *is* defects in the laws that have helped to strengthen and maintain the evils."

Past discrimination, moreover, had been ineffective, had led to massive evasions of the law by Christians and Jews, and had incensed the latter. It was advisable, therefore, not to embitter a population concentrated along the country's western borders, where conflict with Russia's neighbors might erupt. The commission conceded that there was substance to a new kind of charge leveled against the Jews: their prominence in the camp of anarchism and revolution. This had given rise to the belief that Judaism was a natural breeding ground of subversion. Indeed, Jewish socialists and progressives had themselves cited the altruistic teachings of their faith, its injunctions to love and serve mankind, in justification of their missionary calling. The commissioners disagreed. Contemporary Judaism, as had been true for most of its history, was in its deepest essence conservative, egotistical, individualistic, and practical. The radicalism of Jewish youth had simpler, less exalted origins in the failure of many to enter Russian society.

Masses of young Jews "from street and bazaar" had flooded secondary schools and universities and were kept by poverty and inadequate preparation from finishing their studies. Having abandoned religious beliefs, they were then stranded between a world of which they were no longer part and a new one which denied them admission. Angered by the difficulties of their personal situation as well as by the oppression of their coreligionists, they had become recruits for the opponents of the established order. Yet education, particularly at the primary level, remained the only way for Russians and Jews to overcome their mutual fears and hatreds and to engage on equal terms in the normal contacts and conflicts of life. Although they were concerned by what they called the artificial influx of poor Jews into the upper levels of the educational system and were prepared to limit the admission of lower-class students, nine of the commission's members opposed the introduction of general Jewish quotas.

Humanity and common sense, the principles of good government and enlightened self-interest, the majority report urged, demanded that the administration follow a consistent policy toward the Jews. Such a policy would extend to them, as to all citizens, the full protection of laws that would be indifferent to the fact of their Jewishness. The constant enlistment of state aid by the competitors of the Jews had to stop. Russians were not incapable of holding their own against them, and if in free competition they were the losers, it was because they were less agile, less parsimonious, less sober, less enterprising than the Jews and too dependent on the state. Only without its aid could merchants and others become self-reliant, only by their own efforts could they blunt the force of Jewish exploitation. The principle of laissez faire had to apply to peasants no less than to the middle and upper classes. Since the end of serfdom, the "dark people" had been under government tutelage, presumed to be in need of special protection from the Jews. But if they were forced to borrow from the Jew or got drunk in his tavern, it was not the Jew's fault. The best laws against usury and drunkenness would not help a people who would not help themselves, and there was enough proof in the relations between Jews and prosperous Old Believers in the western provinces to show that Russian peasants could stand on their own feet. "Thus, the center of gravity of the struggle against the harmful influence of the Jews must be shifted from the state to society, to all its strata. . . ."

We have no record of the Emperor's reactions to the commission's advice, no specific indication what or who made him reject or ignore it.[11] But it is reasonable to assume that Alexander and the counselors he valued looked upon a relaxation of controls over the Jews as a leap into the unknown. They were as incapable of neutrality or salutary neglect on the question of the Jews as they were incapable of a laissez-faire attitude toward the problems posed by peasants and workers, Poles and religious dissenters, local self-government, higher education, and other areas of life. Neither the Jewish problem nor the others were new; but they must have been given a new urgency by fear of the consequences of the Great Reforms, by the growth of commercial activity and the urban sector, by the beginnings of industrial capitalism and a mobile society of classes rather than fixed estates—and by the dangers all this posed to social stability and the docility of the masses.

The peasants remained special objects of government concern. Laws of 1886 and 1893 tied them still more firmly to their village communes and the institution of the "land captain" (1889) formalized their wardship to the state.

---

[11] Sliozberg, *Dela*, 3:256; Zajončkovskij, *Rossijskoe samoderžavie*, 134.

When so many Russians were still bound by law and custom in order to prevent their doing or suffering harm (as the authorities defined it), it was unlikely that the bonds of the Jews would be loosened. On the contrary, the tendency toward a reaffirmation of controls grew stronger in the late 1880s and the early 1890s as the country embarked on an ambitious industrialization program that speeded the pace of modernization. Those who were most fearful of its unsettling consequences were also those who opposed equal rights for Jews and advocated the rigorous application of existing restrictions.

Their case was stated by Konstantin Pobedonostsev, tutor and adviser to two tsars, philosopher of reaction, and the most articulate anti-Semite in the government until his retirement in 1905. Although he had played a major role in the judicial reforms of Alexander II, Pobedonostsev became quickly disenchanted. As early as 1864 he wrote to Ivan Aksakov's wife: "You will not believe how disgusted we are with the reforms, how we have lost faith in them, how much we would like to stop at something stable."[12] The lively debating and planning in which his countrymen were then engaged seemed but the noise of "cheap and shallow ecstasies."[13] When another fifteen years had passed, he linked the horror, the general corruption, the destruction of honor and duty with the Jews. They were behind the socialist movement and buying landed estates, ruining the old nobility and gaining control of financial institutions, of the press, and even of the principles of science which they were trying to divorce from Christianity. "They have engrossed everything," he wrote to Dostoevsky in 1879, "they have undermined everything, but the spirit of the century supports them." And that was as true in Russia as it was in Rumania and Serbia, a fact that underscored for Pobedonostsev Russia's vulnerability.[14]

His resistance to the Jews as an alien element and as representatives of the radical spirit in science and politics, caused Pobedonostsev to complain of their great numbers in the secondary schools and of the fact that higher education gave them the right to residence outside the Pale as well as access to the professions and the state service. A backward country like Russia, he said repeatedly, had to erect defensive barriers against Jews, and in particular to guard the most backward and defenseless of its people, the peasants. Emancipation had given them freedom, but left them without proper supervision, "which the dark masses require." Left to themselves, with no one to look after

---

[12] "Pobedonostsev and Alexander III," *Slavonic and East European Review* (June 1928):43.

[13] A. E. Adams, "Pobedonostsev and the Rule of Firmness," *ibid.*, 32 (December 1953): 132.

[14] Byrnes, *Pobedonostsev* (n. 3, above), pp. 131, 205–206; Heilbronner, "The Administrations of Loris-Melikov and Ignatiev," (n. 3, above), p. 528. For another unfavorable comparison of Russia with Serbia and Rumania see Pobedonostsev's letter to Alexander III of 3 December 1886, n. 20 below.

them, they had taken to drink and idleness and had fallen into the hands of usurers and Jews. To Jewish visitors he protested that he neither disliked nor hated Jews. He was simply afraid of them, of their superior talents and intelligence, their abstemiousness and industry—qualities that most Russians lacked. The state was obliged, therefore, to redress the balance in their favor.[15]

Deprived of the guardianship of the landlord and without a native middle class in town or country, Pobedonostsev said in 1891, the rural population could only turn to the state for protection, guidance, and aid against Jewish exploitation and deceit.[16] The decline of the commune, the growth of industry and capitalism made it all the more important that the state control and direct the economic forces undermining the old order. It should prevent merchants, Jews, and kulak-usurers, "a great evil for the state and for the local population," from acquiring communal lands; it should establish a peasant class with indivisible and inalienable ownership of property, and supply it and small businesses with capital and credit to restrict the influence of "Jewish usurers," and prevent the growth of a landless and dissatisfied proletariat in the cities. The commune, Pobedonostsev conceded, was doomed; railways and roads had to be built. But the state, as "the guardian of the highest interest," had to minimize the unsettling impact of economic and social change.[17]

Pobedonostsev neither instigated nor approved of pogroms.[18] He feared mobs and demagogues as much as Jews. Nor can specific anti-Jewish legislation be traced to him. But he allowed the synodal press to publish and advertise anti-Semitic literature and himself included material critical of the Jews in the Synod's annual reports and his own publications.[19] In the Committee of Ministers, in the State Council, and in audiences with the Emperor his voice

---

[15] P. L. Alston, *Education and the State in Tsarist Russia* (Stanford, 1969), p. 127; Peretc, *Dnevnik*, p. 39; Sliozberg, *Dela*, 2:252; Byrnes, *Pobedonostsev*, pp. 206–207; Dubnov, *Evrei v Rossii* (n. 1, above), bk. 2:6–7; Jehudah Eppel, *In the Midst of the Beginning of the Great Awakening* (Tel-Aviv, 1936), p. 256. I am grateful to Dr. M. Heymann of the Central Zionist Archives in Jerusalem for making this Hebrew source available to me, and to Professor Amos Funkenstein for translating it.

[16] H. L. von Schweinitz, *Denkwuerdigkeiten des Botschafters General von Schweinitz* (Berlin, 1927), 2:424. By way of illustration, Pobedonostsev told Schweinitz a story which, if he believed it, reveals more than a touch of pathology: In one of the larger districts of Mogilev *gubernija*, the local women did not know how to sew. The making or mending of the most simple articles of clothing had to be done by Jewish tailors. A well-to-do local noble had therefore arranged instruction in needlework for a number of young Christian women and had sent them at his expense into the villages of the district to teach others the use of the needle. Upon this, the Jews set fire to the house and farm buildings of the philanthropic landowner who lost all his property and barely managed to save his life.

[17] Byrnes, *Pobedonostsev*, pp. 301, 302, 331.

[18] *Pis'ma Pobedonosceva k Aleksandru III* (Moscow, 1925–1926), 1:344.

[19] Byrnes, *Pobedonostsev*, pp. 208–209.

must have been heard and his vote cast on behalf of the many measures taken against Jews in the last two decades of the century.[20] Their purpose, to use the language of the official history of the State Council, was to counteract the numerical growth and geographical spread of the Jews. "Because of the difficulty of a radical solution of the Jewish question, it seemed desirable to take certain palliative steps to restrict the in many ways harmful Jewish population."[21]

The army set a quota of 5 percent on doctors and medical assistants (1882). The Ministers of Transport and State Domains limited the number of Jews (and Poles) in their departments. In 1884, the country's only Jewish vocational school was shut down. The argument used to justify the decree might have

---

[20] Among the many letters Pobedonostsev addressed to Alexander, those touching on the Jews were surprisingly few. In November 1886 he opposed shifting Rostov and Taganrog districts from Ekaterinoslav *gubernija* to the Don Cossack Army region because this would, inter alia, mean extending to the two cities and their environs the residence restrictions applicable in non-Pale provinces. As a result, large numbers of poor Jews would have to be moved out, probably at government expense, while a significant number of well-to-do Jewish homeowners and professionals would nonetheless be allowed to enter the Don Cossack Army region. (*K. P. Pobedonoscev i ego korrespondenty* [Moscow, 1923] 1: 569.) In December, Pobedonostsev transmitted to his master a financial specialist's memorandum on how to break Russia's bondage to the Berlin bourse. It was shameful, he said in an accompanying letter, that such small states as Rumania and Serbia managed to keep their currencies stable, whereas the ruble kept falling at the pleasure and for the profit of an unknown power which was exploiting Russian simplicity. Only two names were mentioned in the letter, the Russian bankers Stieglitz and Sack (the latter a Jew), but when Pobedonostsev spoke of the bosses of the Berlin stock exchange his reader would certainly think of the Bleichroeders in the first place. (*Pis'ma Pobedonosceva k Aleksandru III*, 2:122-123.) In March of the next year, 1887, the Director of the Holy Synod complained that the Ministers of Finance and State Properties had failed to defend Russian interests when they approved oil pipeline and processing concessions for which the capital was mainly foreign. If that were allowed, the process of delivering the resources of the Caucasus into the hands of the Rothschilds and other foreigners would soon be completed. (*Ibid.*, 2:146.)

[21] *Dejatel'nost' Gosudarstvennogo Soveta za vremja carstvovanija Gosudarja Imperatora Aleksandra Aleksandroviča, 1881-1894* (St. Petersburg, 1900), p. 135. The following summary of legislative and administrative measures taken before 1900 is based on a variety of sources. For a convenient survey, see A. A. Gol'denvejzer, "Pravovoe položenie evreev v Rossii," in *Kniga o russkom evrejstve* (New York: Union of Russian Jews, 1960), pp. 111-141, and Lucien Wolf, ed., *The Legal Sufferings of the Jews in Russia* (London, 1912). The fullest and most systematic compilation of laws, administrative regulations, and Senate interpretations is in Ja. I. Gimpel'son, *Zakony o evrejakh*, 2 vols. (St. Petersburg, 1914 and 1915). See also Polovcev, *Dnevnik*, 1:143, 2:440, 516; *Istoričeskij obzor dejatel'nosti Komiteta ministrov* (n. 2, above), 4:183, 245, 436; Alston, *Education and the State*, pp. 121-123, 130, 138; Paul M. Johnson, "I. D. Delianov and Russian Educational Policy," unpubl. doctoral dissertation, Emory University (1971), pp. 133-136, 187-191; Sliozberg, *Dela* (n. 2, above), 2:4, 5, 72, 157, 165, 183, 189, 196, 270; Dubnov, *Evrei v Rossii*, bk. 2: 10-18; I. M. Dižur, "Evrej v ékonomičeskoj žizni Rossii," in *Kniga o russkom evrejstve*, p. 178, and S. L. Kučerov, "Evrei v russkoj advokature," *ibid.*, pp. 402-407; *Handbuch des gesamten russischen Zivilrechts*, ed. Klibanski (Berlin, 1911), 1:434; 2:469; Zajončkovskij, *Rossijskoe samoderžavie* (n. 10, above), pp. 131-134.

been supplied by Pobedonostsev: the majority of craftsmen in the southwest were Jews and this situation hampered the development of skills among the indigenous population whom the Jews exploited; since there was no such school for Christians in the region, the existence of a Jewish one would further disadvantage the local people. The Committee of Ministers imposed additional restrictions on landholding by Jews and Poles in nine northern and southwestern provinces (1885). In 1886 it began to fix the number of non-Christians on the boards of local commodity exchanges at a maximum of two and declared them ineligible as chairmen and brokers. The rule was applied to four cities—Baku, Rostov-on-Don, Nikolaev, Odessa—with exceptions made for Odessa when it was found that there were only two Christian brokers who were also Russian subjects.

The families of men failing to answer draft calls were made liable to a fine of 300 rubles in 1886; in addition, individuals enjoying exempt status could be called up as replacements. A year later, the Ministry of Interior interpreted the Provisional Rules of 1882 to apply to changes of domicile from one village to another and closed Rostov-on-Don and Taganrog to newcomers. Educational quotas for secondary and subsequently for higher schools were established by ministerial order in 1887: 10 percent in the Pale, 5 percent in the rest of the country, 3 percent in Moscow and St. Petersburg. They were further reduced in 1889 and 1901. In 1887, Jewish mining enterprises were denied the use of state lands. After 1888, Jewish candidates were not allowed to take officers' examinations in military and cadet schools. The next year, the Minister of Justice suspended new admissions of Jews and Muslims to the bar; the suspension remained in effect for fifteen years. There were expulsions from the border zone in 1890, a number of small towns were declared villages, and the new statutes on local government (1890 and 1892) denied the vote to Jews; in the cities of the Pale, Jewish councilors, not to exceed 10 percent of the total, were appointed by the authorities.

Decrees of 1891 and 1892 abrogated the rights of artisans and of veterans of the army of Nicholas I to reside in the city or province of Moscow. In 1891, also, there began massive expulsions from the old capital and less massive ones from other cities; the prohibition on the purchase, leasing, or holding of peasant land in any form was extended to Poland. Jewish ownership and exploitation of mines and oil wells in certain provinces was inhibited and more strictly regulated after 1892. A year later, a ministerial circular of 1880, exempting Jews who had taken up residence outside the Pale before that date, was repealed. There were new regulations forbidding the use of Christian names (1893), as well as new interpretations of existing rules. Former merchants of the first guild and their descendants were forced back into the Pale (1895) and Jewish soldiers were kept from spending their furloughs outside of it (1896). Beginning in 1899, merchants of the first guild wishing to move to Moscow required special permission from the Minister of Finance and the Governor-General, although the laws did not restrict the residence rights of this category of wealthy Jews. The statutes of new savings and loan associations were screened to make sure they were not dominated by Jews; the ostensible purpose was to protect unsophisticated and inexperienced savers.

What was done was not the end of what some members of the government wished to do. Vyacheslav Pleve, then Assistant Minister of the Interior and head of the conference which had taken over the work of the Pahlen Commission, began in 1890 to circulate within the administration a legislative program of some forty points. What became known of this program shows that its passage would have been a return to the Ignatyev proposals and beyond, to the time preceding the reign of Alexander II and the privileges he had bestowed on selected categories of Jews. The Pleve project was thought to have envisioned the setting up of Jewish quarters in certain large cities, to have aimed at further reducing Jewish commerce and revoking the residence rights of merchants of the first two guilds, of honored citizens, and university graduates. Those Jews whom the Provisional Rules of 1882 had allowed to remain in the villages were gradually to be cleared from them. Young people would have to leave rural localities, even their birthplaces, once they came of age; anyone who had temporarily absented himself from his legal residence in a village was not to be readmitted. Informal or verbal rental agreements concluded in contravention of the 1882 rules against written contracts were to be treated as crimes; and to inhibit contacts between peasants and Jews, things would be made still more difficult for Jewish moneylenders, tavern keepers, traders, and artisans.[22]

Worsening repression and rumors that more was still to come, led a group of rabbis, members of an official advisory commission on religious affairs, to ask the help of a man whom they expected to be receptive to their plea. As Minister of Finance, Nicholas Bunge had led the successful opposition to the Ignatyev project, pointing out the Jews' importance in the rural economy as providers of credit and goods. In the State Council and in reports to Alexander III he had argued that Russia's need for foreign loans and investment capital was not likely to be met unless there was improvement in the treatment and legal status of the Jews. It was also believed that he had helped to prevent pogroms in the south by enlisting the aid of Alexander II.[23]

---

[22] The Pleve project remains undiscovered or, at any rate, unpublished. Descriptions of its probable contents in *ibid.*, p. 135; Sliozberg, *Dela*, 2:165–168; Dubnov, "*Furor judophobicus* (n. 2, above), pp. 27–59.

[23] On Bunge: Peretc, *Dnevnik*, pp. 73, 130–131; Harold Frederic, *The New Exodus* (New York, 1892), p. 116; Gessen in *Pravo*, no. 31; 1679–1681.

A respected scholar and former university professor of economics, he was a humane man who had lightened the peasants' fiscal burdens and tried to shift more of them to the privileged estates. There was good reason to think that on becoming Chairman of the Committee of Ministers in 1886, a position of influence though little power, Bunge had continued to be a voice of reason and restraint. "Your Excellency," the rabbis addressed him in late 1893 or early 1894, "your academic and public activities have left many a bright mark ... as adviser to the Monarch, plead our case."[24] There is nothing to show how Bunge reacted to the letter, whether he brought the plight of the Jews to the attention of the Emperor before his death in October 1894 or to his son, Nicholas, before Bunge's own death in 1895.

There is evidence, however, that the Jewish question occupied him and that he regarded it as one of the gravest facing the Russian state. In his papers a memoir was found which Bunge had prepared either for posterity or for his colleagues in the government, possibly for the new ruler.[25] This survey of governmental activity in the reign of Alexander III covered four areas Bunge considered critical. The first was that of foreign affairs—how to assure Russia's independence of foreign powers. Next was the nationalities problem—or how to satisfy the feeling that Russia must belong to the Russians. The improvement of internal administration came third, and the development of the nation's human and material resources last. In the second category the Jewish question loomed largest. Bunge's discussion of it reflects views shared by other moderates in government, as well as a degree of intellectual confusion, moral lassitude, and perplexity that caused even moderates to despair of breaking out of what Bunge called a vicious circle. "All legislation has led either to the triumph or to the distress of the Jews, and neither has benefited the indigenous population." His counsel of moderation and his call for observing basic legal norms may have helped to slow the rush to persecution; his despair of finding easy or early remedies possibly strengthened the hand of its advocates.

The problem arose, wrote Bunge, with the Polish partitions. The harsh steps taken by Nicholas I to deal with it had been no more successful than their relaxation by Alexander II. As early as 1864 it had become necessary to take note of the power the Jews were amassing. Their right to acquire landed

---

[24] Sliozberg, *Dela*, 2: 128–129.
[25] The Bunge memoir was printed and circulated in government circles after the death of Alexander III for whom, according to Zajončkovskij, it was originally prepared. There is an undated copy in the Harvard Law School Library (*1881–1894 gg. Zapiska, najdennaja v bumagakh N. Kh. Bunge*) which was kindly made available to me by Professor Theodore Taranovsky (University of Puget Sound) who also compared the printed version with the manuscript draft in Moscow. The printed text comprises 130 pages; of these, pages 22 to 41 deal with Jewish affairs.

property was restricted even within the Pale, as was their share in local government (1870) and their keeping of taverns (1874). Yet Jewish influence grew. They entered universities, high schools, and the professions in disproportionate numbers; occupied key positions in banking and railroading; and leased lands and houses when they did not buy them through Christian intermediaries. Large-scale commerce was everywhere in their hands. They nearly monopolized petty trade in the Pale where the rural people were in complete dependence on them as tavern keepers and moneylenders. This abnormal economic situation, not religious intolerance, had caused the pogroms. These in turn had furnished the impetus for the policies initiated in 1882, including such excessively cruel practices as the expulsions from Moscow and such damaging ones (to the peasants) as the closing of Jewish shops by the Governor of Volhynia who had foolishly and vainly advised rural communes to start their own.

In order to judge the effectiveness of the measures taken, Bunge found it necessary to ask what in Judaism accounted for the evil its adherents were doing. Although marked by distinct racial (*rasovye*), religious, and linguistic peculiarities, the essence of Judaism lay in its code of conduct, the Talmud. It was full of savage fanaticism and absurd beliefs concerning Jewry's election as God's people while all others were destined to serve them. Rabbis were civil rather than religious leaders, the *kahal* not a community of the faithful but a unit of government with a worldwide organization, the *Alliance Israélite Universelle*. Everywhere Jews constituted a state within the state, unwilling to become Russians first, as members of other denominations were Frenchmen, Englishmen, or Germans before they were Catholics or Protestants. The purpose of Jewish separateness was to gain dominion over non-Jews; their means was money, which they worshipped as did no other people. Since agriculture and physical labor in general were not sources of quick gain, Jews preferred occupations in which capital could be turned over quickly.

This, then, explained why all that had been done to render the Jews harmless had failed. Discrimination merely intensified their rapacity and fanaticism, their poverty and particularism; in short, it aggravated all the ills it was designed to remedy. Driven out of the villages, masses of poor Jews swelled the proletariat of the cities; expelled from the large towns, they added to the misery of the smaller ones. It was chimerical to think that emigration would substantially reduce their numbers, which Bunge placed at six to eight millions. Only the relatively industrious and well-to-do would leave for England, France, or Germany. The richest and most ruthless would remain and assume leadership of a desperate and parasitical Jewish proletariat. The granting of privileges had equally failed to bring about the fusion of Russians and Jews. Even in the purely Russian provinces it had meant increased Jewish power and influence in every area of economic, intellectual, and public life. Germany and Austria had demonstrated that full equality led to results that were similar or worse and, as in Russia, to an anti-Semitic reaction.

Was it possible to break the vicious circle? Were there means to battle the evil represented by the Jews? Two kinds of measures must be pursued: those guarding the population from the Jews and those directed toward their reformation; the effects might not be visible for years or decades, perhaps not for centuries, and only a consistent policy promised success.

Bunge felt that, to begin with, it was necessary to circumscribe Jewish rights, but no more than absolutely necessary and without tolerating their administrative infringement or Jewish transgression. For the time being, and until the Jewish character changed, the Pale must remain, along with certain constraints upon free movement within it. But the complete removal of Jews from the villages was not desirable, for it would hurt the peasant economy, send a politically and socially explosive proletariat into the towns and, by depriving the Jews of lawful occupations, drive them into a worse exploitation of their Christian neighbors. There could be no doubt that prohibitions on the acquisition of agricultural land must be maintained as long as the Jews did not themselves work it. The ownership of houses and the cultivation of market gardens should, however, be permitted to permanent residents of villages and towns. Finally, Bunge also suggested an unspecified relaxation of the *numerus clausus* in higher education.

Without discussing other restrictions whose purpose it is to safeguard the local people from the pernicious influence of the Jews, it is necessary to state that they all stand in need of revision. They must fit the purpose for which they are intended and not have the character of religious or social oppression which is the case at present and serves no useful goal. Incomparably more difficult is the adoption of fundamental measures to weaken the inherent strength of Judaism.

The fundamental reformation of the Jews must begin with the removal of all that isolates them—their communal institutions, their special schools, their state-appointed rabbis—through all of which Russian laws help to preserve a rigid socio-religious structure fashioned and fixed by Talmudic teachings. In the area of religion, the government neither could nor should create for the Jews a new, less fanatical and more reasonable faith, but it must see to it that the general schools produce enlightened Jews. To that end, primary and secondary schools, especially the former, should become more accessible and give Jewish religious instruction in the Russian language according to state-approved principles by state-approved teachers. If these conditions were observed, the number of Jewish students in the general schools would probably decline, since the fanatical element would not want to enter them in any case.

To overcome their particularism, it was essential also to subject the Jews to the authority of local governments at every level. In the towns, although denied the vote, they participated in municipal affairs and duties. In the villages and rural districts, however, they enjoyed a privileged position vis-à-vis the peasants. The communes could not make them carry their share of village obligations in money and labor services; the cantonal courts could not hear cases involving them, and the cantonal elders lacked authority to punish them. Such an abnormal situation had to end. Since it was not yet possible to let Jews elect or be elected to peasant institutions, a person charged to deal with Jewish matters should be appointed to them. For the rest, the Jews of town and country must be made secure in the possession of those rights which, though fewer than the rights of non-Jews, would allow the lawful pursuit of a livelihood, prevent the creation of millions of restless proletarians, and keep the Jews from the harmful activities their present treatment inspired.

The tortured course of Bunge's argument, which tactics along with prejudice and perplexity may have helped to shape, does not reveal a bold or principled advocate of civil rights and human dignity. A statesman who sees the happy outcome of an issue centuries in the future is, in effect, avoiding it. Bunge did not even give his forthright endorsement to the Pahlen Commission's call for full, if gradually attained, equality before the law, although at times he appeared disposed to embrace it. Yet he confronted with more clarity and courage than did most of his governmental colleagues the fact that the Jewish problem had extra-Jewish sources and that the state, being the chief of these, could choose to aggravate or alleviate it. And in invoking the principle of legality—that arbitrary bureaucrats and scheming Jews alike must obey the law—Bunge had found a firmer and more lasting guide than those who questioned only the utility of persecution.

Bunge's successor at the Ministry of Finance, I. A. Vyshnegradsky, was, like him, a former professor and, in addition, an eminently successful financier. In 1887 he had sided with the minority in the State Council when it held that the regulations of 1882 did indeed forbid changes of domicile from one village to another in the Pale, a view that the emperor adopted.[26] But when in 1890 Vyshnegradsky learned of new anti-Jewish legislation being prepared by Pleve, he intervened with his colleague at the Ministry of the Interior, I. N. Durnovo, to delay its submission to the State Council.[27] In early 1891 he successfully protested to the Minister of Foreign Affairs against new obstacles Durnovo's subordinates were placing in the way of foreign Jews coming to Russia on business.[28] And after the horrors of the Moscow expulsions, and the worldwide outcry to which they gave rise, he decided to risk the emperor's

---

[26] Polovcev, *Dnevnik*, 2:59.
[27] *Ibid.*, p. 314.
[28] V. N. Lamzdorf, *Dnevnik, 1891–1892* (Moscow-Leningrad, 1934), pp. 52–53, 72.

displeasure and to acquaint him with the consequences of the policies his government was pursuing.[29]

In a memorandum of which we have neither the text nor the date—it was in all probability written after the Paris Rothschilds and a number of Jewish banking houses in Germany withdrew from a planned consolidation and conversion of Russia's foreign debt—Vyshnegradsky urged caution upon the tsar, warned him of the financial war that the Jews were capable of waging against Russia, and of the damage the adoption of Pleve's proposals would do to her credit and reputation abroad and her economy at home. The Jews should, of course, be subjected to special laws and controls, the Minister of Finance had said on another occasion, but their excessive persecution only created difficulties at a time when Russia still needed the Jews. The Pleve project, whether at the express order of the Emperor or not, never reached the State Council. It was buried in the archives of the Ministry of the Interior and to this day has not been found. Pleve himself, in leaving the ministry, appears to have lost interest in it.[30]

Vyshnegradsky's victory over Pleve gave renewed currency to rumors that he was in the pay of the Jews. His defense of them hardly helped to strengthen his position. He was dismissed in 1892, when the consequences of the 1891 harvest failure were blamed on his stringent financial policies. High taxes and tariffs to accumulate gold reserves and foster industry had left millions of peasants without reserves to withstand a catastrophic famine.[31]

The Rothschilds' refusal to help the imperial exchequer was not permanent. Until 1901 they took the lead in the issue of most Russian loans. Nor did all Jewish banking houses declare a boycott of the Russian Ministry of Finance. The Rothschilds and others would again decline to participate in Russian credit operations, especially after the pogroms of 1903 and 1905, but some

---

[29] *Ibid.*, pp. 105, 107; Sliozberg, *Dela*, 2:173–174; *idem, Baron G. O. Gincburg, ego žizn' i dejatel'nost'* (Paris, 1933), p. 109.

[30] Zajončkovskij, *Rossijskoe samoderžavie*, p. 135; A. V. Bogdanovič, *Tri poslednikh samoderžca: Dnevnik* (Moscow-Leningrad, 1924), p. 141; Polovcev, *Dnevnik*, 2:312. Professor William Langer in *The Franco-Russian Alliance, 1890–1894* (Cambridge, 1929), p. 179, does not rule out the possibility that the interests of French diplomacy may have had as much to do with the Rothschild withdrawal from the Russian loan as did the interests of their co-religionists. For a conflicting view, see Olga Crisp, "The Financial Aspects of the Franco-Russian Alliance, 1894–1914," unpubl. doctoral dissertation, University of London, 1954, p. 128: "When in 1891 the Rothschilds broke their contract with the Russian Government because of Jewish persecution, the Crédit Lyonnais, apparently with the direct encouragement of the French Foreign Office, undertook the transaction because the national interest demanded it."

[31] Polovcev, *Dnevnik*, 2:280; Hugh Seton-Watson, *Imperial Russia* (Oxford, 1967), p. 518.

Jewish bankers abroad continued to hold or to buy Russian bonds and some Jewish businessmen to deal in Russian goods.[32]

Vyshnegradsky's concern for the reaction of the financial community, and the fact that some of its Jewish members had denied their services in 1891, nourished the widespread belief in the solidarity of Jewish money and its power to control Russia's, perhaps the world's, destinies. Vyshnegradsky himself was not free of it, and he was angered when Baron Horace Ginsburg, the Petersburg banker, told him early in 1892, that it was not within his power to restore good relations with the Rothschilds.[33] Only weeks later, the Minister of the Interior, to illustrate the danger of Jewish influence to the State Council, told that august assembly of ministers and elder statesmen that each time there had been student riots in the capital in recent years, he had stopped them by threatening to banish Ginsburg from the city.[34] When the council received a favorable report on the state of the budget, State Comptroller T. I. Filippov expressed satisfaction that now "we can look with disdain upon the offensive which the European stock exchanges, led by the Jews, are directing against us."[35]

The Grand Duke Vladimir, one of the more intelligent and better educated of the five sons of Alexander II, could not be convinced that the international situation and economic conditions at home had caused a decline in the value of Russian bonds, but insisted that Bismarck's hostility and Jewish machinations were at the bottom of it. State Secretary Polovtsev, the man who had tried to instruct the grand duke in the fundamentals of the international money market and was severely critical of the pseudo-populist chauvinism of the regime, himself saw Jewish money as a connecting link between anti-

---

[32] Crisp, "The Financial Aspects, pp. 114, 308, 316, 463ff.; "Iz dnevnika A. A. Polovceva," *Krasnyj Arkhiv*, 67 (1934):178; idem, *Dnevnik*, 2:390; V. N. Kokovcev, *Iz moego prošlogo: Vospominanija, 1903–1913* (Paris, 1933), 1:59–60; "K peregovoram Kokovceva o zajme v 1905–1906 gg.," *Krasnyj Arkhiv*, 10 (1925):25; *Evr. Ènciklopedija*, 13:693; Zosa Szajkowski, "Paul Nathan, Lucien Wolf, Jacob H. Schiff and the Jewish Revolutionary Movement in Eastern Europe, 1903–1917," *Jewish Social Studies*, 29, no. 2 (April 1967): 75–77.

[33] Polovcev, *Dnevnik*, 2:416–417.

[34] *Ibid.*, p. 433. The prefect of St. Petersburg, General P. A. Gresser, had said much the same thing to an English journalist a few years earlier: W. T. Stead, *The Truth about Russia* (London, 1888), p. 247. In April 1909, the Minister of the Imperial Court, Baron Fredericks, expressed the opinion to the Assistant Minister of War, General Polivanov, that the grant of the Duma had been premature. Twice during the revolutionary disturbances of 1905 and 1906, he said, prominent Jews like Polyakov and Ginsburg, had called on him and had asked that he transmit to the tsar their promise that all disorder would cease with the grant of equal rights to the Jews. A. A. Polivanov, *Iz dnevnikov i vospominanij po dolžnosti voennogo ministra i ego pomoščnika, 1907–1916 godov* (Moscow, 1924), p. 68.

[35] Polovcev, *Dnevnik*, 2:463; and p. 390 for a similar opinion expressed by Alexander III.

Semitic persecution and nihilism. Without the former, the latter would have no funds, and that would be the end of it.[36]

What a man said or what he was believed to think on the subject of the Jews was not always a certain sign of what he did. Dmitry Tolstoy, Minister of Interior from 1882 to 1889, had a well-deserved reputation as a reactionary chauvinist who lost no love for the Jews or what he called the "Hebrew leprosy." But not only did he put a stop to pogroms and pogrom agitation, he also was responsible for the formation of the Pahlen Commission and for appointing as its chairman two men considered liberals on the Jewish question: L. S. Makov, a former Minister of Interior and, after Makov's death, Count Pahlen. These choices testify to the fact that Tolstoy was not committed to a policy of harassment. So does his circular of June 1882 in which he took direct issue with Ignatyev's invitation to the Jews to avail themselves of the possibility of emigration. "The Western frontier is open," Ignatyev had said, whereas Tolstoy threatened to hold to account local officials who induced Jews to leave the country or assisted them in doing so.[37]

Tolstoy's successors at the Ministry of the Interior—I. N. Durnovo, I. L. Goremykin, and D. S. Sipyagin—have left no record of their views on the Jewish question. Of Durnovo, who excluded Jews from the organs of self-government, it has been said that he did so to please the tsar, yet on occasion he prevented harshness and excess in the application of measures his master favored. He appeared to have had no sympathy for Pleve's project and left the day-to-day administration of Jewish affairs to the Director of his Police Department, P. N. Durnovo.[38] The latter, as Minister of the Interior in October 1905, was held responsible "for the riots in the Jewish Pale and the bloody repressions throughout Russia after the publication of the Czar's Manifesto." Other contemporaries described this ultraconservative as "reasonable" on the Jewish question, a defender of the Jews and an opponent of anti-Semitic measures. G. B. Sliozberg, Baron Ginsburg's associate and "lawyer for the Jews," believed that Durnovo was persuaded of the absurdity of the

---

[36] *Ibid.*, pp. 82, 367.

[37] M. L. Peskovskij, *Rokovoe nedorazumenie* (St. Petersburg, 1891), p. 389; *Evr. Ènciklopedija*, 1:130; J. F. Baddeley, *Russia in the Eighties* (London, 1921), pp. 184–190; Gessen, *Zakon i žizn'* (n. 6, above), p. 162; Alston, *Education and the State* (n. 15, above), p. 155, note; Jackson Taylor, "D. A. Tolstoi and the Ministry of Interior, 1882–1889," unpubl. doctoral dissertation, New York University (1970), pp. 48–55; Mark Wischnitzer, *To Dwell in Safety* (Philadelphia, 1948), p. 48. See Alston, pp. 130 and 280 (n. 48) for individual relaxations of the *numerus clausus* by Minister of Education Delyanov; also, German Genkel', "Iz činovnič'ego mira," *Evrejskaja Letopis'* (Petrograd-Moscow, 1923), 1:87–103, and T. Šatilov, "Èpizody iz žizni evreev studentov," *ibid.*, 2:146–151.

[38] Polovcev, *Dnevnik*, 2:429; S. Ju. Vitte, *Vospominanija* (Moscow, 1960), 2:214; Dubnov, *Novejšaja istorija* (n. 2, above), 3:177; Zajončkovskij, *Rossijskoe samoderžavie*, pp. 136, 151, 426; Sliozberg, *Dela*, 2:175; *idem.*, *Gincburg*, p. 139; P. Son-M-k, "K istorii lišenija evreev izbiratel' nykh prav," *Evrejskaja Starina*, no. 4 (1911):109–113.

government's course, discreetly moderated its effects in many instances, and deliberately employed bureaucratic delaying tactics to keep the Pleve project from reaching the stage of formal discussion.[39]

The impetus did not always come from the center. Sometimes a provincial governor—perhaps responding to local complaints, perhaps catering to the known antipathies of the monarch, perhaps expressing his own—reported to St. Petersburg that the Jews were overcrowding schools, dominating municipal councils, or gaining control of certain branches of business. The emperor, in a marginal note, would then request one or another minister "to direct attention" to the problem. The appointment of the Grand Duke Sergey as Governor-General of Moscow and the zeal of the local police have been connected with the ruthless expulsions from that city. P. N. Durnovo told Sliozberg that the May 1882 rules were retained because the police saw them as a lucrative source of income and might stage pogroms if deprived of it. It was wrong to think, he explained, that the central administration had a firm hold over local police forces. It was the center that depended on them, for they could choose to keep order or create disturbances in the provinces.[40]

There was exaggeration, even disingenuousness, in Durnovo's explanation. Yet the police or, more broadly speaking, the security organs of the empire, were intimately concerned with all things Jewish which for many years were under the jurisdiction of the Police Department in the Ministry of the Interior. If the rank and file looked upon Jews as a ready source of bribes, their chiefs considered the Jews—their very numbers, their organizations and activities, the prospect of their free movement throughout the country—as a security problem of the first magnitude. That was certainly the view of Vyacheslav Pleve, the old regime's most famous policeman, Director of the Police Department and Assistant Minister of Interior for a total of fourteen years and head of the ministry from April 1902 until his assassination in July 1904.

Largely as a result of the Kishinev pogrom, Pleve emerges from the literature as the Haman of Russian Jewry, the evil genius to whom its worst sufferings have been traced. Under the impact of Kishinev also—which he plausibly denied instigating[41]—Pleve saw the need for applying palliatives to

---

[39] S. D. Urusov, *Memoirs of a Russian Governor*, trans. Herman Rosenthal (London, 1908), p. vi; Mark Aldanov [M. A. Landau], "P. N. Durnovo—Prophet of War and Revolution," in Dimitri von Mohrenschildt, ed., *The Russian Revolution of 1917* (New York, 1971), p. 73; Sliozberg, *Dela*, 2:143; 175–176; 181.

[40] *Ibid.*, p. 272. Cf. L. Kljačko, "Za čertoju: v Moskve," *Evrejskaja Letopis'*, 1:112–118.

[41] The much-debated question of Pleve's responsibility for Kishinev is discussed in my "Jewish Policy" (n. 1, above). In addition to the literature cited there, see V. I. Gurko, *Features and Figures of the Past—Government and Opinion in the Reign of Nicholas II*, trans. Laura Matveev (Stanford, 1939), pp. 246-248; A. A. Lopukhin, *Otryvki iz vospominanij* (Moscow-Petrograd, 1923), pp. 14–15; Ambassador Alvensleben to Chancellor von Buelow, 18 May 1903. Germany, Auswaertiges Amt, *Akten*, film series I, reel 306, no. 291.

the Jewish problem of which, during his ministry, he spoke often and with unusual expansiveness. After the peasant problem he considered this to be the most important issue facing the state.[42] That fact alone, and his returning Jewish matters to the Police Department, casts doubt on his claim that he entered office as a Judeophile. In May 1902 he told an acquaintance who tried to persuade him of the necessity of gradually granting equal rights, that he agreed with much of what his caller had said, and that the proposals he had drafted as an assistant minister were not his own. "I was then the executor of another's orders. . . ."[43] Who, if anyone, issued these orders—Alexander, the Grand Duke Sergey, Pobedonostsev—must remain a matter of speculation. A man as well versed in the subtleties of power as Pleve would not, in any case, have need of explicit instructions.

Pleve's anti-Semitism has been alternately ascribed to cynical calculation and deep hatred.[44] But whether he was a trimming careerist, a fanatic believer, or both, when at last he became his own man—or as much of one as it is possible for the minister of an autocrat to be—he displayed an unexpected independence on the Jewish question. He had neither sympathy for the Jews nor did he envision or achieve substantial improvements in their status. Yet it was he who with pragmatic flexibility signaled the first correction of course in government policy in more than twenty years.

Much of what is known or believed about Pleve—his part in the Kishinev pogrom, in drafting Ignatyev's rules and the project for their strengthening—comes from the pen of his rival and adversary, Sergey Witte. The differences between the two powerful ministers ranged from the personal to the political, reflecting as well long-standing conflicts between their ministries over policies and priorities. Finance, under Witte's direction since 1892, stood for economic development, for putting restraints on the stifling and arbitrary practices of the bureaucracy so that a climate of legality and predictability might be created in which the enterprise and energy of all loyal citizens could bring private and public benefits. Interior was fearful of giving scope to autonomous social or economic forces; it was preoccupied with stability and control, with maintaining the barriers that safeguarded authority and order. These disagreements extended to Jewish matters as well, but

---

[42] Bogdanovič, *Dnevnik* (n. 30, above), p. 290; on Pleve's return of Jewish affairs to the Police Department after their temporary removal in 1900, see L. Aizenberg, "'Vidy pravitel'stva v evrejskom voprose," *Evrejskaja Letopis'*, 1:37–51.

[43] Kh. Beilin, "Snošenija Prof. Janžula s Pleve po evrejskomu voprosu; 1902 g.," *Evrejskaja Starina*, 9 (1916):329.

[44] Vitte, *Vospominanija*, 2:214–216; Sliozberg, *Gincburg*, p. 107; Zajončkovskij, *Rossijskoe samoderžavie*, p. 153; Louis Greenberg, *The Jews in Russia* (New Haven, 1965), 2:130.

when they were first aired between the two men there was a curious reversal of roles.⁴⁵

In January 1903, the request of a Jewish mutual aid society for permission to open a workhouse in Vilno for indigent Jews came before a meeting of a governmental committee (*Komitet popechitel'stva o domakh trudoljubija*). Seconded by the head of the corps of gendarmes, it was Witte who opposed and Pleve who, together with his assistant P. N. Durnovo, favored granting the petition. There were matters at issue here—Zubatov, his "independents," whether unions of mutual aid should be allowed, which ministry should supervise them—that did not necessarily bear on the Jewish question. But it was against its background that both sides stated their positions in the debate which was all the more interesting for the fact that it was attended by the Empress as patroness of the committee.

Pleve began by reaffirming that he considered the Jews, because of their characteristics and political activities, to be a danger to state and nation. The government therefore had the right and obligation to take protective measures against them and to deny them equality with the Christian population. But this should not mean indifference to the hardships of their situation. People who were poor, unemployed or ill-paid, packed into the unhealthy quarters of crowded cities and towns would naturally be hostile to those they held responsible for their plight. And if the young were particularly restive, it was the breakdown of religious authority and family bonds that had contributed to this. "Therefore, despite everything that I have said, one must ... support all steps towards the relief of the Jews that will through mutual help remove as far as possible their grievous economic burden...."

Witte also opened by outlining his position. He had always, he declared, thought unnecessary and unjust the restrictive measures against the Jews whom as Minister of Finance he valued for their usefulness in trade and industry. The opening of the Vilno workhouse would no doubt be beneficial, but there was more at stake than granting or withholding permission. If it were granted, there would follow a flood of similar petitions which precedent would make it difficult to turn down. And that would create the impression that the government was giving special privileges to the Jews. Turning to the Empress, Witte warned:

The opinion will arise that the Jews, hitherto limited in their rights, enjoy the patronage of the Committee and that of Your Imperial Majesty. The Committee itself will then be taken up chiefly with questions of Jewish mutual aid. In such a state of affairs one cannot but see a certain danger to which I feel obliged to call the Committee's attention.

---
⁴⁵ As a staff member of the journal *Trudovaja Pomošč'*, the jurist A. F. Koni attended the meeting at which, on January 7, 1903, Pleve and Witte aired their views on the Jewish question. His notes in: A. F. Koni, *Na žiznennom puti* (Leningrad, 1929), 5:283-286. Cf.

Pleve denied the danger Witte professed to see, and in reverting to the miserable living conditions of the Pale appeared to suggest where real danger lay. "The government must not overlook the possibility of exerting a conciliatory influence; this is demanded by the interests of the state and of a sensible policy...." The appeal to political interest and good sense lost; the one addressed to the Empress's and the committee's fears of becoming protectors of the Jews won.

Clearly, Pleve was capable of being "sensible" on the Jewish question or at least of accepting the advice of "reasonable" men, like P. N. Durnovo, even before Kishinev and any need he may have felt to counter the storm of protest it aroused at home and abroad. As far as one can tell, being sensible meant just enough concessions, just enough flexibility to reduce the pressures generated by the Jewish problem to manageable proportions and to deprive the revolution of its most dangerous and numerous soldiers. The country's six million Jews had furnished these, Pleve told Count Aehrenthal, the Austrian ambassador, adding that all terrorist attacks of the previous years had, at the very least, been based on Jewish instigation. He also assured Aehrenthal, who craved assurance, that there would be no compromising with the Jews.[46] Yet on May 10, 1903, while prohibiting land purchases by Jews in any of the rural districts of the empire, he also carried out Sipyagin's intention of opening to them 101 localities in the Pale that had lost their rural character and had been closed in 1882. Shortly thereafter he expanded the list by 57 localities and resisted attempts to reduce their number in the Committee of Ministers by arguing that overcrowding in the cities of the Pale was a cause of poverty and potential disturbances. At about the same time, quotas at higher educational institutions, cut a few years earlier, were restored to the level of 1887. In June, 1904, the prohibition on Jewish residence within fifty versts of the western border was lifted.[47]

Pleve may have been happy over the lesson that the pogroms administered to the Jews.[48] But he was also worried by their anger and frustration and wished to create safety valves for them in the form of minimal concessions and emigration. That is why he tolerated the Zionist movement for a time and

---

Jeremiah Schneidermann, "The Tsarist Government and the Labor Movement, 1898–1903: The *Zubatovshchina*," unpubl. doctoral dissertation, University of California (Berkeley, 1966), pp. 452–458. On the Independent Jewish Workers' Party, see Mishkinsky, n. 47 below.

[46] Hans Heilbronner, "Count Aehrenthal and Russian Jewry, 1903–1907," *Journal of Modern History*, 38, no. 4 (December 1966): 394–406.

[47] Gessen, *Zakon i žizn'*, pp. 172–173; Sliozberg, *Dela*, 3:90–91; Dubnov, *Evrei v Rossii* (n. 1, above), bk. 2, 47; Moshe Mishkinsky, "State Socialism and the Policy of the Tsarist Regime Towards the Jews," (Hebrew) *Zion*, 25, nos. 3–4 (1960):245; I. I. Tolstoy, *Der Anti-Semitismus in Russland*, trans. A. Silberstein (Frankfurt, 1909), p. 81.

[48] "Dnevnik Kuropatkina," *Krasnyj Arkhiv*, 2 (1922):43.

twice received Herzl in August 1903.⁴⁹ Herzl's reports of their conversations contain the fullest and most explicit statement we possess of Pleve's opinions on Russia and the Jews; corroborated in most of its parts by other testimony, it is also the most revealing.⁵⁰

During the first interview, Pleve set forth the government's position on the Jewish question which he called an important but not a vital one. The Russian state wished, as a matter of course, for a homogeneity of population. Knowing, however, that this was not fully attainable, it required of all the empire's nationalities, including the Jews, their loyal acceptance and affirmation of the regime. The ultimate goal for the Jews was assimilation, to be achieved through higher education and economic betterment. Whoever fulfilled certain conditions of either kind and of whom it could be safely assumed that education or material wellbeing had made him an adherent of the existing order would be granted rights of citizenship. True, the process of assimilation was proceeding with painful slowness. But educational opportunities could not be made more widely accessible, because there would then be no positions left for Christian graduates, and economic conditions in the Pale were admittedly bad. Moreover, the problem had been complicated in recent years by Jewish adherence to the radical parties. "We were sympathetic to your Zionist movement as long as it worked towards emigration. But since the Minsk Congress we have noted *un changement des gros bonnets*. There is less talk now of Palestinian Zionism than of culture, organization, and Jewish nationality. That is not to our liking."

After opening the second interview with unctuous assurances that the emperor was equally well disposed to all his subjects and had been deeply wounded by charges of inhumanity made abroad, Pleve returned to the question of emigration. It was easy for foreigners to assume a stance of moral superiority and preach generosity, but when it came to accepting two or three millions of poor Jews, they changed their tune and left Russia alone to deal with the problem. The situation of the Russian Jews was, admittedly, an unhappy one, their hostility to the regime understandable, and the government's approach to the problem unavoidable. It would, therefore, welcome the establishment of a Jewish state to absorb several million emigrants while wishing to keep those—the most capable and prosperous—who could be assimilated. "We have no antipathy for Jews as such. . . . "

Could not, Herzl asked, something be done meanwhile for those who were remaining in Russia—extension of the right of residence to Courland and Riga or acquisition of land for agricultural purposes? It would make his work of

---

[49] Schneidermann, "Zubatovshchina," pp. 456–457; Dubnov, *Evrei v Rossii*, bk. 2: 48–49.
[50] *Theodor Herzls Tagebuecher, 1895–1904* (Berlin, 1923), 3: 463–466; 477–483.

pacification easier. To the question of Courland and Riga, Pleve replied, he had already given sympathetic attention. "We have absolutely nothing against letting Jews move where they do not put the population at an economic disadvantage. In the Baltic provinces, where they will have to deal with Germans and Latvians, it should be possible to admit them." Individual land purchases were another matter. An earlier plan of his to allow the acquisition of from three to five desiatinas had run into such fierce opposition that it had to be abandoned. What might be feasible were agricultural communities of Jews—*des bourgs juifs*—within which individuals could acquire in private ownership part of the communal land.

Pleve's readiness to meet so prominent a Jewish figure as Herzl without concealment was motivated by more than the wish to assist the emigration of Russian Jews. It may, in fact, have been the lesser part of his purpose. Believing that Jewish bankers abroad were helping to subsidize the oppositional movement or were needed for the negotiation of a foreign loan, he initiated a number of conciliatory steps in the month of Herzl's visit. A. A. Lopukhin, Director of the Police Department, contacted Baron Ginsburg at Pleve's behest. In exchange for the cooperation of Jewish bankers in Europe and the United States, Pleve was disposed to allow young people who had finished secondary or higher courses of study to live outside the Pale and to propose exemptions from the May Laws—rental of real estate in rural areas, purchase of small plots for agriculture, possibly others.[51]

In August also, Pleve invited the opinions of governors of the Pale on existing Jewish legislation, preparatory to its review and codification. The responses yielded a curious mixture of calls for continued repression and liberalization. It is all the more remarkable therefore, and a possible clue to Pleve's intentions, that the commission which he summoned in January 1904 resolved to improve the legal status of the Jews, beginning with the revocation of the rules of 1882. Such an outcome could not have been predicted from the committee's composition. "It was proposed to start by granting equal rights," Prince Urusov, Governor of Bessarabia and one of the liberal minority recalled in his memoirs, "and to discuss the exceptions, the vital necessity of which was thought to be proved in each case by the personal convictions and experience of the commission."[52]

The outbreak of the Japanese war interrupted the commission's deliberations. It was adjourned on January 27th and never recalled. No other Jewish committee or commission took up its work. Negotiations with Jewish financiers

---

[51] Sliozberg, *Dela*, 3:97, 101.
[52] Urusov, *Memoirs* (n. 39, above), p. 177; *Evr. Ėnciklopedija*, 9-692. Dubnov, incorrectly, I think, viewed the summoning of the commission as the prelude to new repressions: *Novejšaja istorija*, 3:380 and *Evrei v Rossii*, bk. 2:54.

abroad were no more successful. Sliozberg, acting for Baron Ginsburg, met with Jacob Schiff of Kuhn, Loeb and Company in Frankfurt and with Alphonse Rothschild in Paris. The former refused to bargain for Jewish rights and, according to Sliozberg, declined to enter into financial arrangements with a country that denied the protection of the law to any of its citizens. Rothschild made no response at all to Sliozberg's report of the offer and his firm took no part in floating a Russian loan.[53] Pleve's death at the hands of Egor Sazonov in July 1904 put an end to further initiatives on his part and makes difficult a judgment of his ultimate aims.

Was he a genuine believer in the desirability of assimilation for the "better" categories of Jews? In all likelihood, yes, for he spoke of it not only to Herzl and Lucien Wolf, but also in a secret circular to governors.[54] It was for him an essential part of a three-fold program which embraced emigration and improved economic opportunities in the Pale. For a host of reasons, such a program was bound to fail; it could not gain for Pleve the benefits that he expected from it. Selective assimilation, which was in essence a return to the policy of Alexander II, was no longer a real possibility; the benefits of emigration and improved living standards among the poor Jewish proletarians whom Pleve so greatly feared would not be felt for a long time. The more so since the core provinces would remain rigidly shut to their vast bulk. On that point Pleve was particularly firm. "He shares the opinion of those," Lucien Wolf reported him as saying in an interview of which Pleve approved the text, "that it is difficult to give the Jews free access to the Russian interior, because the Russian peasant is himself very poor and would then have to share the little he has with the newcomers who are, for the most part, non-producers."[55]

A problem of such magnitude as Pleve thought the Jewish one to be could no longer be neutralized by partial remedies. On the contrary, partial remedies would intensify it by emphasizing the fact that the Jews remained a special and inferior category of the tsar's subjects. Pleve was unable to see that neither homogeneity nor loyalty based on self-interest could be achieved in a polity that persisted in differentiating its members along confessional and ethnic lines. That inability gave to his program a delusional quality that attaches also to his perception of other challenges to the regime. It is difficult

---

[53] Note 51 above.

[54] Schneidermann, "*Zubatovshchina*," p. 457; A. Braudo, "Beseda V. K. Pleve s L. Vol'fom (1903)," *Evrejskaja Starina*, 9 (1916): 121–125. On Wolf, the "Foreign Secretary of Anglo-Jewry," see Szajkowski in *Jewish Social Studies*, 39, no. 1 (January 1967): 3. The text of Pleve's circular of 24 June 1903, warning against the growth of Zionist tendencies because they were hostile to assimilation, in *Evrejskaja Starina*, 8 (1915): 412–414. There is a mimeographed copy at the Hoover Institution, Okhrana Archives, Index XVIII b, Folder 2.

[55] Braudo, *Evrejskaja Starina*, 9 (1916): 122.

to predict whether his pragmatism or his delusions would have prevailed if, as was certain to be the case, his initiatives did not bring the desired results. The radical changes required in Jewish policy were as difficult for him as was yielding to the many other pressures for change he faced. He once admitted, in private, that the country's oppositional mood had deep roots, that it was not merely the product of artificial stimulation. Russia might indeed be on the eve of great upheavals, but it was precisely for that reason that the state must do battle against the forces threatening its survival. "If we cannot change the course of historical events which will shake the state, then we are obliged to dam it, to hold it back, not to swim with the current or try always to keep abreast of it."[56]

2

The shock of Pleve's death and the joy with which society greeted it, at last convinced even Nicholas that a tactical retreat before the forces of opposition was advisable. To carry this out, he appointed as Pleve's successor Prince Svyatopolk-Mirsky, a former chief of gendarmes, Director of the Police Department and Assistant Minister of the Interior who had resigned that post in 1902 because he disapproved of Pleve's harshness in dealing with dissent. Even before his appointment, which was received as the harbinger of a political spring, Mirsky, then Governor-General of Vilno, had commented in his first annual report to the Emperor on the unhappy consequences of Ignatyev's rules. The misery of the Jewish masses made their further confinement in the cities impossible; in any case, there was no longer any reason to bar them from the countryside. The state liquor monopoly had significantly reduced the potential for Jewish exploitation of the peasantry, while Jewish craftsmen could be of real benefit to villages deficient in their skills. For these and other reasons, Mirsky pleaded for a change in the laws.[57]

For all the good intentions he proclaimed on assuming office, the "liberal" minister, who was distrusted by the Emperor, did as little to aid the Jews as his reactionary predecessor. Mirsky had told a Jewish delegation on leaving Vilno that he regarded the situation of the Jews as the greatest anomaly in all of Russia and that it would have to undergo a radical change. To foreign journalists he stated his intention of abolishing restrictions. In an official declaration, he spoke of expanding the limits of religious toleration and freedom of conscience, of removing all religious and national disabilities insofar

---

[56] "Otryvki iz vospominanij D. N. Ljubimova," *Istoričeskij Arkhiv*, no. 6 (1962):82–83.
[57] Pawel Korzec, ed., "Un document inédit sur la question juive en Russie au début du XXe siècle," trans. Catherine Denis, *Cahiers du monde russe et soviétique*, 5, no. 2 (April-June 1970):278–291. Cf. *Evr. Ènciklopedija*, 5:821; Gessen, *Zakon i žizn'*, p. 172.

as this did not run counter to the interests of the state power.[58] In practice, he was able to accomplish little. There was neither enough time nor support. On the occasion of the birth of an heir, August 11, 1904, certain categories of Jews were exempted from the provisions of the May 1882 Rules and to family members of the most privileged strata the right of universal residence was extended.[59] It was all that Mirsky accomplished before he was dismissed in January 1905, and the ground for it was prepared by Pleve. "The government has not paid due attention to the labor problem," Witte complained in the Committee of Ministers in December. "It has not alleviated the oppressed conditions of the Jews. It has not found a way of pacifying the students."[60]

Of all tsarist statesmen, Witte gave rise to the greatest expectations for the improvement of the Jewish situation.[61] He had on several occasions expressed the view that the whole system of persecution and discrimination was illogical and harmful. As the country's first prime minister and head of a unified cabinet under the new constitutional arrangements of October 1905 of which he was the author, Witte, it was thought, would be able to translate into practice what he preached. It soon became clear that a Russian premier's authority, his ability to pursue policies he thought best, was not very much greater after October 1905 than before. Power, as always, was derived from the tsar and was proportionate to the confidence he reposed in his chief servants and the support he deigned to give them. Witte, having once before fallen from favor and having had to spend two impatient years in relative impotence, was not in 1905 prepared to take great risks. After the success of his supreme effort to persuade a reluctant Nicholas to agree to the issuance of the October Manifesto, he moved with circumspection.

His tenuous hold on office was not, however, the only reason for the caution with which Witte moved on the Jewish question during the months he was Chairman of the Council of Ministers—October 1905 to April 1906. He had long been sensitive to the charge that he was a friend of the Jews or in their pay and once said plaintively to a colleague that he had defended them as a matter of principle and because they, like foreigners and their capital, were

---

[58] Gurko, *Features* (n. 41, above), p. 279; S. E. Kryžanovskij, *Vospominanija* (Berlin, n.d.), pp. 17, 21, 26; Dubnov, *Novejšaja istorija*, 3:383; Bogdanovič, *Dnevnik*, pp. 303, 309; Shmarya Levin, *The Arena*, trans. Maurice Samuel (New York, 1932), p. 277; Dubnov, *Evrei v Rossii*, bk. 2:62.

[59] *Ibid.*, pp. 57–58; Gessen, *Zakon i žizn'*, pp. 173, 175, 186 (n. 106). Sliozberg, *Dela*, 3: 102, gives main credit for these measures to Kokovtsev, as did Kokovtsev himself. Since they affected almost exclusively professionals and artisans (and only as long as the latter plied their crafts), they could not cause a substantial influx into rural districts or lead to land purchases there.

[60] Gurko, *Features*, p. 320.

[61] Szajkowski in *Jewish Social Studies*, 29, no. 1 (January 1967):5–6.

essential to Russia.⁶² He was also excessively conscious of the difficulties and complexities of Jewish emancipation—so conscious in fact that his endorsement of equal rights became, at the critical moment, a qualified one.

Witte's most famous pronouncement on the question of Jewish rights was made to Alexander III. Witte not only recalled it in his memoirs, written many years after the event; he also quoted himself on other occasions such as during an interview with Herzl in 1903. To the tsar's question whether he was friendly to the Jews, Witte reports himself as replying: since one could not drown all Russian Jews in the Black Sea, there was no other way of dealing with them than to give them the same rights as all Russian subjects. This was, of course, to be done gradually—how gradually, Witte did not specify to Alexander, who, as far as is known, made neither a positive nor negative answer to his Minister of Finance. In his memoirs Witte estimated that it would take decades, and more likely centuries, before the problem could be ignored and the Jews treated as they were in most countries. "The racial peculiarities of the Jews can be erased only gradually and slowly." A sensible policy towards them was a prerequisite, and Witte was as unhappy (at least in retrospect) with what had been done by the admired Alexander as he was distressed by what the weak and unstable Nicholas was still doing. If only the removal of exceptional laws begun by Alexander II had been continued, there would no longer be a Jewish question, and the Jews would not have become "one of the malignant factors of our accursed revolution."⁶³

There is a discrepancy between Witte's expectation that twenty more years of a liberal policy would have transformed the Jews, and his abiding belief in the stubbornly racial character of their vices. His feelings toward them were not free of ambivalence.⁶⁴ In that respect, he was not different from most of his contemporaries, in Russia and elsewhere. Although at critical times these contradictions caused inconsistency and hesitation in his conduct, they were never strong enough to overwhelm Witte's basically utilitarian and rational outlook. He did not fight, or even speak boldly, for doing justice to the Jews. Yet when he could do so without great cost to himself or to what he considered to be the interest of the state, he resisted making the Jewish plight worse and favored attempts to improve their condition. He saw the Jewish role in the revolutionary movement as a factor complicating such attempts. Seven

---

⁶² Kuropatkin, "Dnevnik," *Krasnyj Arkhiv*, 2 (1922):26. Cf. Polovcev, "Dnevnik," *ibid.*, 3 (1923):99; Lev Tikhomirov, "25 let nazad," *ibid.*, 39 (1930):55, 57; G. O. Raukh, "Dnevnik," *ibid.*, 19 (1926):90–91; Ernst Seraphim, "Zar Nikolaus II und Graf Witte," *Historische Zeitschrift*, 156, no. 2 (1940):285; *Velikaja vsemirnaja liga* (Moscow, 1906), pp. 3, 17; *Velikij zagovor* (Moscow, 1907), pp. 73–74.

⁶³ Vitte, *Vospominanija*, 2:210–212, and 1:40, 144.

⁶⁴ *Ibid.*, 1:40, 88; Letter to Pobedonostsev, *Krasnyj Arkhiv*, 30 (1928):90.

million Jews, or 5 percent of the population, he told Herzl in 1903, furnished half the membership of the revolutionary parties.[65]

After Witte had delivered himself of this and other remarks about Jewish arrogance, usury, and pandering, Herzl was right to wonder what the enemies of the Jews sounded like if their friends spoke as Witte did. Yet when Herzl asked to what Witte attributed the high incidence of Jewish radicalism, the latter replied: "I believe it is the fault of the government. The Jews are too much oppressed." He had, indeed, as Herzl noted, done very little to alleviate that oppression during the many years he had held high office. He maintained good business relations with Jewish railroad entrepreneurs, employed Jewish technicians, engineers, and managers, pointed out to Nicholas that discrimination made it more difficult to attract foreign and Jewish capital, and protested against closing Siberia to Jews.[66]

Not until late 1904 and early 1905, however, did Witte argue in the Committee of Ministers, which he chaired, for a more comprehensive approach. The active hostility of the Jews, he said on February 11, 1905, was provoked by economic hardship and oppressive laws; it would continue to plague the police until and unless the vague promise of an imperial decree of December 12, 1904, was carried out to ease the lot of national and religious minorities.[67] The committee's May 3 report to the tsar deplored the lack of consistency and clarity in the treatment of the Jewish problem which a "multitude of materials collected at various times" and repeated discussion at the highest levels had brought no nearer to solution. Even so, the committee did no more than propose the formation of still another "inter-departmental conference" which was to submit its proposals to the elected consultative assembly announced in a manifesto of February 18. In that way it was hoped to find a Jewish policy that would gain popular acceptance. Neither conference nor assembly ever met.[68] Just as Witte departed for Portsmouth, New Hampshire, in July to conduct peace negotiations with the Japanese, the electoral law for the future assembly (the so-called Bulygin Duma, named after Mirsky's successor), was being discussed. It was Witte's view, shared and put forward by the Minister of Finance, Kokovtsev, that the Jews should not be denied the franchise. That view prevailed with Nicholas when it was supported by General D. F. Trepov, Assistant Minister of the Interior in charge of the police, who argued that the Jewish population had to be calmed. Witte received word of the decision in

---

[65] Herzl, *Tagebuecher* (n. 50, above), 3:472.

[66] Vitte, *Vospominanija*, 1:40, 144; "Dokladnaja zapiska Vitte Nikolaju II," *Khrestomatija istorii SSSR*, 3 (1952):227; Sliozberg, *Dela*, 2:264-266; idem., *Gincburg*, pp. 135-136.

[67] Dubnov, *Novejšaja istorija*, 3:387.

[68] *Komitet ministrov o evrejskom voprose* (St. Petersburg, n.d.).

America and was able to cite it as proof of his government's good will in conversations with Jewish bankers.[69]

The meetings held with Oscar Strauss, Jacob Schiff, Isaac Seligman, and others at Witte's request, demonstrated to his interlocutors how far he still was from understanding Jewish needs and demands, how much he still thought in terms of favors, exemptions, privileges, and concessions. To the historian it shows, besides, how much this difficult and complicated man willfully or unconsciously misread the reactions of his listeners. Witte cabled Foreign Minister Lamsdorff an account of the evening he had spent with "the main leaders of American Jewry, who have substantial influence on public opinion here, have vast funds at their disposal, and help the Japanese government in monetary operations." He reported his impression that these men knew of the Jewish question in Russia from extremely one-sided sources, notably the immigrants arriving in America in great numbers. The situation of the Russian Jews had been presented to them in a light bound to make them enemies of Russia, and he undertook to set them right.[70]

Witte told his American listeners that all the steps his government had undertaken in the reign of Nicholas, and especially in the recent past, had as their purpose to alleviate the Jewish condition. He had cited facts, Witte reported, which could not be refuted. "My talk, in the opinion of Baron Rosen [the Russian Ambassador in Washington], may have a significant impact on public opinion here and cannot, in any case, fail to alarm the Japanese, since the men who visited me are their bankers." The impression his visitors carried away was quite different. Their letter to Witte of September 5, 1905, reads, in part:

> As we stated to you at our conference, it is our very decided conviction that nothing but the granting of full civil rights to the Jewish subjects of the Czar will entirely remove the conditions which have been the cause of so much disturbance in Russia and adverse criticism abroad. You have answered that the Russian Jew in general is not sufficiently prepared for the exercise of full civil rights, and that the feeling of the Russian people is such that the Jew cannot be placed on an equal footing with them without causing serious internal disorders, and you suggested that it might be advisable and practicable gradually to remove the existing disabilities and thus to prepare the way for an eventual total granting of civic equality. As to this we aver that the million or more of Russian Jews who have come to the United States have become good citizens, notwithstanding their sudden emergence from the greatest darkness into the most intense daylight of political and civil

---

[69] *Petergofskoe soveščanie o proekte gosudarstvennoj dumy pod ličnym ego imperatorskogo veličestva predsedatel'stvom; sekretnye protokoly* (Berlin, n.d.), pp. 112–113, 162–163. Kokovtsev, speaking during the session of July 25, remarked that for some reason it had become the traditional duty of the Minister of Finance to defend the Jews; he would not shirk that obligation. Also see Sliozberg, *Dela,* 3:173–174; Kryžanovskij, *Vospominanija,* p. 40; Dubnov, *Istorija evreev,* bk. 2:72; "Portsmut," *Krasnyj Arkhiv,* 6 (1924):27.

[70] *Ibid.,* p. 33.

liberty, and that they have shown themselves entirely equal to the responsibilities which
have been placed upon them as citizens of this great republic.... While it may be true
that a state of envy against the Jews exists among part of the Russian people, for which
the Russian government is to some extent responsible, still, in our opinion, placing the
Jews at once on a footing of civic equality with the rest of the population would cause no
more friction than each one of the steps leading to the same ultimate end. This very
objection urged by you seems to us good reason why this should be settled once and for all,
instead of allowing it to drag on painfully, creating new disturbances at every stage.[71]

Witte would not or could not see that a piecemeal approach was no longer
adequate. Perhaps he thought that the Emperor would approve no other,
although he appears not to have put this to a clear test. Quite probably, he
was truly fearful of a violent popular reaction. He knew, or learned, after
becoming head of the cabinet in October 1905, that popular excesses against
the Jews were being fanned and abetted by certain officials in the Department
of Police.[72] But he did not doubt, as few educated Russians doubted, the
reality and awesome potential of mob violence. He warned of it repeatedly and
must have been all the more confident of his predictions of mass rage because
he shared some of the prejudices that made it probable. All that happened in
1905 and after, the pogroms and the renewed growth of anti-Semitism in
government and society, confirmed for Witte the caution he had preached and
observed.

To representatives of Russian Jewry who called on him shortly after his
appointment, Witte spoke as he had spoken in America and as he would speak
again to French and German Jews in 1907.[73] The goal for Russia was that of
all civilized countries, full citizenship. But to avoid peasant pogroms it would
have to come slowly and would require Jewish abstention from oppositional
politics. Jewish leaders must publicly declare to the monarch—who alone
could help them—that they asked no more than to receive the same treatment
as his other loyal subjects. They must prove their loyalty by their conduct and
by withdrawing support from the liberation movement and its goal of political
and civil liberty. It did not strike Witte as contradictory that he was asking
Jews to be more loyal than other Russians, but this was not the first attempt
to square the circle on the part of a man who had hoped to preserve autocracy
by issuing a constitution.

---

[71] The text of the letter, signed by Jacob Schiff, Isaac Seligman, Oscar Strauss, Adolph
Lewisohn, and Adolph Kraus, in Cyrus Adler and A. M. Margalith, *With Firmness in the
Right. American Diplomatic Action Affecting Jews, 1840–1945* (New York, 1946). A shorter
version, described as a promemoria, appeared on 20 September 1905 in *Russische Korrespondenz*
in Berlin. This was one of three informational bulletins published by Jewish
organizations in Western Europe to bring the plight of Russian Jews to the attention of
public opinion. (Szajkowski, note 61 above). Cf. Sliozberg, *Dela*, 3:163.

[72] *Ibid.*, 179–180, 188; Lopukhin, *Otryvki*, pp. 82–90; *Russische Korrespondenz*, 31
October 1906.

[73] Vitte, *Vospominanija*, 3:327–329, 2:440.

In view of what he wrote in his *apologia pro officio suo*, it is unlikely (as rumored in a rightist salon) that days before his dismissal in April 1906, Witte at a cabinet session attended by the Emperor, proposed an amendment to the Fundamental Laws on Jewish equality.[74]

As long as the Jewish question is not dealt with in a correct, dispassionate, humane, and statesmanlike fashion, Russia will not find peace. But I am very much afraid that full rights, if suddenly given to the Jews, may create much new turbulence and will once again complicate matters. This, like all political questions touching the masses and what might be called historical prejudices—which are to a certain degree caused by racial characteristics, especially the less attractive kind—can only be solved unhurriedly, by degrees. All hasty or abrupt decisions upset stability.... The state is a living organism, and it is necessary, therefore, to be most careful of performing radical operations upon it. [75]

The services Witte had rendered the monarchy during Russia's first revolution—an end to the Japanese war, the strategic retreat of the October Manifesto, the successful conclusion of a foreign loan just before he left office—enabled Nicholas to rid himself of the man he would forever blame for the diminution of his authority. "I have never seen such a chameleon, a man of such changeable convictions," he wrote to his mother. "Because of that, almost no one trusts him any longer; he has finally undone himself in everyone's eyes, except perhaps for the foreign Yids."[76] Such benefits as Witte, might, in fact, have sought or promised to seek for the Jews were meant to placate both the rich and the radical among them, and to facilitate the job of putting down the revolution and coping with the parliamentary opposition. It was not any concessions to the Jews, however, that gave the government the upper hand over strikes and agrarian riots, but the return of the army from Manchuria and the loan effected through an international syndicate.

---

[74] Bogdanovič, *Dnevnik*, pp. 388–389. In the letter in which on 14 April 1906 Witte asked Nicholas to relieve him of his post, he did, however, give as one of the reasons for his inability to stay the incompatibility of his views with the extremely conservative ones of the Minister of the Interior, Durnovo, on the problem of the Jews, the agrarian question, and others. If Witte thought in this way to give his ministry a more liberal complexion, he miscalculated (*Vospominanija*, 3:338.) A passage in the memoirs of P. L. Bark, Minister of Finance from 1913 to 1917, may stand as a summary of the difficulties that a fair assessment of Witte's words and deeds on the Jewish question presents. "I remember that at a meeting of the Finance Committee [in 1905 or 1906], Count Witte openly declared his deep belief in the necessity of giving equal rights to the Jews and that such a measure would lead to the restoration of normalcy in the Empire. Unfortunately, however, political conditions were such that he thought the realization of this reform impossible. I have no specific information about what steps were taken by the Chairman of the Council of Ministers to ease the plight of the Jews, but do not doubt that he tried to convince the Emperor to take the appropriate steps and that the reactionaries prevented this." P. L. Bark, "Vospominanija," *Vozroždenie* (Paris), no. 172 (April 1966):97.

[75] Vitte, *Vospominanija*, 2:214.

[76] Kryžanovskij, *Vospominanija*, p. 73, note, gives this excerpt in Russian. An English version of the entire letter in E. J. Bing, ed., *The Secret Letters of the Last Tsar* (New York, 1938), p. 211.

Although Witte had helped the regime to recover nerve and strength, the men who inherited his responsibilities were not until another year had passed quite certain that the specter of revolution had been decisively laid to rest and that the Jews were not one of the chief elements keeping it alive. Striking workers and plundering peasants, although less numerous than in 1905, were still troublesome in 1906, and they might once again, as in the previous October, join forces with the political opposition which now appealed to them from the rostrum of the Duma. The Jews were believed to be a factor in this that could not be ignored. There were a dozen of them in the first Duma, which soon took up the question of Jewish rights; pogroms and the government's involvement in them became the subject of parliamentary debate and inquiry; above all, there was still the fear among those in charge of Russia's destinies that the combination of Jewish money and Jewish misery made for a potent and dangerous mixture.

The new premier appointed in July, P. A. Stolypin (he had been Minister of the Interior in the Goremykin cabinet since April and retained that post), is supposed to have said, in words that were almost the same as Pleve had used, that he too would be throwing bombs if he lived as did the Jews.[77] After dissolving the first Duma to call for new elections, he negotiated with a number of moderate political figures in hopes of inducing them to join his government and thus gain for it a measure of public acceptance. In discussions with Prince G. E. Lvov and Dmitry Shipov of the Party of Peaceful Renovation, Stolypin was asked for his program and replied that now was the time for action, not words. To calm all classes of the population and to bring them over to the side of the government, the most urgent needs of each had to be met as quickly as possible. Influential Jews, for example, should be approached and some agreement reached with them on the steps that could and should be taken to combat the rebellious spirit among their coreligionists.[78]

Shipov and Lvov, veterans of the zemstvo movement and the fight for representative government, were appalled at the new premier's readiness to disregard the Fundamental Laws that had just been adopted requiring the assent of the Duma to all legislation. They could not understand, they told him, how after October 17th the government could decide what reforms were to be carried out without consulting the people's elected representatives. Stolypin replied that since he saw clearly what measures were necessary and the Duma had shown little legislative capacity, the government was in the best position to satisfy without delay the pressing needs of the country. Shipov and Lvov declined his invitation. They knew that the country had gone

---

[77] "V Rossii i za granicej," *Russkaja Mysl'*, no. 10 (October 1911): 2.

[78] D. N. Šipov, *Vospominanija i dumy o perežitom* (Moscow, 1918), pp. 461–466.

beyond their cautious brand of liberalism and that Stolypin wished to use them mainly for decorative purposes. For them the Jewish proposal was not a pretext; but in the post–1905 period the obligation to seek Duma approval for any substantial change in the legal status of the Jews became an additional argument for going slow, used by enemies of the Jews as well as by friends of constitutional correctness.

Among the latter were several prominent figures of the right wing of Russian constitutionalism, the Octobrists Alexander Guchkov, Count Peter Heyden, and A. F. Koni, whom Stolypin had also sounded out on their willingness to enter his cabinet. They agreed among themselves that any government they joined must, to disarm the revolution, publicly commit itself to agrarian reform, the extension of local self-government, and the solution of the Jewish question. It was Guchkov—surprisingly, in view of his Great Russian chauvinism—who spoke for the immediate abolition of the Pale, whereas the more liberal Koni conjured up the risks: ten million Jews flooding the heart of Russia and resulting pogroms. Though just, a step of such magnitude and danger should not be taken by the Council of Ministers, but by the nation's chosen spokesmen who might, after all, decide otherwise. Heyden too had expressed sympathy for the principle of civil equality for Jews, peasants, and women during a Duma debate in June, but cautioned against granting it in blanket fashion. Such a complicated business wanted a careful and deliberate approach.[79]

The voices for prudence in the first Duma were in the minority, as Stolypin feared they would be in the second. Before it convened in February 1907, he moved in the direction he had indicated to Shipov and Lvov. A circular of August 24, 1906, announced his intention of removing, as quickly as possible, restrictions that had outlived their usefulness and served only as irritants; questions bearing on essential aspects of the relations between Russians and Jews would be submitted to the national legislature.[80] In October, Stolypin brought the issue to the Council of Ministers. Two participants in the debate— V. I. Gurko, an Assistant Minister of the Interior, and V. N. Kokovtsev, Minister of Finance—differ somewhat in their recollections of it.[81] Gurko tells

---

[79] A. F. Koni, *Sobranie sočinenij* (Moscow, 1966), 2:367; Louis Menashe, "Alexander Guchkov, the Octobrist Party, and the Dilemma of Russian Liberalism," unpubl. doctoral dissertation, New York University (1964), p. 170, note; Sidney Harcave, "The Jewish Question in the First Russian Duma," *Jewish Social Studies*, 6, no. 2 (1944): 162.

[80] Dubnov, *Evrei v Rossii*, bk. 2:83, and *Novejšaja istorija*, 3:405.

[81] Gurko, *Features* (n. 41, above), pp. 504–506; Kokovcev, *Iz moego prošlogo*, (n. 32, above), 1:236–239. The journal of the council's deliberations of 27 and 31 October and 1 December 1906 is available at the Hoover Institution: *Osobye žurnaly Soveta ministrov 1906 g.* (St. Petersburg, 1907). It is no. 157 in the volume and comprises 60 pages; of these pp. 56 through 60 contain the council's specific and very modest proposals. If adopted,

of "further concessions" exempting Jews from military service on physical grounds, admitting them to schools, and widening the categories of those allowed to reside outside the area of Jewish settlement. According to Gurko, he and others were in opposition, but no one objected as the articles of the project were put to the vote, while Kokovtsev, "who often considered matters from the point of view of their reaction upon the stock exchange," defended it in its entirety.

He began by saying that he personally did not like Jews and realized the great harm they were doing. "But," he continued, "I have come to the conclusion that all measures directed against them are ineffective. The Jews are so clever that no law can be counted upon to restrict them. It is useless to lock a door against them, for they are sure to find a passkey to open it. Moreover, a policy of restrictions only irritates the Jews unnecessarily and creates conditions favorable to all sorts of abuses and arbitrariness on the part of the administration and the police. The laws restricting the Jews accomplished nothing except to create sources of revenue for various agents of the administration."

Gurko represents himself as the only[82] one to speak out against the argument that because locks are ineffective, they must be taken off altogether. Either the Jews were harmless, in which case all restrictions must be abolished, or their influence was pernicious, in which case more effective bars should be devised against them. The first course might be the wiser one; deprived of legal protection against the Jews, the population would have to develop its own defenses against them. Partial relief would neither pacify the Jews nor diminish their revolutionary sympathies, but put into their hands a new weapon for fighting the government. "Everybody knows what part the Jews played during the recent upheaval. Now, as a reward, the government is about to give them privileges." After his speech, Gurko relates, others joined in the debate, taking stands for or against the project. "Stolypin seemed at first to side with its defenders; then he became confused and postponed the debate to a later date."

When the council returned to the topic, Gurko was not present, but he reports that its members, at Stolypin's urging, agreed to accept the majority view. The purpose of submitting a unanimous opinion to the tsar, rather than letting him affirm (as was customary) either a majority or minority resolution, was to avoid placing on him alone the onus for either choice. "If the Tsar had adopted a decision to grant the Jews certain rights, it would have antagonized all the Right circles of the public; on the other hand, if he had declined it, it

---

they would have been less important for themselves than as an earnest of the government's intentions.

[82] He had an ally, however, in the state comptroller who made no secret of his views during subsequent meetings. See Hans Heilbronner, "P. K. von Schwanebach and the Dissolution of the First Two Dumas," *Canadian Slavonic Papers*, 11, no. 1 (Spring 1969): 40.

would have increased the antagonism of the Jews, which was not to be disregarded." A majority of the council, Gurko concludes his account, approved the project, with Stolypin himself among the minority, although he himself had placed it before the cabinet. Speculating on the reasons for its rejection by the tsar, Gurko records the rumor that Stolypin had advised him to do so. "There were many other versions, and which was correct I do not know."

In Kokovtsev's shorter account, Stolypin initially asked for a free expression of views. Restrictions, he told the ministers, only angered the Jews, were easily evaded and therefore of no real benefit to the Russian population; they bred a revolutionary spirit among the Jewish masses and provided a pretext for the most outrageous anti-Russian propaganda in the world's most powerful Jewish center, America. Pleve too, Stolypin recalled, had recognized this and had sought to pacify the Jewish masses by certain concessions. Shortly before his death, Pleve had even made some gestures toward reaching an understanding with American Jewry, but had received a very cool response from its leader, Mr. Schiff. "Stolypin added that he had been informed from all sides that at this moment such an attempt might reasonably meet a much better reception if the privileges which we suggested were conceded, even if they did not grant complete equality for the Jews." No objections were raised, Kokovtsev writes; the ministers readily agreed that each should compile a list of those restrictions that fell within his competence. This was done in a very short time and the council agreed that a number of important restrictions should be abolished. Although Stolypin made no mention of having done so, his colleagues all assumed that he would not have raised such a delicate question without first soliciting the Emperor's views.

They were surprised, therefore, that the tsar took so long to act on the council's unanimous recommendation. "We often asked Stolypin what its fate had been and why it had not been returned, and his replies were always assured and confident." Finally, on December 10, Stolypin received a letter from Nicholas and the council's journal containing its recommendation.

I am returning to you the journal on the Jewish question without my confirmation. Long before its submission to me, I thought about this day and night. Despite the most convincing arguments in favor of a positive decision in this matter, an inner voice keeps insisting more and more that I do not take this decision upon myself. So far my conscience has not deceived me. Therefore, I intend in this case also to follow its dictates. I know that you too believe that "the heart of the tsar is in God's hands." So be it. For all those whom I have placed in authority I bear an awesome responsibility before God and am ready at any time to account to Him.[63]

---

[63] Kokovtsev reproduces the tsar's letter in the Russian and English editions of his recollections. The present translation is based on the text in *Krasnyj Arkhiv*, 5 (1924): 105–107, which also contains Stolypin's reply.

Stolypin did not on this occasion insist on having his way, as he would a few years later with the western zemstvo bill, or on pushing through the council's decision by decree, as article 87 of the Fundamental Laws allowed him to do, a practice he followed with peasant legislation. Instead, he wrote to Nicholas, not to change the tsar's mind but to forestall the unpleasantness which his veto of a unanimous cabinet decision might create. It would appear that the Council of Ministers had favored removing certain Jewish disabilities but that the ruler had wished to preserve them. "Your Majesty, we do not have the right to place you in such a position...." To do so, Stolypin continued, was all the more improper since the Emperor himself had pointed out how irrelevant many of the existing laws had become and had merely wished not to remove them before the meeting of the Duma by personal and extraordinary decree. Would His Majesty agree to change his veto message to one of approximately the following content: "Not being in principle opposed to the solution of the question raised by the Council of Ministers, I find it necessary that it be enacted through regular legislative process rather than on the basis of article 87 . . . "? The journal could then be revised to show that the council had not insisted on the issuance of an urgent decree but had sought imperial permission either to take the question to the Duma or to decide it on the basis of article 87. The tsar accepted Stolypin's formula.

Judging from his behaviour as described by Gurko and from the more reliable evidence of his conduct after the tsar's veto, Stolypin's commitment to Jewish reform must be described as qualified, at best. Neither he nor Nicholas showed such a high regard for constitutional proprieties on other issues. Why then had Stolypin, after receiving warning signals from various sides, insisted on bringing up the matter at all? In his letter to the tsar he felt it necessary to explain, perhaps to apologize, something one would expect him to have done earlier in order to secure approval.

The Jewish question was raised by me because the principles of civil equality bestowed by the Manifesto of October 17th give the Jews the rightful expectation of full citizenship. The grant now of partial relief would allow the Duma to put off the full-scale resolution of this problem. Furthermore, I thought to mollify the non-revolutionary part of Jewry and to free our legal system from encumbrances which are the source of innumerable abuses.[84]

Stolypin's is a plausible explanation. He wished to present a smaller target to the opposition in the forthcoming Duma session, to remove this issue from contention in what was sure to be a contentious house, and to split what he assumed to be a powerful Jewish community united in its hostility to the government. There was also advice from Kokovtsev who did, indeed, as Gurko thought, have his eyes on the foreign money market and press. At the

---

[84] *Ibid.*, p. 106.

same time, Stolypin was genuinely fearful of pogroms if more than minimal relief were given to the Jews. As governor of Saratov in October 1905, he had learned with what ease the populace could be inflamed against the Jews in a city where, as he said, there was no cause for a pogrom because there were no Jewish usurers, shopkeepers, or exploiters, no antagonism between Christians and Jews. Asked by a Jewish acquaintance to donate a small sum to a fund for the families of the pogrom's victims to show his disapproval of the perpetrators, Stolypin promised to do so some time in the future. "The rabble is still agitated, and it is necessary to move carefully."[85]

Fear of the mob went together with Stolypin's concern for covering his right flank. The indication Nicholas had given of his feelings toward the Jews, the appearance of anti-Semitic parties and movements, the rumors being spread in conservative drawing rooms that Stolypin was flirting with the Right as well as with liberals and Jews[86]—all this helps to explain the vagaries of his Jewish policy. As the revolutionary wave subsided and a new electoral law, imposed by decree, sharply reduced the number of liberals, radicals, and Jews in the Duma, Jewish reform grew less urgent and politically more costly. The third and fourth Dumas contained a vociferous Right and were dominated by conservative groupings that a minister seeking their support could not ignore. On the Jewish question, the Duma's right wing and most of its center constituted a solid bloc of votes against liberalization, a bloc that was also capable, on occasion, of putting together majorities in favor of discriminatory laws more stringent than those already on the books. Along with the Right the Nationalist Party in particular—which drew its main strength from the western regions of the country and was the premier's main parliamentary ally —was adamantly opposed to any relaxation of constraints upon Jews.[87]

Stolypin's own convictions must have played their part in shaping his political conduct. As landowner, gentry marshal, and governor in provinces (Kovno and Grodno) with heavy Jewish and non-Russian populations, his closeness to the Nationalists was more than mere political calculation. He wished to secure the preeminent and predominant position of the Russian religion and nationality in the empire and did all he could to strengthen that position where it was weak. Yet there remained in his measures concerning Jews an element of inconsistency that makes it impossible to discern in them—

---

[85] Ja. L. Tejtel', *Iz moej žizni* (Paris, 1925), p. 183. In a talk with a French newspaperman in the fall of 1906, Stolypin explained that the postponement of emancipation for the Jews was for their own good. An immediate solution of this complicated question would arouse a storm of public protest. M. Rejsner, "Rossija za granicej," *Vsemirnyj Vestnik*, no. 10 (1906):119.

[86] Bogdanovič, *Dnevnik*, pp. 379, 385, 414.

[87] A. Ja. Avrekh, *Carizm i tret'eijun'skaja sistema* (Moscow, 1966); G. G. Jurskij, *Pravye v Tret'ej Gosudarstvennoj Dume* (Khar'kov, 1912).

or in his two or three recorded expressions of attitude—a clear goal or unifying principle.[88]

During the brief life of the second Duma, its Committee on Freedom of Conscience discussed a government bill removing legal disabilities based on religion but explicitly exempting Jews. Before the committee's version of the bill, amended to include Jews, could reach the floor of the house, the Duma was dissolved on June 3rd.[89] Only days earlier (May 22, 1907), when he had already decided on dissolution, Stolypin issued instructions to governors not to expel from interior provinces, in which they had illegally resided before August 1906, those Jewish families who had established households there and who were neither a danger to public order nor the cause of annoyance to the local population. The circular became the subject of hostile interpellations by Rightist members of the Duma in 1908 and 1910.[90] In 1907 also, a project for the reform of local government would, if passed, have restored the right of Jews to participate in municipal elections, to sit on local boards (*upravy*), and to hold other administrative posts.[91]

In September, Stolypin commented on a letter from the Kiev Union of Russian People that it had at last shown itself capable of seriousness, but that he had long been aware of the subject of its complaint—the improper admission of Jews to the Kiev Polytechnicum—and had already taken appropriate steps.[92] At the same time, the Minister of Education enforced the 10 percent quota at Odessa University. In September 1908 the *numerus clausus*, an administrative rule, became law by imperial decree and in August 1909 it was extended to secondary schools. In Moscow and St. Petersburg the quota was raised from 3 to 5 percent, in the Pale from 10 to 15. In 1911, it was applied

---

[88] Admirers as well as enemies, Jews as well as Russians, have described Stolypin as everything from a friend of the Jews and advocate of emancipation to a rabid anti-Semite. For a sampling of these divergent views see: Frumkin in *Kniga o russkom evrejstve* (n. 21, above), p. 58; A. V. Zen'kovskij, *Pravda o Stolypine* (New York, 1956), pp. 79–80, 85, 108; M. P. Bok, *Vospominanija o moem otce* (New York, 1953), p. 73; L. A., "Stolypin i evrei," *Evrejskaja Letopis'*, 4 (1926):187; A. V. Obolenskij, "Moi vospominanija," *Vozroždenie*, no. 47 (November 1955):98; A. F. Girs, "Svetlye i černye dni, 1909–1911," *Časovoj* (Brussels), no. 330 (April 1953), p. 10; Sergius Gogel, *Die Ursachen der russischen Revolution von 1917* (Berlin, 1926), p. 68; P. G. Kurlov, *Das Ende des russischen Kaisertums* (Berlin, 1920), pp. 166–168; Arkadij Stolypin, ed., *P. A. Stolypin* (Paris, 1927), p. 50; *Russische Korrespondenz*, 4 August 1911.

[89] Dubnov, *Evrei v Rossii*, bk. 2:84.

[90] *Ibid.*, 83; idem., *Novejšaja istorija*, 3:433; A. Černovskij, comp., *Sojuz russkogo naroda* (Moscow-Leningrad, 1929), p. 313. Gessen, *Zakon i žizn'*, p. 177, sees the circular in a more favorable light than Dubnov.

[91] M. S. Conroy, "Stolypin's Attitude to Local Self-Government," *Slavonic and East European Review*, 47 (July 1968):452.

[92] Avrekh, *Stolypin i Tret'ja Duma* (Moscow, 1968), p. 37, no. 41; Dubnov, *Evrei v Rossii*, bk. 2:90.

to "external" students, depriving many Jews of the possibility of qualifying for university admission by examination.[93]

In April 1908, Stolypin decided to ignore the request, made in the Duma's Defense Committee, to bar Jews from the armed forces.[94] In December, he urged the Minister of Justice to refrain, for the time being, from enforcing a law that would have banished some two hundred Jewish businessmen and their families from Moscow. The significant influence of Jews on the money market made it essential to avoid disruptions of industry and commerce as well as damage to Christian and state interests.[95] In 1909, on the other hand, he complained that Jewish merchants who had the right of temporary business visits to St. Petersburg bought merchandise there in which they did not normally deal.[96] In November of that year he kept the Minister of Justice from announcing in the Duma that Jews, baptized Jews, and other non-Orthodox would not be appointed judges, because such an announcement would not be timely. His western zemstvo bill of 1910 specifically excluded Jews as electors or deputies.[97]

It was becoming ever more difficult for Stolypin, who had once appeared so firm in his judgments and actions, to determine what was and what was not politically timely or feasible. He had lost the trust of the Emperor and of the Right; his willfulness now alienated even the Octobrists, and in the spring of 1911, his main allies, the Nationalists, split with the formation of an "Independent Nationalist" group which tried to soften the excesses and narrowness of Stolypin's nationalism and to make it more inclusive, more assimilationist, more national-democratic. In *Lado*, a symposium published in 1911, the "Independents" went so far as to propose the abolition of the Pale.[98] That idea had won the assent of 166 or about one-third of the Duma's members, and the bill introduced by them in May 1910 had been referred to committee by a vote of 208 to 138.[99] Stolypin had told one of the two Jewish Duma deputies, L. N. Nisselovich, that if the legislature took the initiative in this, the government would meet it half way.[100]

It was an ambiguous remark, and one which Stolypin may have made in the confident expectation that the bill would die in committee, as in fact it did.

---

[93] *Ibid.*, 93–94; Greenberg, *The Jews* (n. 44, above), 2:86.
[94] Polivanov, *Iz dnevnikov* (n. 34, above), pp. 44–45.
[95] Copy of Stolypin letter, dated 15 December 1908, to Minister of Justice Shcheglovitov, in Archives, Alliance Israélite Universelle, Paris.
[96] Greenberg, *The Jews*, 2:84.
[97] Bogdanovič, *Dnevnik*, p. 470
[98] Avrekh, *Stolypin i Tret'ja Duma*, pp. 407–415.
[99] Gessen, *Zakon i žizn'*, p. 179; Dubnov, *Novejšaja istorija*, bk. 2:92–93; *Evr. Enciklopedija*, 7:375.
[100] Thomas Riha, "Paul Miliukov's Parliamentary Career, 1907–1917," unpubl. doctoral dissertation, Harvard University (1962), p. 92.

He need not have feared that it would become law, for in the unlikely event that the Duma as a whole would have approved ending the Pale, the State Council would have blocked further action even before the tsar could have exercised his veto. But could Stolypin be certain, in view of changing party and factional alignments, that the bill would never reach the floor of the lower house; and what would meeting it half way have meant in practice? It is inconceivable that he would have agreed to a removal of the barriers that kept the vast mass of Jewry out of the central and eastern provinces. His own inclinations and his dependence on the Right Octobrists and the main body of Nationalists forbade it.

In March 1911, the Nationalist leader P. N. Balashov had asked him to proclaim as an irrevocable principle the existence of the Pale and the total removal of Jews from schools, press, and courts.[101] It is equally unthinkable that that is what Stolypin had in mind when, at the time of his death in September 1911, he was once again preparing to tackle the Jewish question, to "solve it in all its breadth," as one of his associates put it. The governor of Kiev at the time of Stolypin's assassination recalled that the Jewish question, so frightening to the government because of its complexity, was high on Stolypin's agenda.[102] But it is just that complexity and his increasing political isolation that made it a near certainty that Stolypin, if he was indeed ready to confront the Jewish question once more, envisioned no fundamental changes of course.

Stolypin's death at the hands of Dmitry Bogrov, a double agent of Jewish origin, raised apprehensions of a bloody pogrom among the Jews of Kiev; among the Nationalists, the appointment of Kokovtsev as his successor created fears that the new head of government might disavow them and their chauvinism. Kokovtsev, with the Emperor's approval, made certain that there was no pogrom,[103] and before long he was also able to reassure Stolypin's allies that he would not reverse the latter's policies on Finland, Poland, or the Jews. It was his reputation as a moderate on the Jewish question, his close association with Witte, his intimacy with western bankers that worried Nationalists and Rightists and led a delegation headed by Balashov to call on Kokovtsev even before his appointment became official and Stolypin had breathed his last. Could a man be trusted, they wondered, who had helped to extend Jewish rights in August 1904, who had in 1905 insisted that Jews vote

---

[101] "Pis'mo Balašova k Stolypinu," *Krasnyj Arkhiv*, 9 (1925): 291–294.

[102] S. N. Paleolog, *Okolo vlasti* (Belgrade, 1928); A. F. Girs, "Evrejskij vopros," p. 15; undated manuscript in the Archives of Russian and East European History and Culture, Columbia University.

[103] Kokovcev, *Iz moego prošlogo* (n. 32, above), 1:481.

for and serve in the Duma, and who had urged in 1906 that unnecessary restrictions be lifted?

In the memoirs he composed in French exile and in which he ascribes his fall from power in 1914 to a right-wing vendetta, Kokovtsev appears as a determined and angry opponent of nationalist excesses who would not bow to pressure from any quarter. If, Kokovtsev told his callers, their goal was truly the greatness of Russia, her independence of all forms of alien domination, cooperation with them would be more than easy. "But I do not share and cannot serve your policy of oppressing non-Russians (*inorodcy*). That policy is harmful and dangerous." It was one thing to protect and further the Russian element and give it preeminence in the nation, "but to persecute a Jew today, an Armenian tomorrow, then a Pole or a Finn and to see them all as enemies of Russia who must be curbed in every way—with this I have no sympathy, in this I will not go along with you."[104]

Kokovtsev's distaste for the cruder forms of persecution had little practical effect and need not have alarmed nationalist militants. In one of his early appearances before the Duma, he received an ovation from the Right and Center benches as well as a telegram from the Emperor for declaring that he would defend the vital interests, the unity and power of the Russian state and nationality as vigorously as his predecessor had done.[105] And while he did not himself initiate new anti-Jewish measures, he neither resisted what was done by the Duma or his colleagues in the cabinet—the horrible farce of the Beilis trial elicited no word or act of disapproval from him—nor did he repeat the call for a saner, more rational Jewish policy he had sounded in 1906.

Gurko's suspicion that Kokovtsev, then, was influenced by financial considerations was well founded.[106] Early in 1906, on a trip to Paris, Kokovtsev had learned how aggrieved were the Paris and London Rothschilds by Russian treatment of the Jews and that he could not count on them for help in selling Russian bonds. The Mendelssohns of Berlin proved more cooperative,[107] but the Russian need for credit was great and allied France was a more important and desirable source of funds than Germany. When a French banker, writing to Kokovtsev in July 1906, discreetly suggested that the placing of a loan would be greatly facilitated by making the Jews equal before the law, the Minister of Finance replied that he shared his correspondent's view in principle. What he felt it possible and necessary to do sheds light on his and

---

[104] *Ibid.*, pp. 483–486; Avrekh, *Stolypin*, p. 28.
[105] Edward Chmielewski, *The Polish Question in the Russian State Duma* (Knoxville: The University of Tennessee Press, 1970), pp. 114–115.
[106] E. A. Preobražeńskij, ed., *Russkie finansy i evropejskaja birža, 1904–1906 gg.* (Moscow-Leningrad, 1926), pp. 103, 113, 214, 344.
[107] B. V. Anan'ič, "Vnešnie zajmy carizma i dumskij vopros v 1906–1907gg.," *Istoričeskij Arkhiv*, no 81 (1968):178.

Stolypin's motives in bringing the matter to the cabinet in October 1906; the reservations he expressed reflect deep-seated fears and attitudes that sober bureaucrats shared with anti-Semitic zealots inside and outside of government.

> I consider ... that the problem is so complex and its roots so deep, that even if it were possible to devise one measure that would at once transform all Jews from revolutionaries into conservatives, and supposing that measure to be the grant of equal status with the rest of the population, even then not all difficulties would be removed. Those who are familiar with the state of the Jewish question in Russia know that the accusation leveled against the Jews that they exploit the other classes of the population, is far from an exaggeration or based solely on one-sided or prejudiced views. Similarly, it is hardly possible to explain the prominent Jewish part in the revolutionary movement, the Jewish leadership of all revolutionary organizations ... by lack of rights alone. As far as Jewish emancipation is concerned, you know that I am not a principled opponent of granting legal equality, and that it was upon my initiative that certain restrictions upon Jews were lifted in autumn 1904. At this moment too I hold the view—as do most members of the Council of Ministers—that it is high time to abolish the larger part of our exceptional legislation against the Jews. But it would hardly be in their own interest if this were carried to the point of giving them full equality of rights with the indigenous Russian population. There is one area—landownership—in which such equality would do more harm than good to the Jews. It must be remembered that there are seven million Jews in our population of 140 millions. Giving them equal access to the land would arouse the land-hungry peasant masses against them; in view of age-old discords and the exploitation practiced by the Jews, this would lead to inevitable and, for the Jewish landowner, ruinous clashes with the peasants. With this exception, all the fetters now hobbling Jewish [economic] activity must naturally be lifted.[108]

To that end, Kokovstev concluded his letter, he would soon recommend that all restraints on Jewish trade, industry, and participation in joint stock companies be ended and the rules of May 3, 1882, repealed. He hoped that the Council of Ministers would agree to take these steps as immediate and extraordinary measures. Other issues, such as the right of residence outside the Pale, should, because of their importance and difficulty, be submitted to the Duma, with the government preparing and publishing the necessary legislation in advance in order to dispose public opinion in favor of its acceptance. "The latter is exclusively my personal view, and I did not yet have the opportunity of ascertaining those of my colleagues...." How much of Kokovtsev's letter was designed for foreign consumption is impossible to know. But he was clearly convinced that the political and economic exigencies of the moment demanded a liberalized treatment of the Jews. When the crisis passed, so did Kokovtsev's sense of urgency, and the Jewish question did not become the subject of formal deliberation at the highest levels of government until another crisis brought it to the fore.

---

[108] "Perepiska V. N. Kokovceva s Eduardom Neclinym," *Krasnyj Arkhiv*, 4 (1923):129–156; here pp. 134–135.

That crisis was the death agony of Imperial Russia, brought on by a war which hopelessly aggravated all its problems. After an initial outpouring of patriotic enthusiasm by the middle and upper classes, the catastrophic defeats of spring and summer 1915 put an end to the relative immunity from criticism the regime had enjoyed and shocked the government into a horrified realization of its extremity. Forced to retreat before the enemy, the military commanders also forced to the rear millions of noncombatants who taxed the already strained resources of the interior provinces. Among these unfortunates were upwards of half a million Jews whose brutal evacuation as potential spies and helpers of the Germans had begun even before the mass deportations of summer 1915.[109] It was as part of the problem posed by the flood of refugees that the Jews engaged the attention of the Council of Ministers during several of the stormy sessions it devoted to the country's desperate situation in July and August 1915.

To follow these discussions on the basis of notes taken by the assistant head of the council's secretariat, A. N. Yakhontov,[110] is to pass in final review the governing assumptions and standard responses of Russian bureaucrats to the Jewish question. It is also to realize once again how large and threatening that question must have seemed to them to remain one of their central concerns in the midst of a war for survival. Yet the very willingness to yield heretofore inviolable positions testifies that these servants of an old regime retained within their large delusions an element of pragmatic rationality of which Nazi racism during the Second World War was to show itself totally incapable.

Beginning in February 1915, members of the council repeatedly complained of the indiscriminate expulsions of Jews from the war zone without provision being made for their shelter, food, or ultimate destination.[111] By summer,

---

[109] "Iz 'černoj knigi' rossijskogo evrejstva: materialy dlja istorii voiny 1915–1916 g.," *Evrejskaja Starina*, 9 (1916):195–296; Boris Bruckus, "Ekonomičeskoe položenie evreev i vojna," *Russkaja Mysl'* 24 (1915):27–45; Baron, *The Russian Jew* (n. 2, above), pp. 187–200; George Katkov, *Russia 1917: The February Revolution* (New York, 1967), pp. 55–62. E. M. Kulischer, *Europe on the Move* (New York, 1948), p. 31, gives the number of Jews evacuated by the summer of 1915 as having surpassed 600,000. *The Jews in the Eastern War Zone* (New York: American Jewish Committee, 1916) states on p. 11: "A million Jews were driven from their homes in a state of absolute destitution."

[110] A. N. Jakhontov, "Tjaželye dni—sekretnye zasedanija Soveta Ministrov, 16 iuljja–2 sentjabrja 1915 goda," *Arkhiv Russkoj Revoljucii*, 18 (Berlin, 1926):15–136. There is an English translation, *Prologue to Revolution*, with an introductory essay by Professor Michael Cherniavsky, in the Russian Civilization Series published by Prentice-Hall (Englewood Cliffs, N.J., 1967). A typescript of Yakhontov's notes, covering sessions from July 1914 through August 1916 is in the Archives of Russian and East European History and Culture, Columbia University. For Sliozberg's recollections of these events see *Dela*, 3:334–342.

[111] Yakhontov typescript, meetings of 6 February 1915, p. 96; 12 June 1915, p. 150; 10 July 1915, p. 170. All subsequent citations are to the notes as published in *Arkhiv Russkoj Revoljucii*.

there was a stream of refugees of all kinds, and growing anger on the part of civilian authorities against the military's indifference to their fate and the burdens they placed on the strained resources of the interior. In July, the council inconclusively discussed the refugee problem as a whole and that of the Jewish refugees in particular. Its members repeated their objections to the indiscriminate accusations of espionage and treason made by the military against the Jews. They also expressed fears of the revolutionary mood which this mass of hungry and bitter people, driven from their homes, was bringing with them and of the tensions their presence would create among a population already suffering the privations of wartime. But there was little the ministers felt they could do, beyond bringing the matter to the attention of the Emperor in the course of a general review of war plans.[112]

At its meeting of August 4, the question of Jewish refugees took up half the council's time.[113] The representations of Jewish leaders[114] had apparently helped to convince the Minister of the Interior, Prince N. B. Shcherbatov, that while the high command would remain deaf to his pleas, it was both possible and desirable for the civilian authorities to ameliorate the lot of at least those Jews who had already been uprooted. He told his colleagues that the futility of all their interventions with the chief-of-staff, N. N. Yanushkevich, had become obvious, that the general was evidently determined to blame the Jews for his failures, and that it was in any case too late to undo the damage he had done. Hundreds of thousands of Jews were on the move eastward and crowding them into the cities of the Pale would lead to pogroms, starvation, and epidemics. "All this makes it necessary for us to permit the entry of forcibly evacuated Jews to areas beyond the Pale of Settlement, at least on a temporary basis." The barrier of the Pale had anyhow been breached in many places since the beginning of the war; to insist on repairing it would be futile and ill advised. The law of residence had been written for a time of peace; it must be adjusted to the emergencies and demands of war.

More was required, however, than the silent indulgence of occasional transgressions. The Jewish leaders demanded, Shcherbatov told the council, that the presence of Jewish refugees in the interior be legalized. He described their demand as being tantamount to an ultimatum, given force by their declared

---

[112] *Ibid.*, pp. 20, 32–33.
[113] *Ibid.*, pp. 37, 42–46.
[114] The absent Minister of Finance, P. L. Bark, had played an important part in impressing the seriousness of the problem created by the army upon his colleagues. He himself was made painfully aware of it by Jewish bankers and industrialists in Russia as well as by the Rothschilds and others when he attended Allied economic conferences in Paris and London. Jewish ability seriously to impede the flow of funds to Russia was exaggerated by friend and foe alike. See Bark's memoirs in *Vozroždenie*, no. 165 (September 1965): 78; no. 172 (April 1966): 92–99; no. 177 (September 1966): 105–106.

inability to restrain desperate Jewish militants and by their predictions of a drying up of foreign credits. Sliozberg, one of four Jewish notables who called upon the Minister of the Interior, challenged the accuracy of Yakhontov's notes when they were published and denied that there had been an ultimatum or any condition for the abolition of the Pale. But he did mention the effect that the persecutions were having on Jewish loyalties at home and opinion abroad, and he must have done so in full awareness that his warnings would fall on receptive ears. Shcherbatov successfully conjured up the spectre of Jewish financial power and Jewish wrath for his fellow ministers; it is unlikely that he did so with total disbelief in their reality or that his words were merely those of Yakhontov.

What is desired is the issuance of a measure which, by improving the situation of Jewish refugees, would serve to rehabilitate the mass of Jews who have been branded by rumours of treason. I do not doubt that the Minister of Finance will give his full support to my proposal—to issue without delay a governmental decision to suspend temporarily the rules concerning the Pale of Settlement, that is, to formalize what is in fact a common practice. Deciding on such a step, we should also utilize it politically by summoning the Jewish leaders and presenting them with our demands: we are willing to meet you half-way, but you will kindly use your influence to pacify the masses and then we shall also be able to speak about the future.

Shcherbatov, like most of his predecessors and colleagues, seems never to have doubted that Russian, and indeed world Jewry unquestioningly and unanimously recognized the authority of a single group of leaders, that Jewish money and Jewish political activity could be made to stop or start at the behest of a few wealthy men. Nor did he doubt that his proposal would have the desired effect. He merely wondered whether to admit Jews to the cities only or to the countryside as well. Since a weakened police force was barely adequate for the former, he favored keeping Jews out of the villages where there was a likelihood of pogroms and practically no police.

In the ensuing debate, all but one of the ministers agreed with Shcherbatov, but the fact of their agreement is of less interest than their reasons. The Minister of Trade and Industry was as emphatic in his support as in his avoidance of the principles at issue. "We find ourselves, unfortunately, in a time when one has to forgo principles." He tried to have the measure extended to rural districts where many Jewish enterprises useful to the war effort would have to be located, but was overruled. A. V. Krivoshein, the Minister of Agriculture, who was considered a liberal among his colleagues, spoke for himself and the absent Minister of Finance. He related that three Jewish financiers had visited the latter and had made unmistakably clear that the government's shortage of funds would find no remedy without a more humane treatment of the Jews. "Now the knife is at the throat, and there is nothing to be done."

Speedy, decisive, and demonstrative action must be taken while there was still a possibility of influencing events and of profiting from concessions. The Jewish leaders should be given an ultimatum no less blunt than their hints: if we relent on the Pale, you must help us in the money markets at home and abroad and influence the press, which depends on Jewish capital, to moderate its revolutionary tone.

No voice was raised to dispute this fanciful interpretation of the sources of public protest. S. D. Sazonov, the Minister of Foreign Affairs and a member of the council's liberal wing, remarked that the Allies, mentioned as an alternate source of funds, were themselves dependent on Jewish capital and counseled appeasing the Jews. Shcherbatov repeated the need for money to conduct the war, money which was in Jewish hands, and the aged Goremykin, President of the Council, admitted that concessions were unavoidable and spoke of the government's "duty to protect the rural districts from Jewish invasion." There was further debate on this, with Krivoshein declaring that the Jews, wedded to town life, had no interest in settling in the villages. He added that Witte—"who occupied himself much with the Jewish question and tried to reform it basically"—had told him that freely admitting Jews to the towns would, in effect, solve it. Members who had not yet given their opinion were asked for it; expressing little enthusiasm, many reservations, and heavy hearts, they conceded the painful necessity of the proposed step.

S. V. Rukhlov, Minister of Transport and a founder of the right-wing National Union, was the lone holdout. It was wrong to give relief to the Jews while all Russia was suffering. Would this not confirm, by governmental act, the popular belief that money buys everything and risk a bloody popular protest of which the Jews would be the victims? Rukhlov's conscience would not yet allow him to declare himself. "I must think about this and prepare myself for the final answer." No decision would be taken that day, Goremykin assured him. An instruction, taking into account the views expressed, would be prepared by the secretariat for submission to the next meeting. The final words were those of State Comptroller P. A. Kharitonov. The police, he said, might go on strike to protest their loss of income or start pogroms to show that the government's decision offended the feeling of true Russians. "With this kind of joke, which the late State Comptroller was always inclined to make, the session ended."

The council reconvened two days later[115] and bypassing the War Minister's usual report on the situation at the front, heard from Goremykin that the Emperor in principle approved the measure and its limitation to the towns. There was extended argument, but little new was added. Krivoshein expanded

---

[115] *Arkhiv Russkoj Revoljucii*, 18:47–51.

on the benefits the Jews would bring to the sluggish urban economy. The country's economic future could not be built on agriculture alone and Russian business had grown lazy under government protection. The cities were in any case no longer purely Russian; admitting the Jewish masses to them would weaken the hold of the richer Jews. The villages were another matter and had to be guarded in every possible way.

Rukhlov asked to be heard a last time. The action about to be taken by a stroke of the pen was not temporary but a permanent and fateful dismantling of historical defenses against Jewish depredations and corruption; no future government would be strong enough to reverse it. Under the pressure of the Jewish purse the road to further concessions had been entered; it could only lead to equal rights. "How will the army and the whole Russian people look on this? Is there a guarantee that there will not be bloody consequences? After all, rumors of Jewish treason are not pure slander. It is no secret that the majority of spies belongs to the chosen people ... I repeat, I do not have the right to create discord, but I openly state ... that my soul does not accept this. Now I will be silent."

He did, however, speak again on August 9,[116] when ministers were preparing to sign the council's journal providing for the issuance of a special order—to go the road of the Duma was thought too long and uncertain—that would open all the empire's cities to the Jews.[117] The imperial residences of Tsarskoe Selo and Yalta, the Cossack territories, and the villages would remain closed to them. There, as Shcherbatov put it, we are unable to guard them from the clubs. "And there," Krivoshein added, "we do not wish to guard them, for this would be against the national and economic interests of the Russian people." Rukhlov remained unmoved by the Emperor's consent, by appeals to reason of state, to economic advantage, and financial necessity. Unlike Krivoshein, who thought it impossible to fight both Jews and Germans, he wanted to keep the watch against the Jews. He reminded the council of the danger of revolutionary infection their spread throughout the country represented, of the role they had played in 1905 and were still playing in revolutionary agitation and the underground. He struck a responsive chord among several of his listeners who also identified Jews and revolution but bowed

---

[116] *Ibid.*, 57.

[117] The sources disagree whether the council's action was valid only for the duration of the war or until a full review of Jewish laws by the Duma. Perhaps the point was purposely left vague. The order makes clear that it was induced by the exigencies of the military situation and that it did not intend to prejudice future legislation. But it did not otherwise qualify its grant of "the right of residence in cities and towns beyond the Pale of Settlement." Partial text in *Russkie Vedomosti*, no. 187, 14 August 1915, p. 3. What appears to be a full English text in *The Jews in the Eastern War Zone* (New York, 1916), pp. 21-2.

before the inevitable. So did the Emperor, some nine years after his conscience had forbidden him to agree to a much more modest proposal.[118]

The very fantasies of Jewish might, the same sense of Russian inferiority and weakness that lay at the basis of so much discriminatory legislation was now the cause of the most decisive and humane change in tsarist Russia's Jewish policy. Goremykin, who said he did not expect much to come of it, was of course, right—if for the wrong reasons. The roots of Russia's difficulties lay deep; they could hardly be touched by a reluctant, belated, and partial accommodation with a fictitious enemy. But the illusion persisted to the end. In the case of Russia's last Minister of the Interior, A. D. Protopopov, it reached clinical proportions. Convinced that the Pale must be abolished totally and permanently, he thought it possible, only days before the February Revolution, to strengthen his position and that of the regime by attracting the country's commercial classes to the side of the government and by giving the Jewish bourgeoisie new privileges.[119] The Grand Duke Alexander Mikhailovich shared his illusion, but it led him to oppose Protopopov's plan. In January 1917 the Grand Duke wrote to Nicholas:

One has the feeling that some kind of invisible hand guides all our policy in such a way as to make victory impossible. Protopopov told me that it is possible to rely on industry, on capital; what a mistake! In the first place, he forgets that capital is in the hands of foreigners and Jews who wish for the downfall of the monarchy, which would clear the way for the satisfaction of their rapacious appetites. In the second place, our business class is not what it used to be—it is enough to recall 1905.[120]

Past perils and future dangers blunted determination and decisive action to the very end.

---

[118] When the council on 26 August discussed the demands of the Progressive Bloc for further concessions to minority religions and nationalities, its chairman, Goremykin, reported that the Emperor was not prepared to go beyond what had already been done for the Jews, and Prince Shcherbatov pointed out that the Duma too was not likely to pronounce in favor of Jewish emancipation. He believed that what had been granted had already produced beneficial political and financial effects. Selected additional relaxations of unnecessary and antiquated restrictions should, however, be considered. Educational quotas had already been relaxed on 10 August 1915 for invalided soldiers and their children, and in December, admissions to the bar became somewhat easier (*Kniga o russkom evrejstve*, pp. 137, 408–409). At a conference of governors of the central provinces called in May 1916 by Goremykin's successor Boris Stuermer, the participants expressed a desire for the restoration of the Jewish Pale which had been breached by circumstances created by the war. "Soveščanie gubernatorov v 1916 g.," *Krasnyj Arkhiv*, 33 (1929): 160.

[119] A. A. Oznobišin, *Vospominanija člena IV Dumy* (Paris, 1927), p. 243; Protopopov's belief in the necessity of placating wealthy Jews appears to be connected with meetings he had with the Rothschilds in London and Paris during early 1916. See Bark in *Vozroždenie*, no. 177, p. 106. V. S. Djakin, "K voprosu o 'zagovore carizma' nakanune fevral'skoj revoljucii," in N. E. Nosov et al., eds., *Vnutrennjaja politika carizma* (Leningrad, 1967), p. 377; Sliozberg, *Dela*, 3:352.

[120] V. P. Semennikov, ed., *Nikolaj II i velikie knjaz'ja* (Leningrad-Moscow, 1925), p. 120.

3

What is it possible to say, on the basis of our survey, about the motives of conduct and opinion at the top levels of government? What patterns is it possible to discern in the stated premises and concrete forms of official policy toward the Jews? And what revisions or refinements in existing interpretations of Imperial Russia's Jewish policy does our inquiry suggest?

We may, to begin with, see our findings as confirmation of the prevailing belief that Russian policy makers in the period under discussion were anti-Semites of varying degrees of intensity, that they had little sympathy and less understanding for the Jews, and that they were imbued with deep anti-Jewish prejudices. In this respect, tsarist bureaucrats were not, of course, exceptional among contemporaries of comparable background. The sentiments they voiced were also uttered by German and Austrian diplomats, French bankers and officials, English journalists and politicians; they could be heard in most drawing rooms and board rooms, in editorial and government offices all over Europe and America. But in Russia, Jews were thought to be such an unusually difficult and peculiar element of the population that they could not be simply left to the operation of the country's general laws or treated like other subjects of the empire. And anti-Semitism—which has been made to serve for extermination camps and exclusive social clubs—is not a sufficient explanation for the erection and costly maintenance of an extraordinary and cumbersome structure of legal discrimination that embraced some 1400 statutes and regulations plus thousands of lesser rules, provisions, and judicial interpretations.

Even for those who believe that the anti-Semite's obsession bears no relation to reality, that it does not even require a Jewish presence, and that it is a projection of the anti-Semite's own apprehensions and hatreds, the Russian case must give rise to the question: What accounts for its extreme tenacity and virulence?

The answer most often given is that the old regime's treatment of its Jewish subjects in the years after 1881 had for its conscious and deliberate purpose the deflecting onto the Jews of mass grievances and political protests challenging the regime. Bloody pogroms, propaganda, legal discrimination, and administrative chicanery were all employed, in this view, to discredit words and deeds directed against the existing order as the work of Jews who were to be made the substitute target; and when the authorities invoked the need to take protective action, they were, for the most part, merely pretending belief in the existence of a Jewish danger, whether from bankers or revolutionaries. The assumption of a cynically manipulated and officially inspired anti-Semitism becomes the least tenable one, however, when one listens to the views expressed in private or in the secrecy of the council chamber by the men who made and applied the regime's Jewish policies. This was no cold-blooded, hypocritical toying with popular instincts and passions by men who knew better. With very few exceptions they were themselves imbued with deep and genuine prejudices and fears which made their objects appear as a very real, not a pretended, problem or threat. The threat might take a variety of guises—political, economic, demographic, moral, or a combination of these—but it was felt by ministers who were considered moderates no less than by confirmed Jew-haters, without necessarily making them advocates of identical policies.

Another assumption that appears questionable in the light of our evidence sees official Judeophobia as the expression of a determined fanaticism or comprehensive system of beliefs. There is, for example, the thesis, recently advanced by Norman Cohn,[121] of a consistent and systematic drive to clear Russia of Jews. He has written that during the reigns of Alexander III and Nicholas, both fanatical anti-Semites, everything possible was done, with every official encouragement, to achieve that end. This can be shown not to have been so. But more importantly, it raises the question of the meaning of fanatical or ideological anti-Semitism and its incidence among Russian policy makers. If fanaticism is meant to suggest the single-minded pursuit of a single, overriding goal, such as purifying Russia of Jews and doing so in disregard of rational calculations of feasibility and consequences, it was not present among the subjects of our survey. They were not inspired by religious or secular visions of a world free of Jews; they did not have their eyes fixed firmly on a distant Utopia. A few did express the wish to be rid of some or all of the Jews if this could be done at no cost to themselves. But they thought this either impossible or undesirable; they did little to facilitate and less to give positive assistance or support to emigration.[122]

Russia's top bureaucrats were indeed obsessed by Judeophobia, but their fears made them look backward and gave to their Jewish policy, for all its brutality, the same anxious, defensive quality that adhered to all Russian bureaucratic conduct and robbed Russian conservatism of vitality, dynamism, and appeal. The brevity of Ignatyev's tenure of office proves the point. Panslavism (as Hannah Arendt has suggested) may have been, like German political romanticism, a prelude to Nazism by combining the doctrine of racial selection with anti-Semitism.[123] But after Ignatyev, Panslavists were

---

[121] Norman Cohn, *Warrant for Genocide* (London, 1967), p. 52. Cf. *The Jews in the Eastern War Zone*, p. 9: "It was the openly expressed policy of the reactionaries who ruled Russia to solve the Jewish question by ridding the country of its Jews."

[122] There are no studies of official policies and attitudes toward emigration, Jewish or non-Jewish. My article in *Soviet Jewish Affairs* (May 1973) represents an effort to fill that gap.

[123] "From the Dreyfus Affair to France Today," in Koppel S. Pinson, ed., *Essays on Anti-Semitism* (New York, 1942), p. 181.

conspicuous for their small numbers and little influence in Russian government. Although racist notes, echoing German and French theories, began to be clearly audible in official and even more in unofficial Russian anti-Semitism toward the end of the nineteenth century,[124] they did not become dominant, they did not transform traditional dislikes and resentments into a universal mission, or achieve the kind of mad consistency found in Nazi racism.

The bureaucrats' distorted perceptions of the Jews also distorted but did not totally obscure reality, and when they responded to its demands, they were capable of compromising their principles. Their measures, as a result, were riddled with inconsistencies and often they were but half-measures. It is surely significant that the most important policies adopted during our period, beginning with the Rules of May 3, 1882, up to the ending of the Pale in 1915, were issued not as regular laws but as emergency decrees, ministerial instructions, or temporary regulations which were to be in effect only, as the sacramental phrase had it, "until the revision of the laws concerning the Jews." Opposition in the State Council or the Duma cannot alone explain this approach, but the tentative, uncertain, at times almost furtive nature of the actions taken.

Finally, the evidence of the sources makes it necessary to question one aspect of the psychoanalytic interpretation of anti-Semitism as derived from and applied to the Russian case by the late Otto Fenichel. "The Protocols of the Wise Men of Zion," he wrote in 1940, "were forged by the Tsarist police, and they knew for what purpose they forged them. As a result of the general misery, there was a rebellious tendency directed against the ruling powers. If the propaganda succeeds, the Jews will be thought to be the cause of poverty and not the authorities, and the revolutionary tendency will have been redirected against them. The terrible pogroms showed that this intention succeeded."[125] In Fenichel's eyes, officially tolerated or inspired violence was a safe means of satisfying the conflicting drives of average Russians toward rebellion and submission, a displacement of the frustrations of the masses and the projection as well of their anti-Semitic rulers' repressed instinctual drives.

It is impossible to affirm or deny the larger theory developed by Fenichel and other analysts by reference to our subjects alone; but it must be pointed out that for all the ambivalence they may have felt when mob violence was directed against Jews, they were more frightened than gratified by it. The Protocols were the independent production of a subordinate police official, and when Stolypin reported to Nicholas on their spurious origin, the tsar forbade their employment. "Drop the Protocols. One cannot defend a pure cause by

---

[124] Rogger in *Wiener Library Bulletin*, pp. 49–50.
[125] Otto Fenichel, "Psychoanalysis of Anti-Semitism," in Leonard Dinnerstein, ed., *Anti-Semitism in the United States* (New York, 1971), p. 26.

dirty methods."[126] It is, moreover, almost certain that pogroms were not manufactured, inspired, or tolerated as deliberate policy at the highest levels of government.[127] The present evidence suggests rather that an important and continuous aim of policy toward the Jews was not to indulge but to control mob violence. With the possible exception of the revolutionary years 1905–1906, when central authority was divided and especially unsure of itself and the reach of its powers, the men in charge of Russia's destinies tried not to unleash but to restrain the instincts of the masses by removing Jews as their targets, by removing them as competitors for scarce resources (notably land), by reducing the possibilities of contact and conflict (for example, nonadmission to Cossack territories), by raising "protective" safeguards against a people whose impact on the "dark" masses they felt to be deleterious, disruptive, and potentially explosive. Their conviction of the vehemence of popular hostility to the Jews, nourished by their own prejudices, was strong and it was held by men, Populists and Marxists among them, who were not Jew-haters.[128]

It is necessary to conclude, therefore, that the Jewish question was not for the subjects of our study a device or subterfuge, but appeared to them to be a real problem fraught with real dangers demanding protective and preventive measures. We lack the biographical data to examine the psychodynamics of their Judeophobia or to isolate the elements of pathology, of irrationality, of ignorance and moral corruption it contained. Unable to do so, and believing that the commands of ideology were not an important source of conduct, what is it possible to say by way of summary about the motives of Russian policy makers as these are revealed in their words and deeds?

The measures taken were designed to check or minimize the threat the Jews were felt to pose, directly or indirectly, to the regime, to public order, and to social stability. This was as true of the negative and restrictive actions taken as of the few positive or palliative ones for which humanitarian doctrine was rarely advanced. The direct threat was seen as coming, above all, from two directions: the role the Jews played, especially after the turn of the century, in the revolutionary movement, and their role (or potential role) in the professions and public life.

---

[126] Cohn, *Warrant*, p. 115; Sliozberg, *Dela*, 3:283–284.

[127] Rogger in *Wiener Library Bulletin*, pp. 45–47.

[128] For example, Leon Trotsky, "Thermidor and Anti-Semitism" (first published in 1937), in *On the Jewish Question* (New York: Pathfinder Press, 1970), p. 22; Avrahm Yarmolinsky, *Road to Revolution* (New York, 1959), pp. 305–310, for Lavrov and others; *Evr. Ènciklopedija*, 1:820 for the opinion of the liberal War Minister of Alexander II, D. A. Milyutin, that Jews, even if the civil service were opened to them, should not be allowed to become officers in the army since peasant soldiers would lack respect for them. Also see Erich Goldhagen, "Communism and Anti-Semitism," in A. Brumberg, ed., *Russia under Khrushchev* (New York, 1962), for additional references testifying to the belief of Russian radicals in the existence of popular hostility to Jews.

The danger from Jewish radicalism, which some ministers, like some of their critics, recognized to be of their own making, was seen not only in the presence and prominence of Jews in the ranks of the radical and liberal opposition. It was enlarged for them by the concentration of a pauperized mass of Jews in the cities of the Pale, a mass which was believed to be undergoing a process of political radicalization. The accumulated frustrations and bitterness of Jewish proletarians were given an even more menacing aspect by the reality of Jewish money and the unreal assumption that it would join with Jewish misery for a common assault on the regime. That assumption was common to men as dissimilar as Pleve and Witte and led them, and others, to advocate more moderate policies in order to diminish the support supposedly given by Jewish financiers to Jewish revolutionaries. Their expectation that the "leaders" of Jewry could control at will the political behavior of a population of over five million individuals is a striking illustration of the way in which reality and delusion combined to shape action.[129]

The demand for the reduction of the Jewish role in the professions was, of course, in the interest of the competitors who voiced it. But from the state's point of view—and this helps to explain the educational restrictions it imposed—there was concern that the educational qualifications gained by Jews would give them access to state service or public employment or enable them to dominate key sectors of public life in which there were not as yet cadres of Russian specialists. Fear enlarged the threat to unrealistic dimensions, but it was given substance by what was happening in other countries. Here we come to what might be called anticipatory anti-Semitism, a horror of what they saw happening in France, Germany, or Austria expressed by Pobedonostsev and Bunge or by public figures such as Dostoevsky and Yury Samarin. If the press, the bar, the theater, the whole tone and direction of public and intellectual life in countries like these could fall under Jewish influence, how much more careful did undeveloped Russia have to be to preserve its national character and essence![130]

---

[129] It should be noted, however, that some Jews abroad shared the delusions of the tsar's ministers and gave financial aid to the oppositional movement. See Szajkowski in *Jewish Social Studies*, 29, no. 2:75–77, and especially two excerpts from letters of Jacob Schiff, dated 19 July 1904 and 29 March 1905 in n. 121, p. 75: "... Plehwe und seine Genossen fangen endlich an zu fuehlen, dass sie es mit dem internationalen Judentum gruendlich verdorben haben, und ich glaube, dass die russische Regierung jetzt sehr weit gehen wuerde, um den guten Willen des internationalen Judentums zu gewinnen." "Wenn die russische Regierung ueberhaupt etwas lernen kann, so muessen die Erfahrungen der letzten zwoelf Monate die Einsicht gebracht haben, dass das internationale Judentum doch eine Macht ist."

[130] Byrnes, *Pobedonostsev* (n. 3, above), p. 108; Hans Kohn, *Pan-Slavism*, 2nd ed. (New York, 1960), p. 410; Bunge, *Zapiska* (n. 25, above), p. 33.

Simply to dismiss as "faked humility"[131] what Pobedonostsev and others said on this score is to ignore the complex of inferiority and pugnacious boasting that has afflicted many countries in past and present. In Europe, this has been particularly evident in agrarian societies where, as in Russia and Romania, the Jews were the most visible symbols of alien encroachment and power and the most accessible objects of resentment. The comment made to Bernard Pares by a police official in 1904 reflects in its basic premise an attitude too common to be feigned: "As for the Jews, Russia is too young and untrained to admit them to full freedom everywhere. What is wanted, is a period of total exclusion, such as there was in English history. Then they might come back without being dangerous."[132]

Since there was not enough resolve or strength to make it total, exclusion was partial, designed primarily to minimize the Jewish threat to the economic position of the lower classes, especially the peasants.[133] Here was one area, perhaps the only one, in which the patriarchal, conservative populism of the regime and its paternalistic rhetoric could be applied without fear of conflict with key interests. A fundamental reorganization of the economic structure in the countryside—a massive redistribution of private lands, for example, or the regulation of land renting in favor of the peasants—was impossible without alienating the gentry or violating existing property relationships. But agricultural land could at least be kept out of the hands of Jews and the Jews kept out of the villages, where they would not only do economic damage to a peasantry supposedly incapable of competing with them but where they would also inflame mass grievances which would, in turn, endanger public tranquillity and the security of the State.[134] P. K. Schwanebach, a member of the State Council, ex-Assistant Minister of Agriculture and former State Comptroller, said in 1908 that the Jews were one big nest of fleas. "If one were

---

[131] Baron, *The Russian Jew* (n. 2, above), p. 63.

[132] Bernard Pares, *Russia Between Reform and Revolution* (New York: Schocken Books, 1962), p. 154.

[133] An interministerial commission appointed in 1899 to examine the Provisional Rules of 1882 recommended that they be modified to allow Jewish rental of gentry land for non-agricultural purposes. The peasantry, "little developed, lacking in enterprise and capital," was still to be guarded from Jewish competition; rental of peasant and adjacent lands, as well as the subletting of gentry lands to the peasants, would continue to be prohibited. The suggestion was not adopted. *Evrejskaja Ènciklopedija*, 3:85–86; Gessen, *Zakon i žizn'*, p. 171.

[134] Government fears that its forces were not adequate to control the rural population were not confined to periods of war and revolution. Professor G. L. Yaney writes: "Throughout the 19th and early 20th centuries, the ministry was only too well aware of the utter inadequacy of its police force, both in the number and quality of its men, to cope with any serious or widespread disorders in the countryside." "Some Aspects of the Imperial Russian Government on the Eve of the First World War," *Slavonic and East European Review*, 43, no. 100 (December 1964): 72.

to uncover it, the fleas would spread out over the whole country and the peasant population would be ... surrendered to the blood suckers."[135]

Even bureaucrats who were not obviously or rabidly anti-Semitic accepted the notion of the peasants' vulnerability and their need for protection. The notion is so persistent, so little challenged inside the government, so little susceptible to disproof by facts and figures, that deliberate deception seems hardly possible. That peasants in the Pale were better off than those in provinces without Jews was as irrelevant to advocates of exclusion as were arguments proving the economic inferiority of the peasant commune to its advocates. Indeed, the abolition of the commune in 1906 may have made those who saw it as an unspoiled reservoir of national strength and virtue all the more determined to protect the *mir* and its members from the corrupting influence of the Jews. Self-deception this curiously romantic peasantism and anticapitalism certainly was; but it was strong enough to impose, and until the last to preserve, most of the anti-Jewish legislation designed to "protect" the peasants. At the same time, little was done to inhibit Jewish big business and finance, against which anti-Semites inveighed most loudly. This testifies to the contradictions of Jewish policy and to a simple-minded, compartmentalized view of economics. It also confirms that it was to the economically most defenseless that Russian bureaucrats felt obliged to extend their anti-Jewish protectionism.

As the nature of the economy changed in the years after 1881, this protectionism became less and less effective and was recognized as being, at best, a delaying tactic in a difficult and possibly hopeless cause. The plaint of its fearful complexity is heard in all governmental discussions of the Jewish question, the refrain that it may, in fact, not be soluble at all or soluble only in the very distant future. Commissions, committees, and ministers talked endlessly of the pressing need for solving it, yet no attempt at its solution was made, whether negative or positive, that was more than partial or went beyond the stage of discussion. Pleve spoke of the difficulty of a radical solution; Witte warned of performing radical operations; everywhere they and their colleagues turned there lurked unknown obstacles and dangers as great as those that were to be overcome.

---

[135] Heilbronner, "Aehrenthal," p. 398 (n. 46, above). Such opinions were not held exclusively by anti-Jewish ministers of backward Russia. See *Darkest Russia* (London), no. 129 (17 June 1914): "In the remarkable leading article which we discussed last week, the *Times* supported its unworthy championship of the disabilities imposed on the great mass of Russian Jewry by an argument which—to borrow its own phrase—'betrays utter ignorance of the real situation.' According to the writer of that article, the Jews are rightly kept in bondage because otherwise they would exploit the peasants. 'There cannot be much doubt,' it was stated, 'that, were the Jews free to move and trade amongst them at pleasure, they would very soon 'eat up' the tillers of the soil.'"

No radical operation was planned or carried out by the old regime. There was only the recurrent pattern of harshness alternating with minor concessions. It required a world war before Russia's rulers could contemplate even a partial and qualified departure from that pattern. They could not envision killing or expelling the Jews, or making them full and equal citizens. Their biases and fears immobilized them in an incongruous and contradictory position which they lacked the humanity, the courage, the wisdom or the single-minded fanaticism and determination to change decisively either for better or for worse.

THE APPARENT AND THE REAL IN GOGOL'S "NEVSKIJ PROSPEKT"

BY

OLGA RAEVSKY HUGHES

To the memory of Professor Oleg A. Maslenikov

IN HIS REMARKS on the plots of Gogol's stories Andrey Bely points out that when stripped of their typically Gogolian verbal embellishments, digressions and details, they are extremely simple. Gogol's methods of development lead to unexpected results, for the finished work seems to have little in common with the original simple plot; he achieves this mainly through the "luxury" of his images and the "power of sound."[1] In "Ob arkhitekture nynešnego vremeni," an article published in 1835, Gogol himself says that a story should express only one basic idea which, however, should be developed so as to reach enormous dimensions. An inability on the part of the writer to develop a simple story into a complex but unified whole in Gogol's opinion is a sign of a limited talent:

Poèt, ne imejuščij obširnogo genija, vsegda nedovolen odnim prostym sjužetom, i vmesto togo, čtoby razvit' ego i sdelat' ogromnym, on privjazyvaet k nemu množestvo drugikh; ego poèma obremenjaetsja pestrotoju raznykh predmetov, no ne imeet odnoj gospodstvujuščej mysli i ne vyražaet odnogo celogo.[2]

"Nevskij prospekt"—one of Gogol's Petersburg stories published also in 1835—is a good illustration of the application of this view in Gogol's own work. An attempt is made here to demonstrate how Gogol conveys one "dominant idea" through an elaborate development of a very simple plot.[3]

Reduced to its essence, the plot of "Nevskij prospekt" is indeed very simple.[4] One evening on Nevsky Avenue two young men meet and follow two women; both are deceived by their first impressions and in the end are unsuccessful in their pursuits. The title of the story, however, and the narrator's pronouncement that he intends to describe the changes that occur on Nevsky Avenue within twenty-four hours ("Skol'ko vyterpit on peremen v tečenie odnikh

---

[1] Andrej Belyj, *Masterstvo Gogolja* (Moskva-Leningrad: GIKhL, 1934), p. 43. The simplicity of Gogol's plots was noticed much earlier by Boris Èjkhenbaum in "Kak sdelana 'Šinel'" Gogolja." (Reprinted in *Skvoz' literaturu* [Mouton, 1962] and in *O proze* [Leningrad, 1969]). No attempt is made to include here even a selective list of Gogol criticism; only those works that bear direct reference to the subject are cited in the notes.

[2] N. V. Gogol', *Sobranie sočinenij v šesti tomakh* (Moskva: GIKhL, 1952), vol 6:44. All subsequent references and quotations from Gogol's works are to this edition.

[3] This analysis does not exhaust the material of the story and leaves many valid approaches to it untouched.

[4] Gogol's "simple plot" and its "development" correspond to "story" and "plot" respectively, or to the *fabula* and *sjužet* of the Russian formalists.

sutok! Načnem s samogo rannego utra ... ")⁵ might suggest that the description of Nevsky Avenue, which frames the two episodes, rather than the narration of the episodes themselves, is his object. In that case, the two episodes have to be viewed as an illustration of this description, and their structural function as a slowing-down of the account of the changes that Nevsky Avenue suffers within one day.

The story opens with a rather detailed description of Nevsky Avenue presented in a chronological sequence: it begins in the early morning, continues through the day, is interrupted at nightfall by the Piskarev and Pirogov episodes, and resumes after the completion of these two episodes with the picture of Nevsky Avenue at night. In "Nevskij prospekt" Gogol meets his own demand that a story have an essential unity. The description of Nevsky Avenue and the two episodes, despite the striking contrast between the two major characters and their experiences, express one "dominant idea"—a basic disparity between the appearance and the essence, a clash between dream and reality. The romantic Piskarev rejects the repulsive reality for the beautiful dream. When he is forced to separate the heroine of his dreams from the real woman who inspired those dreams, he crosses into the world of insanity and eventually ends his life by suicide. A down-to-earth realist and cynic, the officer Pirogov is likewise misled by the appearance. What he has in mind is an easy amorous adventure, of the success of which he is quite confident; thrashing by the Germans is hardly a part of his plan. Essentially, "Nevskij prospekt" presents a manysided and masterly illustration of the contradiction between the apparent and the real.

The opening description of Nevsky Avenue is given in what at first glance appears to be exalted and exaggerated terms. The narrator seems to be genuinely amazed by everything he sees on Nevsky Avenue, but his attitude changes radically in the course of the story. The tone of the conclusion—the undisguised disappointment of the closing lines of the story: "O, ne ver'te ètomu Nevskomu prospektu!! ... On lžet vo vsjakoe vremja, ètot Nevskij prospekt" (42, 43)—is in sharp contrast to the tone of exaggerated praise of the opening pages: "Net ničego lučše Nevskogo prospekta, po krajnej mere v Peterburge, dlja nego on sostavljaet vse" (7). The two episodes related in the story produce the change and serve as motivation for it: the naive amazement of the narrator is shattered by the illustrations of reality.⁶

However, if we keep the tone of the epilogue in mind, the opening exalted

---

⁵ Gogol', *Sobranie sočinenij*, vol. 3:8. "Nevskij prospekt" is on pp. 7–43 of this volume. The page references to the story given subsequently in the text are to this volume.

⁶ Viktor Šklovskij speaks of the change of tone in this story as an effective device for producing an impression of reality, a device that gives the author a possibility of "reflecting reality" in a short work. *Khudožestvennaja proza* (Moskva: Sovetskij pisatel', 1959), p. 399.

description of Nevsky Avenue acquires a different meaning. The narrator only pretends to be naive, for he knows the value of the beauty and the wealth exhibited on Nevsky Avenue even before he tells the stories of Piskarev and Pirogov. His unlimited excitement about insignificant things is ironic; he mocks those who might take his statements at their face value. "Rather important domestic occupations" are illustrated by an enumeration which does nothing but prove how insignificant and trivial they are:

Malo-pomalu prisoedinjajutsja k ikh obščestvu vse, okončivšie dovol'no važnye domašnie zanjatija, kak to: pogovorivšie s svoim doktorom o pogode i o nebol'šom pryščike, vskočivšem na nosu, ... pročitavšie afišu i važnuju stat'ju v gazetakh o priezžajuščikh i ot"-ezžajuščikh, nakonec vypivšie čašku kofiju i čaju. [9]

The narrator's ironic attitude becomes even more pronounced when another category of people walking along Nevsky Avenue—the government officials—is introduced:

K nim prisoedinjajutsja i te, kotorykh zavidnaja sud'ba nadelila blagoslovennym zvaniem činovnikov po osobym poručenijam. K nim prisoedinjajutsja i te, kotorye služat v inostrannoj kollegii i otličajutsja blagorodstvom svoikh zanjatij i privyček. Bože, kakie est' prekrasnye dolžnosti i služby, kak oni vozvyšajut i uslaždajut dušu. [9–10]

A preoccupation with the external and the insignificant is stressed. The narrator naively expresses surprise and lack of understanding for those who, meeting a person, look at his clothes and shoes:

Est' množestvo takikh ljudej, kotorye, vstretivšis' s vami, nepremenno posmotrjat na sapogi vaši, i, esli vy projdete, oni oborotjatsja nazad, čtoby posmotret' na vašy faldy. Ja do sikh por ne mogu ponjat' otčego èto byvaet. Snačala ja dumal, čto oni sapožniki, no, odnakože, ničut' ne byvalo: oni bol'šeju častiju služat v raznykh departamentakh. [11]

Gogol presents Nevsky Avenue in terms of people walking its sidewalks. These people are caricatured: we see the exaggeration of some characteristic feature of their physical appearance; one element of figure or dress is depicted grotesquely. Gogol consistently uses metonymy; grotesque features represent the whole man, and the reader is informed that on Nevsky Avenue he might meet different kinds of sideburns, moustaches, hats, unusually thin waists, ladies' sleeves, and smiles, rather than human beings:

Vy zdes' vstretite bakenbardy barkhatnye, ... usy čudnye, ... tysjači sortov šljapok, ... tonen'kie, uzen'kie talii, ... damskie rukava, ... ulybku edinstvennuju, ulybku verkh iskusstva. [10–11]

A variety of devices, creating an unmistakably "Gogolian" picture, is used. "Comical alogism," a device based on destruction of logical and causal connections or deliberate discrepancy between syntax and semantics, is applied quite liberally in the description of Nevsky Avenue.[7] Gogol arrives at

---

[7] For a discussion of "comical alogism" as used by Gogol, see A. Slonimskij, *Tekhnika komičeskogo u Gogolja* (Peterburg: Academia, 1923), p. 35.

conclusions which are in no way warranted by what, apparently, should lead to them; nonsensical statements are presented in a most matter-of-fact way. In one instance, we are told that in the morning some people inquire about the health of their horses and children. Placing children in the same category with horses is rather unexpected, but the next statement, as if attempting to counterbalance the reader's surprise at this reasoning, actually underscores its incongruity and destroys all semblance of logic. We are informed that those children, *however*, display great talents: "vpročem pokazyvajuščikh bol'šie darovanija" (9). Thus the talents of the children should compensate in some way for their being accorded as much parental attention as the horses.

Speaking of ladies' sleeves which one might encounter on Nevsky Avenue, the author makes an abrupt logical shift in the middle of the sentence:

Oni [damskie rukava] neskol'ko pokhoži na dva vozdukhoplavatel'nye šara, tak čto dama vdrug by podnjalas' na vozdukh, esli by ne podderžival ee mužčina; potomu čto damu takže legko i prijatno podnjat' na vozdukh, kak podnosimyj ko rtu bokal, napolnennyj šampanskim. [11]

First the sleeves are compared to two aerostats which might lift the lady in the air were she not supported by her escort. Then comes "because" (*potomu čto*) as if by the following Gogol intended to give the logical cause of the preceding. But he concludes by comparing the pleasure of lifting a lady off the ground with the pleasure of lifting a champagne glass. The unmotivated shift in the agent of lifting from the hyperbolic balloonlike sleeves to the delicately supporting escort is alogical. At the beginning of the sentence the gentleman is counteracting the effect of the sleeves, that is, preventing the levitation of the lady, at the end he obviously changes sides and himself becomes the instrument of levitation. Further pondering upon this sentence may lead one to conclude that it is the balloon and not the man who is experiencing the pleasure of lifting both the lady and the champagne glass.

The description of Nevsky Avenue unfolds very slowly; the narrator is in no hurry and takes every opportunity to digress. He focuses the reader's attention on seemingly irrelevant details. Thus, when he mentions the workers who hurriedly cross the avenue in the morning, we suddenly learn about the condition of their boots, which are so dirty that even the waters of Ekaterininsky Canal, according to him notorious for its cleanliness, could not clean them. His similes develop into miniature scenes acted out by several characters. For example, the mention of unusually thin waists becomes a scene in which a passer-by steps aside and almost ceases to breathe so as not to harm the lady, who by now has become a work of art (10). The similes are highly hyperbolic: thin waists are compared to bottlenecks and sleeves to aerostats.

Because of their extent, the enumerations of what one may encounter on Nevsky Avenue leave the reader breathless:

Odin pokazyvaet ščegol'skij sjurtuk s lučšim bobrom, *drugoj*—grečeskij prekrasnyj nos, *tretij* neset prevoskhodnye bakenbardy, *četvertaja*—paru khorošen'kikh glazok i udivitel'nuju šljapku, *pjatyj*—persten' s talismanom na ščegol'skom mizince, *šestaja*—nožku v očarovatel'nom bašmačke, *sed'moj*—galstuk, vozbuždajuščij udivlenie, *os'moj*—usy, povergajuščie v izumlenie. [11, italics here and elsewhere added]

The outgrowth of modifiers and relative clauses combines with the parallel construction to overwhelm the reader by the cumulative force which the list attains towards the end:

Zdes' vy vstretite usy čudnye, nikakim perom, nikakoju kist'ju neizobrazimye; usy, kotorym posvjaščena lučšaja polovina žizni,—predmet dolgikh bdenij vo vremja dnja i noči, usy, na kotorye izlilis' voskhititel'nejšie dukhi i aromaty i kotorykh umastili vse dragocennejšie i redčajšie sorty pomad, usy, kotorye zavoračivajutsja na noč' tonkoju velenevoju bumagoju, usy, k kotorym dyšit samaja trogatel'naja privjazannost' ikh posessorov i kotorym zavidujut prokhodjaščie. [10]

The multicolored and grotesque picture moves before the reader's eyes; the crowds on Nevsky Avenue change with the passing time. By the time this colorful and unhurried description has reached nightfall and the street lanterns are being lighted, it is suddenly interrupted by a short dialogue between two young men walking along the avenue. The attention of the reader is shifted from a general picture of the faceless crowd to two specific personages. And thus we meet the two main characters of "Nevskij prospekt." After a short conversation they part never to meet again in the course of the story. Structurally, the short dialogue between Piskarev and Pirogov serves as a bridge between the description of Nevsky Avenue and the two episodes that follow. The other function this short scene serves is the actual bringing together of the two contrasting characters. This is the only instance in the story when they appear together and this joint appearance serves as motivation for the juxtaposition of the two episodes which develop along parallel lines.

Juxtaposition of contrasting elements is an important structural principle used by Gogol in this story. The striking difference between the two men and their experiences sustain the narrative interest of "Nevskij prospekt." Structurally the two episodes have many parallels, a fact that only underscores the differences between the two characters, their attitudes, and reactions. The parallel episodes develop in the following way: both men, as they walk together on Nevsky Avenue, are attracted by beautiful women (for a moment they even think that they are talking about the same woman); each follows the woman to the house where she lives; several encounters at unspecified intervals follow. From the structural viewpoint it is immaterial that three of

Piskarev's five encounters with his beautiful lady actually take place in a dream. Both men are faced with failure: neither is able to achieve his aim.

After introducing the two men, the author abandons Pirogov completely and tells the story of Piskarev. When we learn of Piskarev's suicide, it is mentioned that even Pirogov did not come to his funeral. This statement serves as a transition from one episode to the other, and once they are bridged in this way the author goes back to the first evening on Nevsky Avenue, where he left Pirogov after briefly introducing him to the reader.

The two episodes illustrate two contrasting attitudes. One is that of a romantic dreamer, for whom dream and reality merge and eventually exchange places: "Vsja žizn' ego prinjala strannyj oborot: on, možno skazat', spal najavu i bodrstvoval vo sne" (25–26). The other is that of self-satisfied mediocrity and complacency, the incarnation of *pošlost'*: "On byl očen' dovolen svoim činom, v kotoryj byl proizveden nedavno, ... vtajne ego očen' l'stilo èto novoe dostoinstvo" (33). The juxtaposition of these two opposing attitudes provides the contrast that enables the author to treat the two episodes on two different levels, to narrate them in a completely different tone and manner. Piskarev's story is tragic; Pirogov's is pure farce.

With the abrupt transition from the description of Nevsky Avenue in general to the two men in particular, the author's tone and technique change radically. The picture of Nevsky Avenue is presented visually, in terms of shapes and colors; when Gogol turns to Piskarev and Pirogov, the grotesquely hyperbolic descriptions disappear. One of the two men is referred to simply as "poručik Pirogov," and the other as "molodoj čelovek vo frake i plašče" (13). They are described in terms of their inner qualities rather than external features. These are Pirogov's thoughts as his attention is drawn to an attractive woman on Nevsky Avenue:

"Znaem my vas vsekh," —dumal pro sebja s samodovol'noju i samonadejannoju ulybkoju Pirogov, uverennyj, čto net krasoty, mogšej by emu protivit'sja. [14]

His feelings of self-satisfaction, self-assurance, and certainty of success are emphasized. Immediately after this follows a contrasting response of Piskarev to the same situation; the author points out his timidity and shyness:

Molodoj čelovek vo frake i plašče robkim i trepetnym šagom pošel v tu storonu, gde razvevalsja vdali pestryj plašč.... Serdce ego bilos'... On ne smel i dumat' o tom, čtoby polučit' kakoe-nibud' pravo na vnimanie uletavšej vdali krasavicy. [14]

Throughout the story Gogol consistently presents Pirogov and Piskarev in terms of their moods and attitudes; he does not dwell on their physical appearance at all.

Whereas the men are characterized by means of their desires, emotions, and mental states, the women, on the other hand, are described in terms of purely external, physical qualities. The usage of diminutives in reference to the foolish little blonde whom Pirogov follows suggests a somewhat vulgar tone: "Èta blondinka byla legen'koe, dovol'no interesnoe sozdan'ice" (31), she is addressed by Pirogov as "moja milen'kaja!... plutovočka, kakie khorošen'kie glazki!... kakie milen'kie ručki" (36). The woman who attracts Piskarev's attention is presented in lofty, exaggerated and superlative terms: "Prelestnejšij lob osenen byl prekrasnymi, kak agat, volosami. Oni vilis', èti čudnye lokony" (16). Thus, if the two men stand for two contrasting attitudes, the two women represent two different types of beauty. Neither men nor women are individualized; they are only representatives of certain types.

Four pages elapse before the beautiful girl and Piskarev, who is following her, reach the house where she lives. In the meantime we learn who Piskarev is. He is described as a member of a certain category of people—the Petersburg artists. After describing them as a group, Gogol adds:

K takomu rodu prinadležal opisannyj nami molodoj čelovek, khudožnik Piskarev, zastenčivyj, robkij, no v duše svoej nosivšij iskry čuvstva, gotovye pri udobnom slučae prevratit'sja v plamja. [15]

This list of his qualities merely recapitulates the characteristics of Petersburg artists.

The same method is used in describing Pirogov and the German Schiller. Pirogov is presented in terms of the society to which he belongs:

No prežde neželi my skažem, kto takov byl poručik Pirogov, ne mešaet koe-čto rasskazat' o tom obščestve, k kotoromu prinadležal Pirogov. [31]

After listing some of the characteristics typical of the members of Pirogov's society, Gogol indicates his intention of describing Pirogov as an individual: "No poručik Pirogov imel množestvo talantov, sobstvenno emu prinadležavsikh" (32). Then he gives some details which illustrate the preceding account and actually tie Pirogov more closely to the group of the middle-class officers described above. As to his individual traits, Gogol announces that a man is such a marvelous being that enumeration of all his merits would be endless.

The German Schiller is introduced as a German first of all: "Šiller byl soveršennyj nemec, v polnom smysle vsego ètogo slova" (38). Later, speaking of Schiller, Gogol passes to Germans in general: "Skoree činovnik pozabudet zagljanut' v švejcarskuju svoego načal'nika, neželi nemec rešitsja peremenit' svoe slovo" (39). Schiller's qualities, which in Gogol's opinion are typical of Germans, are stressed. Thus all three, Piskarev, Pirogov, and Schiller, are depicted as representatives of certain groups rather than as individuals. This facelessness of the characters gives support to the suggestion that the two episodes serve mainly as illustrations of the conflict between the apparent and the real and, as such, help depict the real protagonist of the story—the Nevsky Avenue.[8]

The description of Petersburg artists interrupts and slows down Piskarev's pursuit of the beautiful girl. After this description Gogol returns to the two on Nevsky Avenue. The tension builds up as Piskarev follows the girl. First she looks at him in anger, then she smiles; later she makes a sign to follow her into the house; finally, as he reaches the door of her apartment, he hears her voice (16–17). Each of these instances serves to increase tension. Between the moments when she looks, smiles, makes a sign to, and addresses Piskarev, we follow the flight of his imagination: by the time they reach the door, Piskarev decides that she needs his help, and he vows to be her knight.

The mounting tension of this episode is demonstrated in the verbs that Gogol uses. The accelerating physical movement reflects the increasing emotional strain. A series of verbs denoting motion is used.[9] The context indicates the increasing speed and the forward and upward direction of this movement: "s tajnym trepetom *spešil* on," "trotuar *nessja* pod nim," "on *nessja* po legkim sledam," "nepreodolimaja sila i trevoga vsekh čuvstv *stremila* ego vpered," "neznakomka *letela* po lestnice," "on *vzletel* po lestnice." Finally, the emotional response literally parallels the physical motion as the flight of Piskarev's imagination follows the spiral of the stairway: "Lestnica *vilas'*, i vmeste s neju *vilis'* ego bystrye mečty" (15–17).

After the tension reaches its peak at this point, it subsides much more rapidly than it was built up. By observing the room and the people in it, Piskarev realizes that the girl is a prostitute and flees her house. His departure from the scene is described very briefly: "On brosilsja so vsekh nog, kak dikaja koza, i vybežal na ulicu" (19).

The flight up the stairs was interrupted by Piskarev's doubting: "No ne vo sne li èto vse?" (17). This question points directly to Piskarev's next encounter with the girl, which occurs in a dream. Gogol very carefully preserves a semblance of reality. Imperceptibly reality changes into dream: Piskarev falls asleep, then is roused by a knock at his door. He wakes into a dream. The second encounter is constructed in a way similar to the first. The description of the hall to which Piskarev is taken in his dream resembles the description of Nevsky Avenue. The tone of naive amazement bordering on irony, as well as

---

[8] On the relationship of "Nevskij prospekt" to a physiological sketch, which describes groups rather than individuals, see A. G. Cejtlin, *Stanovlenie realizma v russkoj literature* (Moskva: Nauka, 1965), pp. 15–26. A collective as a protagonist of Gogol's work is discussed by G. A. Gukovskij in *Realizm Gogolja* (Moskva-Leningrad: GIKhL, 1959), pp. 259–268.

[9] On Gogol's use of verbs see Belyj, *Masterstvo Gogolja*, pp. 200–204.

enumerations and repetitions, which characterize the opening pages of the story, return:

molodye ljudi v černykh frakakh byli ispolneny *takogo* blagorodstva, s *takim* dostoinstvom govorili i molčali, *tak* ne umeli skazat' ničego lišnego, *tak* veličavo šutili, *tak* počtitel'no ulybalis', *takie* prevoskhodnye nosili bakenbardy, *tak* iskusno umeli pokazyvat' otličnye ruki, popravljaja galstuk, damy *tak* byli vozdušny, *tak* pogruženy v soveršennoe samodovol'stvo i upoenie, *tak* očarovatel'no potupljali glaza ... [21-22]

This description of the ball delays Piskarev's meeting the girl. When he arrives at the ball, we are reminded of the increasing tension of his previous encounter. Gogol describes the stairway Piskarev ascends using the same verb *neslas'* as in the first encounter: "Vozdušnaja lestnica ... *neslas'* vverkh" (21) The girl's actions and Piskarev's reactions in the dream follow the pattern of their first encounter. First she looks at him: "Obvela glazami ves' krug ... i vstretilas' s glazami Piskareva" (23), then makes a sign to him: "Ona podala znak, ... nikto ne mog ego videt', no on videl, on ponjal ego" (23). Later on she begins to talk to Piskarev, but their conversation is interrupted before she has a chance to explain anything. This interruption helps to sustain the tension already built up. When the conversation is resumed, the tension mounts to a higher level as the girl promises to tell Piskarev a secret that will account for the strange circumstances of their first meeting. But the expected climax does not take place, for their conversation is interrupted again and she is led away by an unidentified man. The tension is sustained while Piskarev runs from room to room in the hope of finding the girl. In this encounter the tension is released in two successive stages, first when Piskarev fails to find her at the ball, and then when he wakes up and realizes that their meeting took place in a dream.

Three more encounters between Piskarev and the girl are described in the story, two in dreams and one in reality. Between the first and the second dream Piskarev begins taking opium. This serves as realistic motivation for his eventual hallucinatory condition.[10]

For Piskarev, dream and reality merge more and more; he comes to believe what he sees in his dreams. Thus, although each successive dream ends in an anticlimax of awakening, the tension after each following dream remains at a higher level than after the preceding one. This is achieved by carrying Piskarev's dream reality over into the everyday reality; the beautiful prostitute is transformed into a different person: "Čerez èti snovidenija samyj predmet [ego ljubvi] kak-to bolee delalsja čistym i vovse preobražalsja" (27). In the

---

[10] For the discussion of the connections of the opium motif with Thomas de Quincey's *Confessions of an English Opium Eater*, see V. V. Vinogradov, "O literaturnoj ciklizacii" in *Èvoljucija russkogo naturalizma* (Leningrad: Academia, 1929), pp. 89-126.

second dream Piskarev sees the girl in simple surroundings; this places her closer to his own situation than did the setting of splendor in the first dream. In the third dream Piskarev's illusory happiness reaches its highest point when she appears as his wife. Now dream and reality merge completely for him; awakening does not produce the expected anticlimax of the return to reality as it did on the previous occasions. By the time of the third dream the borderline between dream and reality is completely obliterated for Piskarev, and the tension built up in the dream does not subside in reality: Piskarev decides to marry the girl. Her refusal and his extreme reaction to it serve as a culmination not only of the fifth encounter, but of the whole Piskarev episode as well. The tension gradually built up through the series of dreams is now finally released and the incident is finished. We learn that Piskarev became deranged, and committed suicide.

The distortion of reality, the confusion of dream and reality, which Piskarev experiences and which is the cause of his tragic end, is alluded to early in the story. Gogol hints at Piskarev's own unreality, for a Petersburg artist in general is "dovol'no strannoe javlenie i stol'ko že prinadležit k graždanam Peterburga, skol'ko lico, javljajuščeesja nam v snovidenii, prinadležit k suščestvennomu miru" (14). When Piskarev decides that the beautiful girl whom he follows on Nevsky Avenue has noticed him, the normal proportions and the usual relationships of objects are changed or reversed:

Trotuar nessja pod nim, karety so skačuščimi lošad'mi kazalis' nedvižimy, most rastjagivalsja i lomalsja na svoej arke, dom stojal kryšeju vniz, budka valilas' k nemu navstreču i alebarda časovogo vmeste s zolotymi slovami vyveski i narisovannymi nožnicami blestela, kazalos', na samoj resnice ego glaz. [16]

The eventual merging of reality and dream is prepared gradually and is not entirely unexpected.

The short account of Piskarev's funeral gives Gogol a chance to return to Pirogov who was abandoned at the beginning of the Piskarev episode:

Daže poručik Pirogov ne prišel posmotret' na trup nesčastnogo bednjaka.... Vpročem emu bylo vovse ne do togo.... No obratimsja k nemu. [30–31]

After reminding the reader of Pirogov, Gogol proceeds with the epilogue to the story of Piskarev, in which he states his own attitude to funerals. The epilogue consists of three parts. In expressing his feelings, the narrator goes from the general to the specific: the narrator dislikes funerals in general and is especially annoyed by lavish funerals, but his annoyance mixes with sadness at the sight of a poor man's funeral unattended by relatives or friends; in the end the feelings of dislike and annoyance merge into sadness.

After this epilogue the narrator returns to Pirogov again. His pursuit of the blonde is, however, interrupted and slowed down by several digressions. First, the woman is described, then the narrator proposes to describe Pirogov, but changes his mind and decides to speak about the society to which Pirogov belonged. While describing this society, he digresses further and we learn, for instance, how to amuse the daughters of the officials whose houses people like Pirogov visit frequently, and what kind of husbands Russian merchants expect for their daughters. After this two-page digression, which retards Pirogov's progress along Nevsky Avenue and thereby slows down the development of the plot, the narrator returns once more—for the third time—to Pirogov: "Itak Pirogov ne perestaval presledovat' neznakomku" (33).

The Pirogov episode is presented as a contrast to the story of Piskarev. The difference between the two is conveyed first of all by the change in the tone of narration. It is first evident when the blonde is presented in diminutive terms and Pirogov's society of "middle-class officers" is described. When the blonde, with Pirogov in pursuit, arrives at her house, the scene that Pirogov witnesses there lowers the tone of the whole episode even further: the husband of the blonde implores his friend to cut off his nose. The whole scene is written for the eye to see:

Udivilo ego [Pirogova] črezvyčajno strannoe položenie figur. Šiller sidel, vystaviv svoj dovol'no tolstyj nos i podnjavši vverkh golovu; a Gofman deržal ego za ètot nos dvumja pal'cami i vertel lezviem svoego sapožničeskogo noža na samoj ego poverkhnosti. [34]

In Gogol's fanciful world everything is turned upside down: Schiller and Hoffmann become here Petersburg artisans. The idea of giving famous literary names to farcical characters contributes to the comicality and incongruity of the scene. Gogol does not mention the names of Schiller and Hoffmann casually, but makes a point of distinguishing the two Petersburg artisans from German writers. By a most unexpected and alogical turn the artisans rather than the writers become famous:

Pered nim sidel Šiller, ne tot Šiller, kotoryj napisal "Vil'gel'ma Tellja" i "Istoriju Tridcatiletnej vojny," no izvestnyj Šiller, žestjanykh del master v Meščanskoj ulice. Vozle Šillera stojal Gofman,—ne pisatel' Gofman, no dovol'no khorošij sapožnik s Oficerskoj ulicy, bol'šoj prijatel' Šillera. [34]

This comical tone is sustained throughout the Pirogov episode. The elements of farce are numerous: Pirogov kisses the wife while her phlegmatic husband looks away; Schiller's plan to get rid of Pirogov actually works against him; and in the concluding scene, Pirogov is flogged by the drunken Germans. Pirogov's calls at the house of the blonde are given mainly in the form of dialogue and appear like miniature dramatic scenes. This also serves as a contrast with the first episode, for Piskarev's utterances are few and mostly limited to exclamations. His thoughts and emotions are presented largely by means of inner monologues. The scarcity of dialogue helps to sustain the general air of unreality about Piskarev.

Pirogov visits Schiller's house several times; five of these visits are described. This follows closely the scheme of Piskarev's five encounters. The development of the plot is interrupted and slowed down by several digressions. At the time of the first visit the comical scene between Schiller and Hoffman serves this purpose. During the second visit Pirogov orders spurs from Schiller; this provides motivation for his following visits. After the second visit a digression on the beauty and stupidity of women is included. Between the third visit and the next two, which follow without interruption, Gogol inserts a description of Schiller.

Reality, which intruded into Piskarev's dream world and destroyed it, appears in Pirogov's case disguised as the pretty blonde's husband: very real and as inescapable as one's fate. He cuts short Pirogov's encounters with his wife either by making him leave or by sending her out of the room. When it seems that Pirogov has cleverly escaped the husband's presence, he suddenly and unexpectedly reappears and ends the whole episode by physically punishing Pirogov.

The epilogue of the Pirogov episode is, like Piskarev's, presented in three stages, his rage at the Germans diminishing by degrees with each successive stage and in the end being replaced by his usual self-satisfaction. First: "Odna mysl' o takom užasnom oskorblenii *privodila ego v bešenstvo*. Sibir' i pleti on počital samym malym nakazaniem dlja Šillera. On *letel domoj*, čtoby, odevši', ottuda idti prjamo k generalu," then: "Po doroge on *zašel v konditerskuju*, ... s"el dva sloenykh pirožka, pročital koe-čto iz 'Severnoj Pčely' i *vyšel* uže ne v stol' gnevnom položenii," and finally: "K devjati časam on uspokoilsja ... i otpravilsja na večer k odnomu pravitelju kontrol'noj kollegii.... Tam s udovol'stviem *provel večer*" (41-42).

In the description of Piskarev's pursuit of the girl the verbs helped to reflect the mounting emotional tension of the protagonist which paralleled the increasing speed of his physical movements; here they depict the opposite development: Pirogov's subsiding excitement accompanied by the slowing-down of his movements.

After concluding the Pirogov episode, the narrator returns to the interrupted description of Nevsky Avenue. It serves as the epilogue to the whole story. The evaluation of the splendor exhibited on Nevsky Avenue is quite different from what it was in the opening pages of the story. The narrator stresses the absurdity of life ("Vse proiskhodit naoborot") and the discrepancy between the apparent and the real ("Vse obman, vse mečta, vse ne to, čem kažetsja" [42]). Although the language is as hyperbolic as at the beginning of the story ("rot veličinoju v arku glavnogo štaba" [42]), "miriady karet valjatsja s mostov" [43]), the tone is different; now the narrator is not amazed any more, but knows and stresses the falsity of everything on Nevsky Avenue: "On lžet vo vsjakoe vremja, ètot Nevskij prospekt" (43).

The change in the narrator's tone can be observed several times in the course of the story. At the beginning of the Piskarev episode the ironic tone of the opening pages is dropped. The narrator becomes less prominent and at times merges with Piskarev. When Piskarev runs away from the girl, however, the narrator pretends to consider him ridiculous and simple as a child, and a spark of irony can be detected again:

On byl črezvyčajno smešon i prost, kak ditja. Vmesto togo, čtoby vospol'zovat'sja takoju blagosklonnost'ju, vmesto togo, čtoby obradovat'sja takomu slučaju, ... on brosilsja so vsekh nog, kak dikaja koza, i vybežal na ulicu. [19]

The tragic story of Piskarev ends on a highly subjective and lyrical note; the narrator is prominent again: "*Ja* ne ljublju trupov i pokojnikov.... *Ja* vsegda čuvstvuju na duše dosadu, ... no dosada *moja* smešivaetsja s grust'ju" (31). To indicate the abrupt change of mood and to mark the break with the personal and lyrical tone, Gogol changes from the first person singular to the first person plural as he begins the Pirogov episode: "*My*, kažetsja, ostavili poručika Pirogova na tom" and "No prežde neželi *my* skažem, kto takov byl poručik Pirogov" (31). When Pirogov's individual qualities are listed, the narrator's assumed naiveté, which was evident in the descriptions of Nevsky Avenue and the ball in Piskarev's first dream, comes to the fore again. Reciting poetry and making elaborate smoke rings are placed next to each other: "On prevoskhodno deklamiroval stikhi ... i imel osobennoe iskusstvo puskat' iz trubki dym kol'cami" (33).

The narrator's point of view is repeatedly identified with the point of view of the character who is being described. This becomes especially noticeable when his musings on beauty and vice are compared. He readily agrees with Piskarev on the incongruity of beauty embracing vice. "Takaja krasavica, takie božestvennye čerty—i gde že? v kakom meste!" thinks Piskarev upon realizing that the beautiful girl is a prostitute and the narrator continues:

V samom dele, nikogda žalost' tak sil'no ne ovladevaet nami, kak pri vide krasoty, tronutoj tletvornym dykhaniem razvrata. Pust' by ešče bezobrazie družilos' s nim, no krasota, krasota nežnaja ... ona tol'ko s odnoj neporočnost'ju i čistotoj slivaetsja v našikh mysljakh. [19]

On the other hand, when speaking of Schiller's wife, the narrator makes the following statement:

Krasota proizvodit soveršennye čudesa. Vse duševnye nedostatki v krasavice, vmesto togo čtoby proizvesti otvraščenie, stanovjatsja kak-to neobyknovenno privlekatel'ny, samyj porok dyšit v nikh milovidnost'ju. [37-38]

For *pošlyj* Pirogov and primitive Schiller stupidity in a woman becomes a virtue, and beauty makes even vice attractive; now the narrator goes along with this view, which is in obvious contradiction with the view of Piskarev to which he subscribed before.[11]

Gogol makes skillful and consistent use of words denoting bright light in the depiction of Piskarev's beautiful girl and in contrasting dream and reality. The beautiful girl is described in terms of blinding, flashing beauty; the "blinding whiteness" becomes her dominant feature: "*oslepitel'noj belizny lob*" (16), "*sverkajuščaja belizna* lica ee ešče *oslepitel'nee* brosalas' v glaza" (22), "tonkij sirenevyj cvet ešče vidnee označil *jarkuju beliznu* ètoj prekrasnoj ruki" (23), "ee obnažennaja, *jarkaja, kak zaoblačnyj sneg*, ruka" (25).

Piskarev's first dream which stands in sharp contrast to reality is also presented in terms of bright light:

I *osveščennaja* perspektiva domov s *jarkimi* vyveskami poneslas' mimo karetnykh okon... Kareta ostanovilas' pered *jarko osveščennym* pod"ezdom, i ego razom porazili... *jarko osveščennye* okna.... Lakej... provodil [ego] v seni... s *oblitym zolotom* švejcarom, ... s *jarkoju lampoju*. Vozdušnaja lestnica s *blestjaščimi* perilami.... *Sverkajuščie* damskie pleči,... *ljustry, lampy*... vse bylo dlja nego *blistatel'no*. [21, italics added]

The bright illumination of this dream is contrasted with the dull light of Piskarev's awakening: "Dosadnyj svet neprijatnym svoim *tusklym sijaniem* gljadel v ego okna. Komnata v takom *serom*, takom *mutnom* besporjadke" (25). Later in the story, when the borderline between dream and reality becomes less distinct for Piskarev, the sharp contrasts of brightness and gloom disappear. In the second and the third dreams the striking whiteness of the girl's beauty is not mentioned and references to bright light are entirely absent.

Gogol's subtle hints at the constant presence of evil in life and at the corrupt nature of the beautiful girl are other instances of his careful choice of words in this story. The allusions to the role that demonic forces play in subjugating beauty to evil were noticed by Vasily Gippius, who cited two instances of this in the text of "Nevskij prospekt": "Ona byla kakoju-to užasnoju voleju *adskogo dukha*, žažduščego razrušit' garmoniju žizni, brošena s khokhotom v ego pučinu" (20), and in the concluding lines of the story: "Sam *demon* zažigaet lampy dlja togo tol'ko, čtoby pokazat' vse ne v nastojaščem vide" (43).[12] There is one more reference to the "demon" as the source of confusion and destruction of meaning in life. When Piskarev in his dream enters the ballroom, it appears to him that "*kakoj-to demon* iskrošil ves' mir

---

[11] The changes in the narrator's attitude are discussed by Vinogradov in "Romantičeskij naturalizm" (*Èvoljucija russkogo naturalizma*, pp. 192-201) in connection with the poetics of the "frenetic school" and the work of Jules Janin.

[12] Vasilij Gippius, *Gogol'* (Leningrad: Mysl', 1924), p. 52.

na množestvo raznykh kuskov i vse èti kuski bez smysla, bez tolku smešal vmeste" (21).

It is possible to detect some elements that point to the presence of evil and destructive forces in the beautiful girl herself: "ta li èto, kotoraja tak *okoldovala . . . ego*" (19), "krasavica, tak *okoldovavšaja* bednogo Piskareva" (19), "v ee *sokrušitel'nykh* glazakh" (23). The girl is first identified by her bright cloak: "[Piskarev pošel] v tu storonu, gde razvevalsja *jarkij plašč*" (13), which immediately becomes a symbol of duality:

Razvevalsja vdali *pestryj plašč*, to otkidyvavšijsja *jarkim bleskom* po mere približenija k svetu fonarja, to mgnovenno *pokryvavšijsja t'moju* po udalenii ot nego. [14]

This seemingly minor detail points to the main theme of the story—the contrast between the way things look and what they are in reality. These references, however slight, are nevertheless indicative of Gogol's intention of showing that the beautiful girl was touched by evil. The bright cloak reappears in the epilogue; but now the narrator refuses to be enticed by it: "Kak ni razvevajsja vdali plašč krasavicy, ja ni za čto ne pojdu za neju ljubopytstvovat'" (43). It is significant that both the motif of duality and of the devil as the hidden source of the distortion of reality reappear in the epilogue. At night, Nevsky Avenue—the true protagonist of the story—shows its real face.

Although relatively short and simple, upon careful reading "Nevskij prospekt" reveals a complex structural whole. The disparity between the appearance and the essence is illustrated by means of different episodes, descriptions, and details. The language—both figures of speech and the precise selection of words—is skillfully used to reflect the change in the narrator's point of view, to represent the moods and emotions of the characters, and to create vivid visual impressions. Employing parallels and contrasts, Gogol masterfully develops a very simple story in two structurally similar, but essentially contrasting episodes, which are framed by a hyperbolic and colorful, typically Gogolian description of Nevsky Avenue.

THE NARRATOR AND THE HERO IN CHEKHOV'S PROSE

BY

THOMAS EEKMAN

1

WHO TELLS CHEKHOV'S STORIES? Whose point of view is represented? Whose voice is being heard? Is the same voice heard throughout a story, or are there shifting, alternating voices? Is an evolution, a change, in the use of these procedures discernible in the course of Chekhov's literary career? An attempt to answer these questions might help us to understand better the artistic, creative processes that directed Chekhov (or which Chekhov applied) when writing his short stories and novellas.

Since the study of the structural aspects of literary works, now *en vogue* in the West, has also become acceptable in the Soviet Union,[1] some studies on the technique and structure of literary texts have been published there. In the case of Chekhov, there is the book by A. P. Chudakov, *Poètika Čekhova* (Moscow, 1971).[2] This is certainly a valuable study on which, I think, all further research in this field will have to be based. Later on in my article I shall return to it.

Chekhov began to write his fiction in the early eighties of the nineteenth century, when there existed a rich tradition of short-story narration, developed and established by a vast number of writers through the ages; various techniques and approaches had been tried, applied, and worked out. Boccaccio was the great predecessor in the early Renaissance period (although he, for his subject matter, partly utilized existing medieval stories). He did not establish a tradition: in the romantic period, the art of the novella and short story was, as it were, newly discovered. It was then cultivated in several European

---

[1] Cf. B. A. Uspenskij, *Poètika kompozicii* (Moscow, 1970). See also the critical review of this book by Frans de Valk in *Russian Literature*, no. 2 (The Hague, 1972):165–175.

[2] And his study "Ob èvoljucii stilja prozy Čekhova," in *Slavjanskaja filologija* (Moscow, 1963), 5:315ff., in which the main lines of the book are already staked out. Among publications in Western countries, the book by Nils Åke Nilsson, *Studies in Čechov's Narrative Technique* (Stockholm, 1968) should be mentioned. More recently, there was H. Hamburger's article "The Function of the Viewpoint in Čexov's 'Griša'" in *Russian Literature*, no. 3 (The Hague, 1972:5–15). This is an interesting study; two remarks should, however, be made. The author calls viewpoint "a grammatical category" (p. 14) and treats it as such; there is a danger here that questions of grammar and of artistic method get confused. Viewpoint as a literary category uses grammar as a tool! Secondly, an elaborate comparison is made between the author of a literary work and a camera(man), following an article by L. M. O'Toole. Such a parallel is always defective, as it neglects the primary, intrinsic function of the author as the active, creative, constructive force of the narrative. An excellent general work on problems of narration is Bertil Romberg's *Studies in the Narrative Technique of the First-Person Novel* (Stockholm, 1962).

countries and the United States (by Goethe, Tieck, von Kleist, Hoffmann, by Poe, Melville, Hawthorne, by Hardy, Conrad, to mention just a few names).

In Chekhov's time these genres reached a new high watermark with Guy de Maupassant in France, somewhat later Hugo von Hoffmannsthal in Germany, Katherine Mansfield in England, and others. Famous Russian short-story writers from Pushkin and Gogol to Turgenev, Tolstoy, Leskov, and Garshin had drawn on this tradition, applying the various procedures that had been developed in the past and introducing new ones. A story, for instance, could take the form of a first-person narrative as a variety of the more usual third-person type; of a framed story (*Rahmenerzählung*); of a story in letters, or in diary form; it could be told by a narrator other than the author himself, by somebody speaking a special dialect or jargon; or it could have two or more levels of narrative viewpoint.

It was quite natural that a young and inexperienced prose writer like Chekhov would follow in the footsteps of all these predecessors. But it was equally natural that the gifted artist Chekhov was would add new traits to the tradition, widen the possibilities, and enrich the genre of short-story writing. It is generally known that he introduced the story with the zero ending, the story that finishes (and also starts) at a more or less arbitrary point in the lives of the heroes, that tells us about seemingly ordinary happenings or presents an eventless slice of life, in which, however, the atmosphere—as it is called *faute de mieux*—the typical Chekhovian mood or a certain subtext (*podtekst*) in the dialogue is clearly perceptible. It should be added that by no means all of his stories are eventless and that some of them have a rather elaborate, "Turgenevian" conclusion. Chekhov, in his turn, invigorated and fertilized the short-story tradition and became a model for many Russian and Western writers in this genre after him. What was particularly admired was his economy, the scantiness of his artistic means, and the lack of superfluous detail with which he reached a maximal effect.

It is not surprising, then, that a good deal of attention has been paid to the character and structure of these Chekhovian stories. In recent years especially, several detailed studies of his narrative technique have been published both in the Soviet Union and in the West. One has, therefore, to overcome a strong hesitation before venturing to embark on another paper in this field, however specific and limited in scope it may be. But it seems to me that some facts have not been stated, some conclusions have not been drawn, which might be relevant in this context.

2

When we ask, who tells a Chekhov story? the immediate answer an ingenuous reader is inclined to give is, the author himself, of course—the author as the omniscient, omnipresent, and omnipotent narrator, the superior master of his own story, which he can direct and mold any way he wants. But is the answer quite so simple?

Let us take some of the innumerable short stories and sketches from his early years. Certainly, in stories like "Tolstyj i tonkij" ("Fat and Thin") or "Tragik" ("The Tragic Actor") from 1883, and in many others, one can see him at work as such a superior narrator. Let us look now somewhat closer at a story like "Nalim" ("The Burbot," 1885), which, according to Chekhov's brother Mikhail, was based on a real happening.[3] In it he describes two peasants, village carpenters, standing in the water near the bank of a river (one of those innumerable rivers on which every town and every country estate in Chekhov's works seem to be situated), trying to catch a huge burbot.

There is an—obviously concise—introductory description of the surrounding scenery: two short impressionistic sentences. There is an equally brief indication of the situation and a cursory description of the two heroes. Then follows the actual story, which is almost entirely in dialogue. Up to here the narration could have come from a superior author, but just as well from a person present at the scene, who could have seen and heard everything that was going on. Or rather, not quite everything: strictly speaking, he would not be able to see the under-water tree stump Lyubim puts his foot on and the object he then grabs under the surface, something that is described as "čego-to sklizkogo, kholodnogo" ("something slippery, cold"),[4] which must be the burbot, but which a spectator cannot yet see. He "uže zalezaet pal'cami pod 'zebry'" ("gets him with his fingers under his gills"), Chekhov reports, which only an omniscient narrator would be able to notice; however, here he adds the word *povidimomu* (apparently) and, recovering himself from the slight deviation from the illusion of a describing onlooker he made a few lines earlier, he indicates with this little word, one of those modal adverbs that served this purpose in nineteenth century fiction,[5] that the spectator-narrator only *presumes* what is going on.

A little later, a shepherd, the landowner's coachman, and the landowner himself, Andrey Andreich, join the fish catchers. Andrey Andreich, "to his great satisfaction, feels how his fingers get under the burbot's gills" ("k velikomu svoemu udovol'stviju, čuvstvuet, kak ego pal'cy lezut nalimu pod žabry"). Here the omniscient author seems to speak, knowing what Andrey

---

[3] M. P. Čekhov, "Čekhov na kanikulakh", in *A. P. Čekhov v vospominanijakh sovremennikov* (Moscow, 1960), p. 87.

[4] A. P. Čekhov, *Polnoe sobranie sočinenij i pisem*, 20 vols. (Moscow, 1944–1951), 4:8. Subsequent references, by volume and page number only, are to this edition; the translations are my own.

[5] B. A. Uspenskij, *Poètika kompozicii*, p. 113.

Andreich was feeling with his fingers and in his heart; although one might argue that an attentive observer could notice these sensations by the way the hero behaved, or maybe the hero shouted something, expressed his thoughts in words, but they have not been rendered in the text. However this may be, the greater part of the story, up to the final, fatal turning point when the fish suddenly jumps back to freedom, is presumably told either by the author himself or by an attentive spectator-reporter.[6]

The formalists have introduced the idea of the narrator as a constant intermediary figure between the author and his heroes. Often, however, there is no indication that such a narrator has been called in, and no reason to believe that it is not the author himself who is writing (telling) the story. The assumption of the existence of a narrator other than the author himself is solely warranted when his presence is clearly felt, let us say because of a special, characteristic word usage, or when the author alludes to his existence (for example, when the person telling the story remarks that he does not know exactly what happened or what has happened later on, as he was not able to witness it, or when he apologizes for not knowing what a hero was thinking). Such remarks occur in many nineteenth-century prose works; they are frequent in Dostoevsky, for instance. But in Chekhov's prose, there is often no reason to assume that the narration is conducted by anybody other than the author himself, reporting in a neutral, objective way what is to be seen and felt and what is going on.

Here we come across another difficulty of terminology. Some theoreticians have called this purely authorial point of view "subjective," because the writer gives his own evaluation of the situation, the characters, and the events. They contrast this attitude with the "objective" approach, when the author lets his characters think, describe, and express themselves from their own viewpoint.[7] I do not think these terms are quite satisfactory. In a way, of course, all fiction writing is "subjective," just as much as poetry or any other art form, because it originates in the imagination of the creator. He can choose his subject matter, his landscapes, his heroes, their conduct, and characters at will. But when a writer depicts scenes, characters, and developments, he can either insert or refrain from personal comments; he can take up the position of an involved, partisan, prejudiced, prepossessed commentator, or strive after a painfully balanced, nonbiased, objective attitude, although this is

---

[6] It is, therefore, not quite correct when A. P. Chudakov writes (*Poètika Čekhova*, p. 46) that in this story "the narrator penetrates directly into the conscience of almost all the characters."

[7] See, e.g., Chudakov, *Poètika Čekhova*, pp. 10ff., 51ff., 61ff. On the question of objective and subjective narration, see Lubomír Doležel, "The Typology of the Narrator: Point of View in Fiction," in *To Honor Roman Jakobson, Essays* (The Hague-Paris, 1967), 1:esp. pp. 547–552.

perhaps only a seeming, relative, conditional, agreed-upon objectivity. By the same token, the "objectivity" of the heroes and their viewpoints and opinions is no less subjective, as they are all created by the author. In fact, one could argue that their viewpoints and opinions are often more subjective than the author's own professed point of view, because the author has to make it clear to the reader that these opinions belong to the heroes, not to him, so he has to show their very personal character.

When, for example, doctor Ragin in "Palata № 6" ("Ward No. 6," 1892) argues that "if physical and moral uncleanliness are being removed from one place, they will pass to another.... If people have founded this hospital and tolerate it, they obviously need it; prejudices and all this filth and meanness of life are necessary, because in the course of time they will be made into something sensible, like dung turning into black earth,"[8] then we know quite well that these are Ragin's subjective, strictly personal opinions. They do not have to be shared by the author at all, and Chekhov will never fail to point this out, usually by simply inserting a so-called *verbum sentiendi*: "on čuvstvoval," "ona ponjala," "emu pokazalos'," "oni dumali (znali)," or, as in the passage from which I quoted, "rassudil" (he argued). This has not prevented many commentators from drawing far-reaching conclusions about Chekhov's opinions and world view from statements by his heroes, which sometimes may, but by no means have to, be identified with Chekhov's own ideas. Even when a Chekhov story is told in the first person, this does not mean that the "I" of the story can be equated with Chekhov himself, although formal indicators like *verba sentiendi* or modal adverbs might be lacking here. Let us remember Chekhov's irate sentence in one of his well-known letters to A. Suvorin:

If I present you with the professor's thoughts, then you should believe me and not look in them for Chekhov's thoughts.... Do you really value opinions in general so much ... that only in them you see the main point, and not in the way they are being expressed?[9]

In this connection it is not inappropriate to cite two other well-known passages from his correspondence: the letter to Lidiya Avilova in which he urges her to be "cooler," because

that gives somebody's suffering a background, so to speak, against which it stands out in greater relief. As it stands now, both your heroes cry and you are sighing. Yes, be cool.[10]

And in the next letter to her:

You may cry and moan over your stories, you can suffer together with your heroes, but I think you should do it in such a way that the reader does not notice it. The more objective, the stronger the impression will be.[11]

---

[8] 8:19.
[9] October 17, 1889.
[10] March 19, 1892.
[11] April 29, 1892.

About the problem of objectivity, Chekhov writes in a letter to Suvorin, equally often quoted:

You blame me for my objectivity.... You want me to say, when I depict horse thieves: the stealing of horses is bad. But that is well known without my saying so. Let the jurors judge them—my task is only to show what kind of people they are.... If I add a subjective note, the image will get blurred, and the story will not be as compact as all short stories should be.[12]

These words indicate clearly that Chekhov himself advocated the author's objectivity, that is, his nonintervention in the mental, psychic, and emotional processes of his heroes. In order to avoid the apparently somewhat confusing terminology of "subjectivity" versus "objectivity," I suggest using the word "neutral(ity)" here, to indicate an attitude of, or at least a striving after, impartiality on the part of the author, his quiet, dispassionate description and registration of what is to be observed. The story "Nalim," then, is narrated in a neutral way; in only one instance, as we saw, a personal feeling of one of the characters is mentioned, and it cannot be said with certainty whether an onlooker would be able to reconstruct or interpret it correctly.

Such dispassionately narrated stories are not numerous in the first five or six years of Chekhov's literary career. Very often the author in one way or another interferes, adds a comment, an exclamation, a subjective remark, a comparison, betrays his presence in the story. Sometimes he addresses to the reader a sentence or even a whole paragraph of a subjective nature.

In a short anecdotal piece like "Kleveta" ("Slander," 1883), the whole content seems, at a first and not too careful reading, to be narrated in a straightforward, neutral way. There is, to be sure, an abundant admixture of the hero's personal emotions, thoughts, and feelings. This hero, Akhineev, at the wedding of his daughter makes a smacking sound in the kitchen on seeing the sturgeon that will be served. A friend hears it and says jokingly that the host is kissing the cook. In order to prevent the friend from spreading this joke as a rumor among the wedding guests, Akhineev tells everybody about the little incident, stressing the absurdity of the friend's assumption. However, a week later, first his superior and then his wife appear to know he is living with the cook; although the friend did not say a word to anybody. That is in short the *fabula* of the story.

When describing the wedding, Chekhov inserts a direct allocution to the reader: "The conversations were, as you see, horrible, but very agreeable." He goes on: "From the street, people who, because of their social status, had no right to enter, looked through the window,"—certainly a satirically meant remark. Then Akhineev enters the kitchen and "makes with his lips the sound

---

[12] April 1, 1890.

of an ungreased wheel"—a personal impression from the standpoint of the author or an imagined narrator.

After the wedding the hero "fell asleep like a child that is innocent of anything, and the next morning he did not think any more of the episode with the sturgeon. But, alas! Man proposes, God disposes. An evil tongue had done its evil work, and Akhineev's smartness did not help him!" Here we find one of those general human truths inserted in the narrative, as so many nineteenth-century writers loved to do (but the tradition goes back to the eighteenth century and can even be traced back to antiquity).

Akhineev goes home "as if bitten by a whole swarm of bees at a time and as if scalded by boiling water." This is the tone of comic exaggeration, so habitual in humorous writing, not only by Chekhov or in Chekhov's time and literary milieu. The hero goes to his friend, who "started to blink and wink with all the fibers of his dilapidated face": another instance of the author's abandoning of the point of view of a neutral reporter. And finally, echoing Akhineev's desperate question: "But who then, who?" (could have spread this awkward false rumor), the author ends his story with another apostrophe to the reader: "Yes, who? We, too, ask the reader."[13]

Chudakov has demonstrated[14] that such authorial interpolations decrease in the course of the first six years of Chekhov's literary activity. It did not take the young Chekhonte long to become thoroughly disgusted with the constant, obligatory putting on of a mask, usually a fool's mask, although one gets the impression that at least during the first years he did it with a lot of gusto. As we know, among his early products not a few were satirical and parodistic; and when a writer parodies other writers, he must know them, he must have a pretty good idea of what is going on in literary life, read other authors, and feel in himself the desire and the ability to imitate them. He cannot have been the wholly indifferent ink-spiller he pictures himself in the well-known letter to Grigorovich of March 28, 1886: "As reporters write their reports on fires, I used to write my stories: mechanically, half unconsciously, not bothering at all about the reader nor about myself." He was an interested, conscious young man of letters just as much as he was a gay, sprightly student and a serious prospective physician; and he must have given thought to his own literary products, their form and their style.

3

As early as 1882 a volume of his stories was planned, but it was never realized. On that occasion Chekhov, for the first time, read through the stories

---
[13] 2:30.
[14] *Poètika Čekhova*, cf. the tables on p. 18.

thus far published and made corrections; and it is interesting to see that what he removed from the texts were a number of exclamations, aphorisms, longer digressions, and author's meditations.[15] In this context another unrealized plan may be worth mentioning: the one he made while preparing the publication of his *Collected Works* at the end of his life, when he brought together a series of seventeen short stories from the years 1883–1886, intending to publish them under the title "From the Notebook of Ivan Ivanovich (Thoughts and Notes)" ("Iz zapisnoj knižki Ivana Ivanoviča [mysli i zametki]"). By this common title he indicated his feeling that at least some of the early stories belonged together; they could be reduced to the same denominator, as if they came out of one notebook, to wit that of a most ordinary man-in-the-street, Ivan Ivanovich. In other words, Chekhov later felt he had been wearing a comical mask and, by calling in an unspecified narrator, through the well-known device of a diary or notebook, he made an abortive effort to disassociate himself from this narrator, to create a distance between them.

The years 1886 to 1887 mark a definite change in the nature of Chekhov's literary work and in his attitude toward it—a change that was, however, as we saw, gradually prepared during the preceding years. I propose to pay somewhat closer attention to the stories from 1886 onward and the role in them of the author, the narrator, and the hero. Chudakov divides Chekhov's prose production into three periods (which inevitably brings to mind Chekhov's mocking remark that one critic had divided his works into three periods; why in three, and not in, for example, four, Chekhov wondered). Of course, Chekhov, as an artist, had every right to be distrustful of attempts at classifying, grouping, pigeonholing his writings; but to us, readers and students of these writings at a certain historical distance, a sensible classification or periodization of his literary output may be expedient and helpful. However, at closer scrutiny, Chudakov's division does not appear to be quite convincing.

After an early period of seven years (through 1887), he construes a middle period from 1888 to 1894 and a final period from 1895 to 1904 (which actually should be 1903, in which year Chekhov wrote his last story, "Nevesta": "The Betrothed"). During the first period, we witness, according to Chudakov, an increasing tendency to eliminate the author's or narrator's voice and to supplant it with that of the main hero; also the position from which the story is viewed is more and more often that of the hero instead of that of the narrator. Supposedly, the first-person narration is also on the wane during this period.

The second period is that of the hero as "objective" holder of the point of view. Between 1888 and 1890, for example, all stories belong to this type,

---

[15] *Ibid.*, p. 23.

Chudakov states. Unlike the "subjective" Turgenev, he points out, Chekhov in these years wanted to be an "objective" author, speaking in the tone and spirit of his heroes. Consequently, the scenery, the interior, the outward appearance, and the inner life of the heroes are presented directly from the hero's vantage point. During the third period, however, the narrator resumes his leading role, the hero's voice disappears or, at least, recedes into the background. The first-person narration of this period, according to Chudakov, is a form only; these stories reveal nothing personal of the narrator.

The main distinguishing mark in Chudakov's periodization is the predominance of the hero's point of view in the middle years and its mysterious, almost complete disappearance during the last period, coupled with a new intrusion of the "subjective" narrator. In other words, after Chekhov had allowed his heroes more and more to take over and present their judgments instead of the author's or narrator's, he changed his approach around 1894 to 1895. From these years on, "the judgment and orientation of the hero are by no means necessarily expressed in his own words"; instead, Chekhov "only pinpoints the hero's general position; when rendering this position, the narrator now prefers the forms of his own speech."[16]

The explanation Chudakov gives of the change in Chekhov's working method after 1894 is that "in these years the scale of social problems dealt with in his work broadens," and he "comes to think of the necessity of more directly expressing his author's attitude towards the negative phenomena he is presenting, of more actively stating his positive ideals."[17] This might be true; however, we should be careful not to regard the evolution as absolute: as we shall see, the changes were far from sweeping or all-embracing; and we should not try to explain presumable changes in his artistic methods too easily by possible evolutions in his thinking.

I should add here that to present the hero as the observer, reasoner, and feeling organ of a narration to the exclusion of an author's or narrator's point of view was not common in prose fiction before Chekhov or in his time, although I do not imply that he was the first to experiment with this method.[18] It was applied more often in twentieth-century prose—maybe under the direct influence of Chekhov's work. This would be the theme of a separate study.

---

[16] *Ibid.*, p. 88.
[17] "Ob èvoljucii stilja prozy Čekhova," p. 331.
[18] Cleanth Brooks and Robert Penn Warren in their *Understanding Fiction* (New York, 1959^2), when discussing the focus of narration (point of view), distinguish only narration with an internal analysis and with an external observation of the events, not even mentioning the possibility of the hero as holder of the point of view and the opposition author/narrator/hero (cf. pp. 146–150, 659–664).

4

The method I propose to check Chudakov's statements and findings is to classify Chekhov's stories in diachronic groups. First, those stories in which we are clearly confronted with the point of view of one main hero, as manifested by the voicing of feelings and judgments that are obviously his or hers, not anybody else's, and by the viewing of situations and events from the viewpoint (or, to use another terminology, through the photographic filter) of the hero(ine).[19] Second, we may discern a category to which belong stories presenting the viewpoint of not one hero, but at least two. Third, a group of stories in which the hero's angle of vision is only rarely or occasionally expressed, while the dominating viewpoint in the story is that of the author-narrator. This mixed type is very common in Chekhov's prose, notwithstanding Jean-Paul Sartre's contention that in a good narrative only one "privileged observer" can act and that "the novelist can be their [the heroes'] witness or their accomplice, but never the two at the same time."[20]

A fourth category, which in my view has to be distinguished from the previous ones, shows a more intricate interplay of the author-narrator's voice and those of one or (often) more hero(es). The fifth is the one in which no hero's viewpoint is represented, but neutral narration is paramount. And finally there is a group of first-person narratives; in them no distinction of different points of view is possible: the narrator can, by definition, merely speak for himself.

It should be remembered that many of Chekhov's stories abound in dialogue, and that this dialogue (or monologue) each time interrupts and obliterates the point of view. Direct speech renders, of course, the viewpoint of the speaker, who can be anybody in the story and who does not have to be the bearer of the story's main viewpoint. Notably, texts from the period of very short stories and sketches sometimes consist almost entirely of direct speech.[21]

As the statistics in the accompanying chart show, it turns out that the stories with a clear hero's point of view do increase from 1886 through the middle period in Chudakov's periodization and decrease again in his third period; but the differences are by no means startling, and this type never reigns supreme. The stories in which two or more heroes see, feel, and

---

[19] Hamburger, "The Function of the Viewpoint," p. 10.
[20] These opinions are disputed by Tzvetan Todorov in his "Poétique," in Oswald Ducrot a.o., *Qu'est-ce que le structuralisme?* (Paris, 1968), pp. 159–160.
[21] Among the stories consisting almost totally of dialogue are "V lando," "Tëšča-advokat," "Opekun" from 1883; "Bespokojnyj gost'," Dlinnyj jazyk," Proizvedenie iskusstva," "Ty i vy," "Dramaturg" from 1886; "Moroz," "Polin'ka," "Kritik" from 1887, and many others.

	1886	1887	1888–1894	1895–1903	Average
Hero's viewpoint[22]	24 = 25%	21 = 34%	14 = 41%	6 = 23%	65 = 30%
Two or more heroes' viewpoints	5 = 5%	4 = 6%	1 = 3%	—	10 = 4%
Reduced hero's viewpoint	11 = 11%	8 = 12%	5 = 14%	—	24 = 10%
Mixed viewpoints	9 = 9%	4 = 6%	5 = 14%	12 = 46%	30 = 13%
Neutral	29 = 30%	17 = 25%	2 = 6%	2 = 7%	50 = 22%
First-person narrative	18 = 19%	9 = 14%	7 = 20%	6 = 23%	40 = 18%
	96 = 100%	63 = 100%	34 = 100%	26 = 100%	219 = 100%

think fade out altogether, but they were not numerous in the early work either. Also dwindling is the category in which the hero is only slightly represented. Neutral stories with no noticeable hero's angle of vision are less numerous in the last period, but they had already decreased during the middle period. An increase is to be found only in the stories with a more complicated, sometimes inextricable, relation of narrator's and hero's points of view. But this type is very close to the second and third groups; its increase in the last period is connected with the fact that Chekhov's prose works during these years are, by and large, longer and structurally more elaborate.

Chudakov's statement that the first-person narratives were steadily on the decrease does not tally with the figures shown here: their percentage is pretty stable and tends even to increase toward the end; and a first-person narrator "without a face" occurred also in earlier stories. It is also incorrect to say that the hero's-point-of-view stories reached 100 per cent in 1888: out of the nine stories written during that year, five bear a clear imprint of the hero's view, two to a small degree only, whereas one does not at all ("Bez zaglavija": "Without a Title"), and one is a first-person narrative ("Krasavicy": "Beauties," actually consisting of two short impressions).

Even during the years in which, according to Chudakov, most stories are from the hero's angle of vision, namely 1888–1894, in seven stories (over 20 percent) this is the case only to a very limited extent, and in two (6 percent) it is not the case at all. From 1889 to 1890 not all the stories are from the hero's-point-of-view, as Chudakov claims: two are, one ("Gusev") evinces only partly and occasionally a hero's viewpoint, and the fourth ("Skučnaja istorija": "A Dreary Story") is a first-person narrative. Consequently, the hero's point of view does not disappear in Chekhov's last works: there is a certain change or evolution, but it is more complicated, less rectilinear than it appears from Chudakov's survey.

---

[22] A breakdown of these stories according to the viewpoint will be found in the Appendix.

5

In the stories of the extremely fecund years 1886 and 1887, we frequently find a mixture within one story of the author's and the hero's viewpoint. In "Khudožestvo" ("Art"), for example, in which two men are at work to create an artful Bible scene on the ice, the main hero, Seryozhka, "is in fact a good-for-nothing, a lazybone, a soak and a spendthrift, but when he has red lead or a pair of compasses in his hand, he is something higher, a servant of God,"[23] says the author, and by calling him a good-for-nothing, and so on, he obviously appraises him and gives him a verdict or a valuation. The same can be said of the sentence from the same story "The soul of the lazybone fills with a feeling of glory and triumph": here we are also allowed to have a glimpse into the hero's soul; his inner feelings are revealed to us, however briefly and superficially it may be. But in the famous "Toska" ("Misery") the poor cabman's viewpoint is sustained throughout the story: we see the world through his eyes. The only exception is a sentence in the beginning, where the author exclaims: "He who is torn away from the plough ... and thrown into his whirlpool here ... cannot but think ... ,"[24]

A few words in the text of "Misery" suggest Chekhov wanted to let his hero express himself, even in his thoughts, in the way a simple cabman of peasant extraction would, using expressions like " ... a on eščë putëm ne govoril ni s kem," "Te [= "baby": the women] khot' i dury, no revut ot dvukh slov."[25] But otherwise we can safely assume the man would never be able to formulate his thoughts and feelings in such an articulate, distinct, eloquent, literary way, in sentences that would, in his ears, sound highly sophisticated and highfalutin'. In other words, Chekhov transposes the wordless emotions and more or less vague, inarticulate thoughts of his hero, who belongs to a lower social and intellectual level, into his own literary style. And this is what usually happens in a Chekhov story.

Chekhov was not the type of prose writer who would in the first place strive after a careful rendering of all the speech characteristics of each hero, something N. S. Leskov, for example, wanted to achieve. He would not attempt to reproduce his hero's thoughts the way this hero would think and express them. It is true that he wanted "the objective writer" to "speak in their [his heroes'] language."[26] But he was more inclined to let a certain unity of style and speech prevail throughout a prose work, whether it be in the author's or narrator's voice, or in the inner monologue of the characters, or to a certain extent even in the dialogue, especially in that of the more educated among his heroes. Peasants and simple people, to be sure, were put upon the stage with their own speech, so in their dialogue Chekhov did try to be true to reality.

---

[23] 4:124, 125.   [24] 4:135.   [25] 4:139.   [26] 4:118.

Compare stories like "Zloumyšlennik" ("The Malefactor," 1885), "Khudožestvo," "Mečty" ("Dreams," 1886), "Sčastie" ("Happiness"), "Svirel'" ("The Pipe"), "Vstreča" ("The Encounter")—all from 1887.

This stylization of the hero's language is even stronger in children's stories than in the case of the cabman Iona. The small world of Grisha, the title hero of another story from 1886, is seen through his eyes, as an adult author imagines a two-year-old child would see it, and his observations are transformed into and rendered in normal nineteenth-century literary Russian. "Žitejskaja meloč'" ("A Trifle of Everyday Life") features another boy, who is caught in the matrimonial problems of his parents, who are separated; at the end, the author abandons his neutral position and speaks about his little hero, who for the first time "in such a rude way was confronted with the lie,"[27] "not knowing that . . . ." In other words, the hero (this boy) has only limited visibility while the author is, of course, omniscient. When the hero of "Van'ka" thinks of his grandfather, the latter is not presented to the reader in a childish way. Not only is the story not narrated in the boy's words but the images are clearly those of the author (grandpa, "with drunken eyes," "cracks jokes with the cooks"); and things are related which Van'ka did not see.[28]

A boy's point of view is also rendered through an adult writer's filter in "Beglec" ("The Fugitive") and "Na Strastnoj nedele" ("In Passion Week"), both from 1887. In one of the best children's stories of these two years, "Detvora" ("Kids"), a group of children is being observed, but their own viewpoints are not expressed. An extreme case of author's interpretation and voicing of a primitive point of view is "Kaštanka," in which the world is seen through the eyes of a dog.

In a more elaborate story from 1886, "Košmar" ("A Nightmare"), we observe the landowner Kunin in his conversations with the local priest, father Yakov, and share his thoughts about him. However, here we find a general remark at the end, thrown in by the author, a comment on the main hero and a pronouncement of a psychological and social nature: "Thus began . . . the sincere effort of one of those well-meaning, but all-too-sated people."[29] Such generalizations are not frequent in Chekhov's prose, but they do occur in different periods.

In some products of these transitional years there can be no doubt that the world is viewed through the perception of the main character—a good example being "Veročka" and its hero, the agronomist Ognyov.[30] In other

---

[27] 5:176.   [28] 5:259.   [29] 4:229.

[30] Chekhov is not consistent in this story either, because, whereas he starts by telling us that Ognyov "remembers" all this, he soon talks about him from an outside observer's viewpoint: "He spoke with a melodious seminarist's voice" (6:61).

stories it is hard to establish whether what we hear is being narrated and depicted through the hero's perception or whether all this should be attributed to the author himself.[31] The viewpoints of at least two characters are shown in another series of stories.[32]

Sometimes the hero's point of view is not consistently sustained throughout the story. In "Aptekarša" ("The Pharmacist's Wife," 1886) the author steps back and lets things happen as they occur to the story's heroine: we watch her first in her bedroom, then follow her going down the steps to the shop and receiving the two nocturnal customers. Then, however, the author mentions the words of one of them, the doctor, at a moment when the lady had disappeared behind the store and apparently could not hear what was being said. In "Učitel'" ("The Teacher") the same thing happens: although the story is told in a rather neutral tone, we feel it comes to us as it is directly experienced by the hero; however, at the end, in the last three lines, the scene is shifted to "a neighboring room," where the hero is not present, so he cannot know what is going on. Such minor inconsistencies can probably be found in greater numbers; this is true of many writers in all literatures.

Our third category includes stories of which it is difficult to verify whose angle of vision is represented: the author's, or a narrator's, or the hero's, or perhaps that of more than one hero. When daddy in "Ser'ëznyj šag" ("A Serious Step," 1886) "for some reason shrugs his shoulders," he is apparently seen from the outside: it is not known why he shrugs his shoulders. But the very next sentence says: "'This is impossible,' he thinks"; so here we *are* told what he thinks, which would imply that his mind is in the center of the story and his viewpoint is rendered. At the end daddy mutters: "The flies don't let one sleep!"; and the author adds one little sentence from his viewpoint as an all-understanding contemplator: "But the flies are not guilty: happiness is...."[33] This shows that we should not assume, each time we read, for instance, "on dumal," "emu pokazalos'," that the viewpoint completely changes and is transferred to that hero: such an occasional, short thought or impression in the hero's mind is just one little fact that, together with other facts, descriptions, actions, reflections, and characterizations makes up the story as told by the author.

In "Dreams," for example, in the beginning the thoughts of one of two constables escorting a tramp are presented, and at the end "all three are

---

[31] E.g., "Aktërskaja gibel'," "Učitel'," "Talant," "Neobyknovennyj," "Tsss!...," "Vragi," "Otec," "Kholodnaja krov'," "Poceluj," "Rano!"

[32] Among others, in "Anjuta," "Ivan Matveič," "Ved'ma," "Muž," "Tina," "Čužaja beda," "Vyigryšnyj bilet," "Pis'mo," "Sledovatel'," "Sčastie."

[33] 5:347–349.

thinking."[34] But the story as a whole is descriptive, related by the author, except that a large part of it is taken up by the tramp's talk, which brings it close to a *skaz* story. This mixed type is not infrequent during the years 1886–1887, but becomes relatively more frequent toward the end of Chekhov's career.

As an example of stories with a less clear, more complicated viewpoint we might have a look at another story from 1886, "Neobyknovennyj" ("An Unusual Man"), in which we witness the confrontation of a most parsimonious gentleman with a midwife. Initially, it seems as if we follow the gentleman's movements and thoughts as he enters her apartment:

> He enters the living room. The green light of a small lamp shines sparingly upon the cheap furniture ... the miserable flowers.... It smells of geraniums and carbolic acid. The wall clock ticks shyly, as if it feels embarrassed in the presence of an unknown man.[35]

This passage has an undeniable subjective tone; but are these the hero's or the author's impressions, or are the two viewpoints mixed? Later in the story the gentleman is viewed from the outside; however, here we find the midwife's thoughts and, presumably, her observations mentioned a few times. There is no clear, single, unequivocal point of view upon which the whole story is based.

6

In some cases the story by its nature simply does not lend itself to such a simple viewpoint conception. In "Tina" ("Ooze," 1886) the first lieutenant Sokolsky arrives at the house of a queer Jewish lady, Susanna Moiseevna, and has an unusual encounter with her. It seems that his point of view is given; sometimes, we must assume, it is combined with that of the author. The second chapter, however, does not show a distinct point of view at all, except that the author is narrating. The reason is that the nature of the story has changed: there is no longer one hero occupying the center of our attention, facing the other characters and events, but two equivalent people, Sokolsky and his cousin. Then, however, the situation changes again: the cousin, the landowner Kryukov, now becomes the acting personage, and thus we are given his point of view (he "wondered how ...," "thought," and so on).[36]

The hero of the story Chekhov wrote next, "Tsss!" a newspaper man who turns out to be a little tyrant at home, is partly shown by the author, we must assume, from the outside; but the man's own viewpoint, his thoughts and dreams are also rendered:

> Oh, with what a delight would he go back to sleep, what dreams would he have, how voluptuously would he turn in his bed, if he had become a famous writer....[37]

---

[34] 5:231.   [35] 5:198.   [36] 5:217–219.   [37] 5:223.

However, the author could not but insert in the story a subjective remark, which no doubt comes right from Chekhov himself:

Affectation and pedantry with regard to himself... despotism and tyranny over the little anthill that fate has placed under his power, constitute the salt and the honey of his existence. And how little the despot resembles that petty, humble creature we are accustomed to see in the editor's offices. . . . [38]

Cringing humility on the one hand, undue, selfish despotism on the other—there seems to be no human vice and no characteristic of Russian life that Chekhov unmasked and condemned more vigorously.

An interplay of the author and two equivalent heroes is also shown in a somewhat longer and more significant story from 1887, "Vragi" ("Enemies"). In the beginning the visitor, Abogin, is viewed through the eyes of the doctor, Kirilov, who just lost his son, but who is now forced to accompany Abogin to his sick wife. However, the doctor, in his turn, is seen through the author's eyes: and the latter has comments on "the beauty of human grief": "Kirilov and his wife were silent, they did not weep, as if . . . they also realized all the lyricism of their situation."[39] Abogin "felt himself" that anything he was saying turned out to be "stilted."[40]

The points of view interchange between the three throughout the story: there is a complicated relationship. In some instances we have to assume the author is presenting his own viewpoint. He is the spirit above the scene and can look through the prism of each character. In some nineteenth-century novels this "synthetic point of view"[41] is more elaborate than in this Chekhov story, which has, after all, a very simple structure. At the end, the author appears before the footlights and submits his comment: the doctor, he writes, hated and despised Abogin and people like him, and this conviction, "unjust and unworthy of the human heart," will remain with him until his death. This ending is not quite convincing, not at the level of Chekhov's best stories: in fact, it is much weaker than the simple zero endings of such stories as "Temnota" ("Darkness") or "Polin'ka," which appeared just a few days later in the columns of the same *Peterburgskaja Gazeta*.

The point-of-view structure is even more "synthetic" when two or more characters, first separately observed, toward the end of a story appear collectively, for instance in "Vyigryšnyj bilet" ("The Winning Ticket," 1887), where the husband and wife are partly seen separately, but then "They thought only

---

[38] 5:222.
[39] 6:29.
[40] 6:30 ("khodul'nymi").
[41] Uspenskij, *Poètika kompozicii*, p. 130.

about numbers . . . ," and "I.D. and his wife began to believe. . . . " There are more stories with a similar collective viewpoint.[42]

All these are still "early stories." In the following years, which constitute the "middle period," according to Chudakov's periodization, no striking shifts in the viewpoint construction of Chekhov's stories take place. It is true that a type of narration in which the point of view of the main hero is presented predominates more strongly than in the previous or following years, as the statistics show; but other types continue to be used. Two stories from 1888, "Imeniny" ("The Name-Day Party") and "Pripadok" ("The Nervous Breakdown"), are entirely and consistently told from the vantage point of the heroes: Olga Dmitrievna in the first case, the student Vasilyev in the second; although in the first, the heroine's husband, Pyotr Dmitrich, is sometimes thinking (and his thoughts are rendered), or he "lied" (7:156), which she actually could not know, although she could perhaps suspect it.

In "Spat' khočetsja" ("Sleepy") of the same year the story is partly narrated by a neutral voice; but the girl, Varka, "wants to sleep," "understands," "she is glad . . . ,"[43] and thus emotional, intellectual, and physical experiences are disclosed that cannot be observed from the outside. We learn also about her dreams; if there is no change of viewpoint from a neutral one to that of the little heroine here, we must assume this is the voice of the omniscient author. In "Neprijatnost'" ("An Unpleasant Incident") we hear mostly the doctor's voice, but his antagonist, the medical assistant (*fel'dšer*) is also said to be "irritated and ashamed,"[44] so there is no complete consistency.

Finally, in the longest story from this year, "Step'" ("The Steppe"), the situation is again more complicated. The question of narrator and point of view in this work has been analyzed in detail by Nils Å. Nilsson, and I therefore refer to this study.[45] As he points out, this relation of a trip through the South Russian steppe has "a unifying link: the nine-year old boy Egorushka. He is the central figure of the story, a silent observer of the people, the scenery, and the events that present themselves to him during the journey" (p. 7). Nevertheless, unlike the "active hero" Huckleberry Finn, Egorushka is a "passive reflector" (p. 22). "Čechov does not always seem able to make up his mind who should tell the story—Egorushka through his view of the events as they unfold themselves, or the narrator himself" (p. 25). In the organization of the point-of-view question in his first elaborate prose work, "Čechov is, of course, not absolutely consistent," writes Nilsson (p. 32).

---

[42] 6:100, 103.
[43] 7:12, 15, 16.
[44] 7:114.
[45] *Studies in Čechov's Narrative Technique* (n. 2, above), esp. pp. 5–48.

Whether we can agree with him that various, at least three, different narrators can be discerned in this text (pp. 42–44) is of less importance here. But he makes it perfectly clear that Egorushka is not the only thinking, perceiving mind in "Step'"; this function is sometimes assumed by the author or narrator, sometimes by minor figures in the story; sometimes the narrator is a neutral observer, sometimes he gives subjective comments. There are "different approaches to the story, which makes the narrative structure rather complex and somewhat confusing" (p. 36).

"The Steppe" presents the same approach to the problem of children as heroes that we witnessed in previous, shorter stories: Chekhov does not attempt, at least not consistently, to render a child's thoughts, feelings, and observations in a language that is on the child's level. Perhaps we can agree that "we see the impression it [the steppe] makes on the boy's mind";[46] but the contents of Egorushka's thoughts and feelings are presented in a general literary language, and some of these thoughts would never occur to a nine-year-old boy. At times we see Egorushka's mind at work: when it is said, for example, that a windmill "resembles a little man," or when "Egorushka already wholeheartedly hated his [the wagoner Dymov's] fair-haired head ... and was thinking of the abusive word he would say to him in revenge."[47] Wholly within the boy's frame of mind is the paragraph on page 85 where he thinks of marriage and women and then of the countess Dranitskaya he had met:

he would probably be glad to marry her, if that were not such a shameful thing to do.... The quiet, warm night descended upon him and whispered something in his ear, and it seemed to him that this beautiful lady was bending over him, looked at him with a smile and wanted to kiss him.... [48]

But usually the author expresses and phrases the boy's feelings and thinking, or inserts thoughts, philosophical parentheses, and whole lyrical passages (on pp. 52 and 72, for instance) that cannot be called but strange to Egorushka's mind. In at least two instances the little hero is even asleep while the story goes on; and a whispered conversation takes place, which he cannot hear (p. 109). Sometimes other characters are thinking or observing;[49] the subject of this thinking and observing can even be a group.[50]

---

[46] Karl D. Kramer, *The Chameleon and the Dream, The Image of Reality in Čexov's Stories* (The Hague-Paris, 1970), p. 91.
[47] 7:23, 61.
[48] 7:85.
[49] Like Father Khristofor on p. 102.
[50] E.g., p. 79: "All were silent and thought of ... however horrible a story one tells in Russia, ... it will always resound in the listener's soul as a true story"; and p. 80: " ... all saw at the first glance they cast at him ... his smile before anything else." Another deviation from the concept of Egorushka as the perceiving mind is the phrase: "Egorushka

So, from the viewpoint of narration, "The Steppe," this significant, serious literary product by an author who had rid himself of some typical imperfections of his juvenile work, is the continuation of a type that existed in his previous stories.

7

In the following years Chekhov continued to write prose works with different solutions of the point-of-view problem. If we exclude, for the moment, the first-person narratives (like "Skučnaja istorija"; "Ogni": "Lights," 1891; "Rasskaz staršego sadovnika": "The Story of the Senior Gardener," 1894), we see that a number of stories (not a large number, but a higher percentage than in previous years) are constructed from the position of the main hero: "Knjaginja" ("The Princess," 1889) from that of the egotistic lady; "Vory" ("Thieves," 1890) from that of the robbed medical assistant; "Sosedi" ("Neighbors," 1892) from that of the man who visits his sister and the neighbor she lives with; "Student" ("The Student," 1894) and "Učitel' slovesnosti" ("The Literature Teacher," 1894) from that of the title heroes. But next to them are stories like "Gusev" (1890), which initially shows Gusev's vantage point, but in the last chapter, when he dies, the author-narrator takes over.[51] Or "Baby" ("Peasant Women," 1891), which is partly a *skaz* narration, told in the first person by the merchant Matvey Savich; subsequently we are confronted with the viewpoint of one of the listening women, presumably Sofya. However, this becomes less and less clear, and toward the end there is only a general, neutral, author's point of view. Or "V ssylke" ("In Exile," 1892), which presents basically a neutral narration, although at one point[52] one is led to believe that of the two interlocutors it is the Tatar who is represented; but this seems only occasionally to be the case.[53] There is also a long monologue by the other personage, Tolkovy.

If these stories do not provide an unequivocal answer to the question, Who tells a Chekhovian story? this is still less the case in works with a somewhat more complex construction, like "Duèl'" ("The Duel," 1891), "Poprygun'ja" ("The Grasshopper," 1892), "Palata № 6" ("Ward No. 6," 1892), and "Černyj monakh" ("The Black Monk," 1894); to maintain a single point of view would be technically difficult here. This brings us to a general and, I think,

---

now ... believed in every word, but later he would think it strange that somebody would tell things that did not exist" 7:79). Here the present is apparently linked with the future about which the boy has no idea yet.

[51] Earlier in the story, the fiction that only the main character's experiences are being rendered is abandoned when another character, Pavel Ivanych, is speaking and Gusev does not listen (7:306).

[52] The paragraph starting with "Tatarin..." on p. 8:80.

[53] Also later, when the Tatar is left alone and is thinking (8:84).

rather obvious conclusion: that Chekhov did not use different approaches at different periods, changing back and forth during his career; rather the technical exigencies of prose works with various types of interplay among the narrator, the heroes, and the action, with different organization of the narrative material, decided for him how the question of point of view was to be worked out in each case.

Notably, "The Duel" and "Ward No. 6" are more complex in this respect than most preceding prose works. They both consist of about twenty small chapters, and although it is not quite correct that "each chapter (of 'The Duel') is given from the aspect of one of the personages,"[54] it is true that the situation somewhat changes with every new chapter, or at least with a group of chapters. The first chapter of this story, which is the longest Chekhov wrote, pictures the main hero Laevsky and doctor Samoylenko; it consists mainly of dialogue: nobody's viewpoint is really represented, only toward the end do we seem to be presented with Samoylenko's vantage point. Chapter 2 is seen from Laevsky's angle of vision. The third and fourth chapters, at Samoylenko's, again consist mainly of dialogues between him, von Koren, and the deacon, without showing anybody's particular point of view. Chapter 5 is seen from Nadezhda Fyodorovna's standpoint (the bathing scene), but the sixth chapter, the picnic, consists of a neutral description with much dialogue, and only at the end do we briefly get the deacon's viewpoint. Chapter 7 (the end of the picnic) presents first Nadezhda Fyodorovna's, then Laevsky's viewpoint, but not clearly or strongly: the scene is rendered in a predominantly neutral tone. Chapter 8 initially shows Laevsky's and Nadezhda Fyodorovna's viewpoints, but later (in the discussion between von Koren and Samoylenko) nobody's particular viewpoint is noticeable. Chapter 9 also starts from Laevsky's point of view, but in his conversation with Samoylenko there is a general descriptive narration again. Chapter 10 starts with Nadezhda Fyodorovna's point of view in her conversation with her friend Marya Konstantinovna, and later we see briefly Laevsky's point of view, although the scene between him and Samoylenko is predominantly neutral in tone. The chapters 11 and 12 mainly consist of dialogue without any particular hero's point of view, but toward the end Laevsky's standpoint is clearly represented, and subsequently Nadezhda Fyodorovna's. They both interchange in chapter 13, too (the chapter in which Laevsky has a fit of hysteria). In chapter 14 we notice first Nadezhda Fyorodovna's, but later her suitor Achmyanov's viewpoint. In chapter 15 it shifts to Lacvsky again, except that for a moment it rests with Samoylenko. The latter's viewpoint is also briefly shown in the next chapter, which otherwise consists of a neutrally rendered conversation between

---

[54] Chudakov, *Poètika Čekhova*, p. 73.

the deacon and von Koren. Chapter 17 is completely told through Laevsky's mind, rendering his thoughts the night before the duel. Chapter 18 shows us the deacon on his way to the duel, and his thoughts. Chapter 19 starts with Laevsky's viewpoint, but then the prelude to the duel is depicted in a neutral way. There is a little sentence in the middle of it: "Moles! remembered the deacon, sitting in the bushes"; and later: "In a moment I am going to kill him, thought von Koren"[55]—which is the first time this prominent character is presented with his own viewpoint, not as seen through other characters or by the author.

After the twentieth chapter, which first renders a neutral, author's point of view, and later on Laevsky's, there follows a concluding chapter 21, in which von Koren is shown from his point of view, although at the very end Laevsky's thoughts are communicated.

This dry survey of the story evinces (and it is given here solely for that purpose) how often Chekhov shifts the position of the central hero, the person who is seeing, hearing, thinking, and feeling, and how all the characters in the story get their turn. For "Ward No. 6" a similar breakdown into chapters, with alternating vantage points, could be made. In these stories the author and more than one hero share the point of view, although this is the period in which, Chudakov claims, the "objective" narration, that is, the hero's point of view, is strongly predominant.

As an example of this type he especially dwells on "The Grasshopper," although he admits that we find in it "a not completely homogeneous narration," "a complicated case, not quite typical of the second period."[56] What is characteristic of "The Grasshopper," however, is not the "objective," that is, in this case, the heroine's, point of view, but the voice of a narrator. Whereas in many Chekhovian stories, as I mentioned before, the assumption of a narrator other than the author himself is not justified, in this case it seems that we can clearly distinguish such an inserted storyteller. Especially in the beginning, one feels the story is not told in the neutral way that characterizes many of Chekhov's more mature narratives. After some matter-of-fact information about Olga Ivanovna's husband, the medical man Dymov, on the first page, we are told: "That's all. What else can be said about him?"[57] This colloquial tone is not quite usual for Chekhov's narrative style at this stage of his development. The text continues: "Meanwhile, Olga Ivanovna and her friends and good acquaintances were not quite usual people."[58] There follows a description of some of these friends.

---

[55] 7:421.
[56] *Poètika Čekhova*, pp. 78ff.; the quotations are on pp. 84 and 85. Cf. also his "Ob èvoljucii stilja prozy Čekhova," pp. 313–315; the story, Chudakov states, "contains already elements of his poetics of the third period" (p. 314, footnote).
[57] 8:51   [58] *Ibid.*

It is an error to take these sentences for Olga Ivanovna's words, as Chudakov does: they must originate with an observer who is very close to the described circle, forms part of it, but at the same time keeps some distance, because there is a slight, but unmistakable irony in his words: for example, when he mentions "the opera singer, a good-hearted, fat man, who used to assure Olga Ivanovna that she was ruining herself ...," or "the violoncellist, whose instrument wept, and who publicly confessed that of all the ladies known to him only Olga Ivanovna knew how to accompany him."[59] Olga Ivanovna took herself and the company much too seriously to make such detached comments. Compare also the following:

In this artistic, free company, spoiled by fate, delicate and modest, it is true, but remembering the existence of doctors only when somebody fell ill, and for whom the name Dymov sounded just as indifferent as Sidorov or Tarasov, in this company Dymov seemed an outsider, superfluous and small, although he was tall and broad-shouldered.[60]

Another indication that Olga Ivanovna's own viewpoint is not presented is the added "kak by" (as if) in the second sentence of the story. The insertion of a modal adverb indicates that somebody is *guessing at* her motives for marrying this man.

In the second chapter it seems, at first, hard to decide who is the narrating medium: the author, the narrator, or Olga Ivanovna herself, telling about the way she used to spend her day. One feels a slightly sarcastic tone again in sentences like:

But nowhere her giftedness manifested itself so strikingly as in her ability to get immediately acquainted and become close friends with famous people ... ; but she would soon get accustomed to them or become disillusioned in them, and then she would begin eagerly to look for new and still newer greater men, she would find them and search again. What for?[61]

The last question clearly indicates it is not the author who is speaking (he is supposed to be omniscient and know the answer), nor is it the heroine, who would never ask herself this question, totally dedicated as she is to this kind of life. There remains only the narrator, whose irony is perceptible again on the next page, where he intimates that Olga Ivanovna "considered all ladies, except the actresses and her dressmaker, dull and vulgar."[62]

As has been remarked, the narrative situation is "ineluctably ironical. The quality of irony is built into the narrative form as it is into no other form of literature."[63] The word irony is used in a most general sense here,

---

[59] 8:52.
[60] *Ibid.*
[61] 8:54.
[62] 8:55.
[63] Robert Scholes and Robert Kellogg, *The Nature of Narrative* (New York, 1968) (paperback ed.), p. 240.

as "the result of disparity of understanding," arising "in any situation in which one person knows or perceives more—or less—than another" (ibid.). But both in Chekhov's prose and in his letters, irony in a narrower sense is often discernible, a detached, slightly mocking tone (usually not sharp or aggressive), either amused or subdued-irate, sneering or tongue-in-cheek. This tone is absent from many of his mature stories, where there is no need of it, because the subject matter is too serious or the author wants to restrict himself to a neutral attitude. But in other stories one perceives this ironic tone, usually when a narrator is included. The most obvious examples are the first-person narratives of the trilogy: "Čelovek v futljare" ("The Man in the Case") and "Kryžovnik" ("Gooseberries") of 1898.

In the third chapter of "The Grasshopper" the narrator's voice has disappeared: the further development of the story does not allow or call for an ironic attitude. Dymov visits his wife in the *dača* where she is with the painter Ryabovsky and other *bohémiens*. From the words "he felt hungry and tired all the time and dreamed of how he ... would have supper with his wife ... "[64] we infer that the scene is visualized through Dymov's eyes. The next two chapters, in which Olga Ivanovna and Ryabovsky are the actors, show, at least partially, her point of view: as so often, part of the narrative is kept in a neutral tone and could also be attributed to the author. In the next chapter Dymov "began to surmise that he was being deceived";[65] but the vantage point shifts from him to Olga Ivanovna, and it stays with her throughout the last two chapters.

Refraining here from any attempt at analyzing the story "Ward No. 6" of the same year, we can easily establish that again, at least in part of this work, a narrator is present and follows, describes, and sometimes comments upon, the main characters and events. There are remarks like: "They say.... In how far this is true I do not know, but...."[66] This narrator's voice alternates with the viewpoint and thoughts of Dr. Ragin, and this remains the pattern up to the end of the story; however, here, too, there are passages where the neutral author takes over.

8

Most of the remaining stories of the early nineties do have a central hero whose viewpoint is presented. This is clearly and unequivocally the case in "Učitel' slovesnosti," in which the events are viewed through the prism of the key figure, the high school teacher Nikitin; the second chapter even starts with

---
[64] 8:57.
[65] 8:65.
[66] 8:117.

a fragment from his diary and has, consequently, the form of first-person narration. In "Volod'ja bol'šoj i Volod'ja malen'kij" ("Big and Little Volodya," 1893), "Bab'e carstvo" ("A Woman's Kingdom," 1894) and "Skripka Rotšil'da" ("Rothschild's Violin," 1894) the hero's viewpoint is sustained, although there are some departures from it. We may assume that Sofya Lvovna's relationship to the two Volodyas is primarily seen through her own eyes, but sometimes (for example in the first paragraphs) one clearly notices the viewpoint of her husband, the colonel Vladimir Nikitich, and sometimes there is just neutral narration. Anna Akimovna in "A Woman's Kingdom" yields her point of view in one instance to her footman Misha (8:314), and in another instance, when we learn that the lawyer Lysevich "once even won forty thousand, but kept it concealed from his acquaintances,"[67] the omniscient author must be speaking. Such exceptions we find also when the viewpoint of Yakov in "Rothschild's Violin" is alternated with his wife's (8:339).

Likewise, in "The Black Monk" the main hero Kovrin's view is predominantly represented, but sometimes we may assume a neutral narrator's voice, and sometimes Tanya is present as the thinking and feeling medium.[68]

The short story "V usad'be" ("In the Manor") from the same year is more complex in its viewpoint structure. First we have the words of a narrator-informant, describing the scene and the personages in the first paragraph—a viewpoint that at times coincides with that of those present in the room ("One could hear that the table was being set").[69] The next paragraph brings a monologue by the main hero, the landowner Rashevich, advocating the superiority of blue blood. In the third paragraph the observer is speaking again, who could, however, just as well be the only other person present, the visitor Meyer. But the next two paragraphs contain Rashevich's thoughts (about himself, about Meyer), which could, of course, also derive from the omniscient author. When we are told: "The interest to the bank was not paid for two terms, and various arrears and fines ran up to over 2000 rubles,"[70] this reminds us of the way Chekhov sometimes introduces his stage characters, communicating things they know very well and would not think or speak of so concretely, but about which the listener or reader has to be informed; so again, we perceive this information more as given by the author than by Rashevich himself.

After another monologue, in the seventh paragraph, observations are again made by a narrator or maybe by Meyer. When the host resumes his harangue

---

[67] 8:316.
[68] "Tanya ... understood his mood" (i.e., her father's, 8:281); "Tanya felt as if ..." 282; "His face seemed ugly to Tanya," 290.
[69] 8:373.
[70] 8:374.

Meyer interrupts him—the first time he says anything. Also, these monologues are sometimes provided with a remark or observation by the narrator. We are informed about Meyer by this narrator, invisibly present at the scene, or by the author, who observes and records, but does not transport himself mentally into the character's mind (". . . he [Meyer] looked at Rashevich with bewilderment and alarm, as if he only now began to understand him").[71]

In the next paragraphs Rashevich's daughters are pictured, from the outside; but they look irritated at their selfish father, "to whom apparently the joy of talking . . . was more valuable and important than the happiness of his daughters."[72] This is what they think, so their viewpoint or the voice of the author is given, who is the mind-reader not only of the main figure, but also of secondary characters.

In the remaining paragraphs Meyer is again observed only from the outside; Rashevich, however, is presented with his thoughts and feelings—the daughters merely inasmuch as they are seen by their father. Yet we wonder whether Rashevich was really thinking as it is described here, which is rather the way an observer, standing aside or above him, would put it: " . . . what was most amazing: he criticized science, the arts and morals in a most sincere way. . . . He was a sensitive, tearful man indeed."[73]

The narrative form in which this story is told is, of course, not exclusively Chekhovian: many writers have clothed their short stories, novellas, or novels in a similar narrative structure, alternately keeping the point of view for themselves, conveying it to the main hero or to one or more other characters, or, if so desired, calling in an anonymous observer-narrator. And in many cases it is hard to establish exactly from whose angle of vision a passage is being narrated. Whether an author describes directly or through his hero or a narrator, depends largely (I repeat) upon the nature, the special requirements of the prose work in question.

"Tri goda" ("Three Years") was published in 1895, but written in 1894, and should therefore mark a transition between the period characterized by "objective" narration, according to Chudakov, and the third one, in which the hero's voice is supposedly rarely heard and the narrator takes over. However, it is difficult to see any substantial or obvious differences in Chekhov's narrative technique before and after 1895. In the majority of the seventeen chapters of "Three Years" we visualize reality, in all probability, through the eyes of Laptev, the heir-in-spite-of-himself to a large enterprise in Moscow. But his wife Juliya is the central intelligence in several other chapters or parts of chapters. Twice the viewpoint switches to his sister Nina Fyodorovna;

---
[71] 8:377.
[72] *Ibid.*, 377–378.
[73] 8:380.

briefly the standpoints of Laptev's friend Kostya and of another friend, Yartsev, are represented. Moreover, there are a few chapters of a descriptive informative character told by the author without recourse to the vantage point of any hero.

The other stories of 1895 are similar to "Three Years" in this respect. In "Supruga" ("The Spouse"), "Anna na šee" ("Anna Around the Neck"), and "Ubijstvo" ("The Murder") the point of view is divided between the hero(ine) and the author-narrator; in the latter story, next to the main hero, Matvey, his brother Yakov is also occasionally given the viewpoint position. When we leave out the first-person narratives, which are relatively numerous during these years, we move to "Mužiki" ("The Peasants") of 1897. In this story, it is true, the heroes (the sick Moscow waiter Nikolay, his wife Olga, and their daughter, who come to live with their relatives in a poor peasant village) do not clearly show their own point of view, which is indissolubly connected with the author's. This is particularly evident in Olga's inner monologue at the end, which could hardly be thought in exactly this way by a rather primitive character, but is totally put in the literary form, language, and style of the author. When Nikolay and Olga watch "how the sky, golden and purple, was reflected in the water, in the church windows and in the whole air, which was delicate, quiet, ineffably pure, as it never is in Moscow,"[74] there is no doubt that this is the author's word usage, because the couple would not phrase, and probably not perceive the situation in this way, except for the concluding subordinate clause.

In "Pečeneg" ("The Pecheneg"), "V rodnom uglu" ("At Home"), and "Na podvode" ("On the Cart") from the same year, there is again an unmistakable central hero who is the recording consciousness of the story, although in each case the author himself steps forth to provide the necessary neutral information; this seems frequently to be the case in the first of these stories, and perhaps also in the second one, but it is not easy to separate his voice from that of the heroine Vera.[75] In "On the Cart" there is a rather unexpected interruption by the author, in which Chekhov, generalizing, comments on people like his heroine, "teachers, impecunious doctors, medical assistants ... work-horses, like this Marya Vasilyevna" (9:248). This subjectivity is rather unusual, but, as we have seen, something similar can be found in earlier stories, whenever the subject matter was somehow close to his heart and his own experience; and after the years in Melikhovo this was certainly the case with the medical and educational workers in the countryside.

---

[74] 9:193–194.
[75] If we read: " ... said she, as if she wanted to mitigate the harshness of her decision" (9:242), this is somebody else (the author or a narrator), giving his comment, not Vera.

9

Let us try to summarize what can be concluded from the stories written in Chekhov's last years. In several of them there is, contrary to what Chudakov attempts to demonstrate, an uncontestable hero's point of view: that of the doctor, Korolyov, in "Slučaj iz praktiki" ("A Doctor's Visit," 1898), of the visitor Podgorin in "U znakomykh" ("With Friends," also 1898), of Gurov in "Dama s sobačkoj" ("The Lady With the Dog," 1899), of bishop Pyotr in "Arkhierej" ("The Bishop," 1902), and of Nadya in "The Betrothed." There are only a few passages where the viewpoint shifts to the author (in "With Friends," for instance, a passage on p. 458: "There were two human beings in him ... ," also a description on p. 467; in "The Lady With the Dog" a few informative words about the hero: "He was not forty yet, but he had already a twenty-year-old daughter ... ";[76] and a similar neutral passage in the first short chapter of "The Betrothed").

In "Po delam služby" ("On Official Business," 1899), after an introductory external description, we see the two main characters, the country doctor and the deputy prosecutor Lyzhin, on a trip to the site of a suicide or maybe a murder. At a certain moment they think collectively: " ... they both thought of how little all this resembled real life .... "[77] Then follows the story by the *sotskij* (police assistant), which has a *skaz* character. The ensuing scenes are all viewed from Lyzhin's angle; he is gradually cast "in a new role: the investigator has now become a witness."[78] Included here is the well-known scene in which Lyzhin in his dream hears the voices of the police assistant and the dead Lesnitsky, moaning: "We go on, go on, go on.... "[79] It is evident that Lyzhin has become the central character in the story, through whose prism everything is viewed; this is along the same lines as many stories from earlier years.

We find a more mixed viewpoint in "Ionyč" (1898), "Dušečka"(" The Darling," 1898), "Na svjatkakh" ("At Christmastide," 1899), and "V ovrage" ("In the Ravine," 1900). "Ionyč" opens with some introductory remarks, but soon we are confronted with the main hero's thoughts: " ... such good, quiet thoughts entered his mind all the time—he did not want to rise from his chair."[80] Occasionally the author's voice enters into the narrative ("she had already told all the guests that he was an extraordinary, remarkable doctor";

---

[76] 9:357.
[77] 9:344.
[78] Kramer, *The Chameleon and the Dream* (n. 45, above), p. 47.
[79] "My idëm, my idëm, my idëm ... " (9:357). On the significance of dreams in Chekhov's works see Gleb Struve in his study "On Chekhov's Craftmanship: The Anatomy of a Story," *Slavic Review*, 20 (October 1961); 465–476, esp. pp. 466–471; and Kramer, *The Chameleon and the Dream*, chapter "Dreams," pp. 76–92.
[80] 9:288.

or, in an informative way: "once an Italian opera company was *en route* in S., one of the female singers died . . . ").⁸¹ And in the last, fifth chapter the author-narrator evidently takes over characterizing the hero ironically: " . . . it is an impressive sight, and it looks as if a heathen god, not a man were driving..."⁸² As in several of Chekhov's other, later, more elaborate stories there is a conclusive ending, reminding one of the typical Turgenevian story- or novel-endings.⁸³

In "The Darling" there is an alternation of the author's (or neutral narrator's) and heroine's point of view, and the same situation is to be found in "At Christmastide," where the author shares his viewpoint with the simple woman Vasilisa, and in the second chapter with her son in the town.⁸⁴

The nine chapters of "In the Ravine" show a frequent change of viewpoint. The story starts with some general information, as usual, but the feelings of the old merchant Tsybukin are also rendered.⁸⁵ The standpoint of the son Anisim is reproduced in the scene of his wedding with Lipa and when he leaves the house in chapter 4.⁸⁶ When Lipa, her mother Praskovya, and Kostyl return from a pilgrimage, the facts, observations, and emotions that cross their minds are rendered in a literary style and language; but then again, collectively and at the same time more personally: " . . . and they felt joyful and happy, and there was restlessness in their hearts." One finds a mixture in one sentence of their own feelings and the conjectures of an observer on the next page: "maybe it seemed to them for a moment that . . . they, too, were a force . . . ; they liked to sit up here, they . . . forgot . . . ."⁸⁷

In chapter 5 the viewpoint of Lipa and Praskovya seems to be central again; in chapter 8, in which Lipa returns from the hospital with her dead child, her viewpoint is shown. The concluding chapter takes us to the present and is narrated by a neutral voice; Tsybukin, Lipa, and her mother are viewed from the outside.

Only one story remains which is totally narrated by the omniscient author and in which even the principal heroes are regarded from the outside: "Novaja dača" ("The New Villa") from 1899.⁸⁸

---

⁸¹ 9:291, 294.   ⁸² 9:302.

⁸³ The same applies, e.g., to "Novaja dača." The communication of facts about the heroes which are in fact of no direct relevance to the story, in the Turgenevian manner, although usually considered nontypical of Chekhov's narration, can be found in some of his other stories as well, for example, in "On the Cart."

⁸⁴ The son "remembered how . . . " (9:377).

⁸⁵ " . . . he regretted that his eldest son was not married to her"; "he loved his family" (9:379).

⁸⁶ "Deep emotions filled his heart, he felt like crying" (9:387). See also 393.

⁸⁷ 9:396, 397.

⁸⁸ In a few instances the author pretends not to be omniscient, he adds modal adverbs to indicate that the heroes are viewed by an observer: "The engineer apparently became irritated . . . ," 9:338; "the girl, too, judging by her face, had . . . " at the very end.

We may conclude by repeating what we mentioned earlier: Chekhov displays in his third-person narratives a variety of approaches, depending on the theme and the situation, the size and the "tone" of each story. The type in which the hero is the perceiving and commenting medium occurs relatively infrequently in his early prose, it becomes more frequent from 1887 on, and loses some ground after 1894, but it never dominates strongly and never disappears. On the other hand, the type of story with several viewpoints, among which is also the author's, or possibly a narrator's, becomes proportionally more important in his last years, but again, never predominates.

10

There are other narrative types, which I have so far disregarded in this paper. As our statistics show, a considerable number of Chekhov's stories are written in the first person. In them the question of viewpoint has a very special aspect: it is always, and has to be, with the "I" who tells the story. Still we can distinguish at least two main types of *Ich-Erzählungen*: those in which the "I" is passive and those in which he (or she) is an active participant— an observer and recording intelligence or one of the acting characters, maybe *the* main hero.[89] Both types, with various degrees of first-person participation, are represented in Chekhov's prose. As examples of the more or less passive "I" (commenting on, but not participating in the events) one can think of the two stories from the trilogy of 1898: "The Man in a Case" and "Gooseberries." An example of the involved "I" type would be "A Dreary Story" (which, for the rest, begins with a paragraph where the "I" speaks about himself in the third person). The passive attitude can be observed in some of the earlier stories as well, for instance in "Svetlaja ličnost'" ("An Enlightened Personality") or "Kto vinovat" ("Who Is Guilty"), both from 1886.

Often the first-person narratives take the form of a frame story, in which we are first introduced (if it follows the traditional pattern) to a group of people, one of whom takes the floor and tells his story. It sometimes occurs that the embracing, framing story is also told in the first person (like "Ariadna," for example), in which case we have a double "I" narrative. Within this type we can also discern different varieties: the framed, inner story may be just a fragment within a larger narrative whole, an inserted piece of narration, or, at the other extreme, the framework can be reduced to just a few lines in the beginning, or even to a mere title or subtitle.

Some of Chekhov's stories have this character: the title indicates that we have to do with a tale narrated by a certain person or a certain type: such as, "Rasskaz gospoži N. N." ("The Story of Mrs. N. N."), "Rasskaz staršego

---

[89] Cf. C. Brooks, R. P. Warren, *Understanding Fiction* (n. 18, above), pp. 140–150.

sadovnika" ("The Story of the Senior Gardener"), "Rasskaz neizvestnogo čeloveka" ("The Story of an Unknown Man," usually translated as "An Anonymous Story"). Still more numerous than the titles are the *sub*titles of this kind: such as, "Rasskaz domovladel'ca" ("The Story of a Houseowner"), "Rasskaz podsudimogo" ("The Story of a Defendant"), "Rasskaz starogo vorob'ja" ("The Story of an Old Sparrow", that is, a cunning fellow), "Rasskaz očevidcev" ("The Story of Eyewitnesses"), "Plač oskudevšego" ("The Lament of an Impoverished Man"), "Iz zapisok vspyl'čivogo čeloveka" ("From the Notes of a Quick-tempered Man").

Examples of a story-within-a-story of relatively modest proportions and significance are the tramp's story in "Dreams," and the police assistant's story in "On Official Business," both mentioned before: they are told in the special jargon of the hero. In "The Student" there is the student's relation of a passage from the New Testament. Engineer Ananyev's story in "Lights" carries somewhat more weight. Another *skaz* narrative is "Peasant Women," containing the merchant Matvey Savich's story. Examples of *Rahmenerzählungen* in the classical style, reminiscent of Turgenev's and Leskov's stories, are "Sil'nye oščuščenija" (Strong Emotions") and "Svjatoju noč'ju" ("In the Holy Night"), both from 1886. And "To byla ona" ("That Was She") from the same year is an example of a story in which the framed inner narrative is well integrated in the enclosing larger whole.

In first-person stories it can easily happen that the author for a moment forgets his limited horizon and provides information he cannot actually possess if he keeps to the rules of the game. This occurs relatively rarely in Chekhov's stories. In "Khorošie ljudi" ("Good People," 1886) the main hero, Lyadovsky, is introduced to the reader and depicted by the "I," which is not common in Chekhov's short stories. However, we should not forget the theme of the story: the hero is a "colleague," a fellow-writer, but Chekhov wants to express here his aversion for a certain type of superfluous, ungifted litterateur or scribbler, a type that he must have encountered often: a man who repeats himself, although he has nothing to say, and who immediately after his death will be "completely forgotten." Next to the derisive profile of this man he pictures his sister in a quite appreciative way. She is the idealistic type that leaves the safe fireside and goes out to work for the suffering people, to vaccinate peasants. In a way, she is predecessor of figures like Misail in "Moja žizn'" ("My Life") and Nadya in "The Betrothed" from later years. The reason I mentioned this story here is that the narrator intimates a few things about Lyadovsky he can hardly know, although he supposedly is a good and close friend.[90]

---

[90] "He wanted . . . ," 5: 239; also 242.

Another slight flaw in the first-person structure can be seen in "My life." Can the "I", Misail, really know everything he is reporting? For example, when he tells us that his wife Masha " . . . was often at the watermill. . . . When she returned, each time a village simpleton would . . . shout. . . . "[91] As I mentioned, these instances are rare, and there seems to be no reason for Chudakov's statement that the narrator in the 1898 trilogy "not only renders what he himself directly saw, but also reproduces in detail conversations at which he was not present and thoughts of heroes which he could not know."[92]

In his early years Chekhov used the first-person narrative procedure rather frequently: in 1883, for example, when his total production amounted to approximately eighty-eight stories (not including short non-narrative texts, feuilletons, and so on), he wrote twenty-four "I" stories, which is over 27 percent. In the last nine years of his active period as a short-story writer he produced only six first-person narratives, but this is 23 percent of his entire output of these years, which shows that he never turned away from this device.

There exist not only first- and third-person-singular narratives (*Ich*- and *Er-Erzählungen*), in fact, there are as many types of narration as there are personal pronouns, and Chekhov in a way used all of them in his work.

There are, it is true, no complete second-person-singular (*ty-*) stories in Chekhov's oeuvre (one cannot include here the many instances in which he uses this person as a syntactic form, equivalent to English *one*, French *on*, German *man*; it occurs primarily in first-person narration, where the author talks to the reader.[93]) "Žizn' prekrasna" ("Life Is Beautiful," 1883) is a text almost entirely written in the "you" form; however, it is a comic piece, but not a real story. Similarly, the text "Rukovodstvo dlja želajuščikh ženit'sja" ("Guide for Those Who Are Desirous of Marrying," 1885) consists largely of singular imperative forms (such as, " . . . obraščaj vnimanie," "pay attention," 4:421). In all such stories, Chekhov is turning to the reader, the person who is the object of the narration, or the *narrataire* in Gerald Prince's terminology.[94]

There are a few instances of "we" ("my") stories. In 1883, for example, when Chekhov wrote, as we have seen, twenty-four first-person stories, there are four more in which the collective first person is used throughout the story: "V počtovom otdelenii" ("At the Post Office"), "Edinstvennoe sredstvo" ("The Only Remedy"), "Rasskaz, kotoromu trudno podobrat' nazvanie" ("A Story for Which it is Hard to Select a Title"), and "Benefis solov'ja" ("The

---

[91] 9:166.
[92] Cf. *Poètika Čekhova*, p. 95.
[93] See, e.g., "A Dreary Story," 7:234–235, 277; "An Anonymous Story," 8:175.
[94] Gerald Prince, "Introduction à l'étude du narrataire," in *Poétique*, Paris, 4, no. 14 (1973):178–196. An example of the consistent *you*-story is I. Bunin's "Cifry" (1906).

Nightingale's Benefit Night"). In the latter, I (*ja*) is also used. In all these cases the narrator identifies himself with a group of men. A good example of the use of "my" in his later production is "The Man in the Case," where it is used several times to indicate the collective teachers' body as opposed to the solitary teacher of Greek. There are several stories in which "we" is only occasionally mentioned. A complete and consistent "we" story is "Zloumyšlenniki" ("The Malefactors," 1887), in which "we" watch two suspicious individuals, who then turn out to be solar eclipse observers.[95]

The second person plural or polite singular is found in some other stories (for example, in "V Moskve, na Trubnoj ploščadi": "In Moscow, on Trubnaja Square," 1883, in which it is the author's aim to acquaint his readers with this place).[96] In later years, such addresses are less frequent, but they still occur. Extending this procedure, Chekhov sometimes developed a full second-person narrative. His "Novogodnjaja pytka" ("A New Year Torture," 1887) starts: "Vy oblačaetes' vo fračnuju paru...." ("You don an evening dress...."); and this tone is sustained for five and a half pages, up to the end of the story, except that to a large extent it consists of dialogue, in which this second-person narrative is, of course, absent.[97]

Classical writers like Gogol and Turgenev liked to apostrophize their readers, following, in their turn, an older European tradition. Compare in Gogol's "Nevskij prospekt": "At this time, whatever you will put on, even if you would have a cap on your head instead of a hat, . . . nobody will notice it," or in one of Turgenev's *Sportsman's Sketches*, "Les i step'" ("Forest and Steppe"): "You come out on the porch. . . . You ride and ride. . . . You are somewhat cold...." It is somewhat surprising to find Chekhov using the same procedure at the beginning of "Ward No. 6": "If you are not afraid of

---

[95] A collective "we" is also used in "Mest'" ("The Revenge," 1882, 2:80), "Čtenie" ("Reading," 1884, 3:29), and others.

[96] Other examples can be found in stories like "Patriot svoego otečestva" ("A Patriot of His Fatherland," 1883) ("Good beer ... you can find in the hotel ...," 2:162); and "Baron" ("The Baron," 1882, 2:71). In "Toržestvo pobediteľja" ("The Triumph of the Victor," 1883), a first-person narrative, there is an address to the reader in which the first and second person occur (2:21). "Ispoved'" ("The Confession," 1883) ends with a whole harangue by the narrator directed at his acquaintances (2:113). Cf. the texts from 1886 "Vesnoj" ("In the Spring"), 4:207; "K svedeniju mužej" ("For the Information of Husbands"), 4:579; "Akh, zuby!" ("Oh, My Teeth!"), 5:374; "Predloženie" ("The Proposal"), 5:383.

[97] Less consistent is "Na reke" ("On the River," 1886), a *causerie* about the breaking up of the ice in second-person narrative; but later the subject of the action as well as the heroes with the story's point of view are the floaters (*splavščiki*), who are watching "kartiny odna drugoj krače" ("views, one even more beautiful than the other," 5:290). "No ne dumajte ... " ("But you should not think ... "), continues the narrator, as if he were still speaking, but that is not quite possible, as he does not belong to the floaters about whom we are told now.

being pricked by the stinging nettle, let us go . . . "; "Then you enter a big room . . . ".[98] Noteworthy are the sentences on the next page which form part of the description of the psychopathic patient Gromov: "When he speaks, you recognize in him the lunatic and the human being. . . . He speaks about . . . the wonderful life that in the course of time will come on earth. . . . "[99] We hear this supposedly insane character express thoughts similar to those of Vershinin and other Chekhovian personages. Gromov is apparently not in his right mind, but at the same time Chekhov intimates that he is *human*, too.[100]

Even more like Gogol and Turgenev is the opening paragraph of "At Home," a lyrical-descriptive introduction about the steppe, in which *vy* (you) takes the place of "one" (or "I").[101]

The foregoing pages have, of necessity, the character of a dry enumeration: their aim is to show that Chekhov in the structure of his stories, far from being dry, was inventive and evinced a rich variety of procedures and approaches.

APPENDIX

Here is the breakdown of Chekhov's stories according to the point of view from which they are written (see the chart on p. 103).

Hero's viewpoint:
1886:

(24)   "Toska"   "Aptekarša"
       "Perepolokh"   "Lišnie ljudi"
       "Panikhida"   "Khoristka"
       "Košmar"   "Nesčast'e"
       "Pervyj debjut"   "Talant"
       "Otkrytie"   "Mest'"

---

[98] 8:107-108. Entirely in the polite address form is Tolstoy's "Sevastopol' v dekabre."
[99] 8:110.
[100] Which does not mean Chekhov tries to idealize this man! He thus concludes his portrait of Gromov: "The final impression is that of an incoherent, jumbled medley of old, but not yet died off songs" (*ibid.*).
[101] A third-person plural story is most uncommon. Closest to it come some collectivist novels in Soviet literature from the twenties and thirties, e.g., A. Serafimovič's *Železnyj potok* (*The Iron Stream*, 1924). Among Chekhov's short stories there are only imperfect examples of this category: in "Na gvozde" ("On the Nail," 1883), e.g., an undifferentiated, small group of men (apparently employees) constitutes the collective hero. In "Mal'čiki" ("Boys," 1887) we see the two boys on the one hand, the three sisters on the other as collectivities. "Bez zaglavija" ("Without a Title," 1888) figures an unspecified group of monks. Sometimes Chekhov renders the words or thoughts of a collective hero, e.g., at the end of "Moroz" ("Frost," 1887) (6:18-19). "O ženščinakh" ("About Women," 1886) has "women" as its theme and heroines, but it contains no narrative, rather a mocking *causerie* about female stupidity.

"Glupyj francuz"   "Van'ka"
"Persona"   "Na dače"
"Otrava"   "Ot nečego delat'"
"Volk"   "Skuka žizni"
"Griša"   "Rozovyj čulok"
"Damy"
"Znakomyj mužčina"

1887:
(21) "Veročka"   "Beglec"
     "Doma"   "Zadača"
     "Tif"   "Intrigi"
     "Žitejskie nevzgody" "Dorogie uroki"
     "Proisšestvie"   "Lev i solnce"
     "Volodja"   "Beda"
     "Drama"   "Kaštanka"
     "Bezzakonie"   "Dobryj nemec"
     "Svirel'"   "Odin iz mnogikh"
     "Mstitel'"   "Neprijatnaja istorija"
     "Počta"

1888–1894:
(14) "Neprijatnost'"   "Posle teatra"
     "Imeniny"   "Sosedi"
     "Pripadok"   "Student"
     "Sapožnik i nečistaja sila" "Čërnyj monakh" (in most of the story)
     "Pari"   "Bab'e carstvo"
     "Knjaginja"   "Skripka Rotšil'da"
     "Vory"   "Učitel' slovesnosti"

1895–1903:
(6) "V rodnom uglu" (with occasion-   "Dama s sobačkoj"
        ally the narrator's viewpoint) "Arkhierej"
     "Slučaj iz praktiki"   "Nevesta"
     "Po delam služby"

Two or more heroes' viewpoints:
1886:
(5) "Anjuta"   "Muž"
     "Ivan Matveič"   "Čužaja beda"
     "Ved'ma"

1887:
(4) "Vyigryšnyj bilet" "Sledovatel'"
     "Pis'mo"   "Sčast'e"

1888-1894:
(1) "Poprygun'ja"
1895-1903:
None

Reduced hero's viewpoint:
1886:
(11) "Khudožestvo" "V sude"
     "Neudača" "Mečty"
     "Aktërskaja gibel'" "Sobytie"
     "Bespokojnyj gost'" "Den' za gorodom"
     "Nakhlebniki" "Nedobraja noč'"
     "V potëmkakh"
1887:
(8) "Moroz" "Nenast'e"
    "Niščij" "Mal'čiki"
    "Neostorožnost'" "Rano!"
    "Nedobroe delo" "Kazak"
1888-1894:
(5) "Spat' khočetsja" "Istorija odnogo torgovogo
    "Baby" (partly first-person *skaz*)   predprijatija"
    "V ssylke" "V usad'be"
1895-1903:
None

Mixed viewpoint:
1886:
(9) "Roman s kontrabasom" "Tina"
    "Učitel'" "Na puti"
    "Stradal'cy" "Na reke"
    "Tjaželye ljudi" "Neobyknovennyj"
    "Tsss!"
1887:
(4) "Vragi" "Kholodnaja krov'"
    "Svad'ba" "Poceluj"
1888-1894:
(5) "Step'" "Palata № 6"
    "Gusev" "Volodja bol'šoj i Volodja malen'kij"
    "Duèl'"
1895-1903:
(12) "Supruga" "Na podvode"
     "Anna na šec" "Ionyč"

"Ubijstvo" "Dušečka"
"Tri goda" "U znakomykh"
"Mužiki" "Na svjatkakh"
"Pečeneg" "V ovrage"

Neutral:
1886:
(29) "Detvora" "Orator"
"Vesnoj" "Proizvedenie iskusstva"
"Mnogo bumagi" "O ženščinakh"
"Novogodnie velikomučeniki" "V pansione"
"U telefona" "Ser'ëznyj šag"
"Beseda trezvogo s p'janym "Ty i vy"
  čertom" "Nyt'ë"
"O brennosti" "Akh, zuby!"
"V Pariž" "Predloženie"
"Sčastlivčik" "Žilec"
"Pervyj ljubovnik" "Kalkhas"
"Dlinnyj jazyk" "Na mel'nice"
"Žitejskaja meloč'" "Dramaturg"
"Khorošie ljudi" (actually a "Beda"
  first-person narration) "Zakaz"
  "Jubilej"

1887:
(17) "Temnota" "V sarae"
"Polin'ka" "Sirena"
"P'janye" "Vstreča"
"Nakanune posta" "Udav i krolik"
"Bezzaščitnoe suščestvo" "Kritik"
"Tajna" "Obyvateli"
"Skoraja pomošč'" "Pered zatmeniem" (actually a
"Otec"   dialogue)
"Khorošij konec" "Doktor"

1888–1894:
(2) "Bez zaglavija" "Ryb'ja ljubov'"
1895–1903:
(2) "Belolobyj" "Novaja dača"

First-person narrative:
1886:
(18) "Noč' pered sudom" "Tajnyj sovetnik"
"Šutočka" "Strakhi"

"Agaf'ja"   "Passažir pervogo klassa"
"Noč' na kladbišče"   "Pustoj slučaj"
"Rasskaz bez konca"   "To byla ona"
"Moj razgovor s počtmejsterom"   "Ljubov'"
"Grač"   "Svetlaja ličnost'"
"Svjatoju noč'ju"   "Moj domostroj"
"Sil'nye oščuščenija"   "Kto vinovat"

1887:
(9)* "Šampanskoe"   "Staryj dom"
     "Na Strastnoj nedele"   "Rasskaz gospoži N.N."
     "Iz zapisok vspyl'čivogo   'Vesnoj"
        čeloveka"   "Zloumyšlenniki"
     'Perekati-pole"
     "Zinočka"

1888–1894:
(7) "Krasavicy"   "Strakh"
    "Skučnaja istorija"   "Rasskaz neizvestnogo čeloveka"
    "Ogni"   "Rasskaz staršego sadovnika"
    "Žena"

1895–1903:
(6) "Ariadna"   "Čelovek v futljare"
    "Dom s mezoninom"   "Kryžovnik" (in these frame stories
    "Moja žizn'"   the "I" has a very limited role)
                                    "O ljubvi"

---

* Not listed is the second-person story "Novogodnjaja pytka."

OSIP MANDELSTAM AND AUGUSTE BARBIER*

Some Notes on Mandelstam's Versions of *Iambes*

BY

GLEB STRUVE

To the memory of Boris Unbegaun and Michal K. Pawlikowski

1

IN THE SECOND VOLUME of her remarkable memoirs which were circulated clandestinely in the Soviet Union (in the so-called *samizdat*) before being published in the West,[1] Nadezhda Mandelstam, the poet's widow, says that of all his verse translations the poet himself attached most value to "Gogotur and Apshina," the long narrative poem of the Georgian poet Vazha Pshavela (pseudonym of Luka Razikashvili, 1861–1915),[2] and to the poems of the French poet Henri Auguste Barbier (1805–1882).

Of the seven poems chosen by Mandelstam in Barbier, five were from his famous *Iambes*, and the other two from Barbier's later poetry, namely from *Lazare*, his book of poems about England and Ireland. Four of the five from *Iambes* had to do, directly or indirectly, with the July Revolution and belonged to 1830 and early 1831. They were "la Curée (written in August

---

* This article represents a somewhat expanded version of a paper read at the Twelfth Congress of the International Federation of Modern Languages and Literatures held in Cambridge, England, from 20 to 26 August 1972. A very brief abstract of it was published in the Proceedings of the Congress: *Expression, Communication and Experience in Literature and Language*, ed. Ronald G. Popperwell, The Modern Humanities Research Association (London, 1973), xviii, 310 pp.

[1] The first volume of Nadezhda Mandelstam's memoirs was published, both in Russian and in English, in 1970: *Vospominanija* (New York: Chekhov Publishing Corporation), 432 pp.; *Hope Against Hope: A Memoir*, translated from the Russian by Max Hayward (New York: Atheneum), 432 pp. The second volume was published in Russian in 1972: *Vtoraja kniga* (Paris: YMCA Press), 712 pp. The English version, entitled *Hope Abandoned*, also in Max Hayward's translation and with some explanatory comments by him, appeared in February 1974 (New York: Atheneum), xii, 688 pp. There had been, in the meantime, translations into some other languages. These memoirs are one of the most remarkable nonfictional works to come out of the Soviet Union in over fifty years of its existence. See my review of *Vtoraja kniga* in *The Russian Review* (October, 1973), vol. 32, no. 4, pp. 425–428. To this day the books remain unpublished in the Soviet Union.

[2] This poem will be found in the three-volume edition of Mandelstam's *Sobranie sočinenij* (Collected Works), ed. G. Struve and B. Filippov (Washington, D.C., and New York: Inter-Language Literary Associates). See vol. 1, rev. ed. pp. 321–333. The first editions of vols. 1 and 2 were published, respectively, in 1964 and 1966; the revised and improved editions in 1967 and 1971. Volume 3 was published in 1969. Vazha Pshavela's poem was also translated by two other well-known modern Russian poets, Boris Pasternak and Nikolay Zabolotsky. Subsequent references to vols. 1 and 2 are to the revised editions.

1830), "Quatre-Vingt Treize" (January 1831), "l'Emeute," and "la Popularité" (February 1831). The fifth was "l'Idole" (May 1831), the famous exposure of the revived Napoleonic cult. Of the five, Mandelstam translated only two in their entirety: "la Curée" and "Quatre-Vingt-Treize."[3]

"La Curée" was the first and the most famous of Barbier's poems inspired by the July Revolution. Published first in the *Journal des Débats*, it made him a celebrity overnight. Except for a short "Prologue," it was to open the 1831 separate edition of *Iambes*. In his well-known *History of French Literature under the July Government*, the conservative literary historian Alfred Nettement, who had no sympathy with the July Revolution, described Barbier as "a satirical poet of the first order." Speaking of "la Curée," he wrote:

"La Curée" qui nous est apparue sur le seuil de la Révolution de 1830, comme un prélude poétique où vibrait le pressentiment d'une autre révolution, était surtout consacrée à glorifier la multitude et à flétrir ces hommes de lendemain qui flairent un triomphe et dévorent la proie qu'ils n'ont pas abattue. Jamais la poésie française n'avait montré la hardiesse cynique d'images et l'énergie brutale d'expressions qui respirent dans cette malédiction démocratique. C'est l'hyperbole de Juvénal avec une sincérité de colère que n'a pas le rhéteur romain, et un tout autre mouvement d'idées et de sentiments.[4]

Comparisons of Barbier with Juvenal were fairly common among the critics of the time. On the other hand, it has been rightly pointed out that Barbier renovated the satire as a genre by introducing into it some elements of the ode.

All of Mandelstam's translations from Barbier appeared in 1923 and 1924. This is also apparently when they were written. "La Curée" was the first to be published. It appeared in the magazine *Prožektor* (No. 13, August 15, 1923), a weekly (and later, bi-weekly and monthly) literary supplement to *Pravda*. This magazine was at the time edited by Aleksandr Voronsky who was also editor of the major monthly review of those days, *Krasnaja Nov'*, and as a literary critic played an important part in Soviet literature in the 1920s and early 1930s, when some of Mandelstam's poetry was published in his journal.

---

[3] Mandelstam's translations from Barbier will be found in the Struve-Filippov edition under nos. 467, 468, 469, 470, 471 (in vol. 1) and 491a (vol. 2). Since the publication of our edition, a Soviet one-volume edition of Mandelstam's poetry, which had been announced several times since the late fifties, was at last published at the very end of 1973 in the "Biblioteka poèta" series: O. Mandel'stam, *Stikhotvorenija* (Leningrad: Sovetskij Pisatel', 1973), 334 pp. It was prepared for the press by N. I. Khardzhiev, with his commentary. It contains two translations from Barbier which were not in our edition and is also said to embody corrections, based on the poet's autographs, of some mistakes in the original magazine publications. The two Barbier poems added in the Soviet edition are: "Bronza," a translation of the initial section of the poem called "l'Idole," of which Mandelstam also translated another section, and "Irlandskie kholmy" ("les Belles collines d'Irlande," from *Lazare*). Section iii of "l'Idole," originally published as "Kobyla" ("The Mare"), is given in the Khardzhiev edition under the title "Napoleonic France."

[4] A. Nettement, *Histoire de la littérature française sous le gouvernement de Juillet (1830–1848)* (Paris, 3e éd. 1876), p. 140.

The other translations appeared in 1924 in *Zvezda*, in *Krasnyj Žurnal dlja Vsekh*, in the almanach *Naši Dni*, and in the literary supplement to the Berlin "Change-of-Landmarks" newspaper *Nakanune*, sometimes in two of those publications at short intervals.[5]

Nadezhda Mandelstam, in the first volume of her memoirs, translated into English as *Hope Against Hope* (in Russian the book is called simply *Vospominanija*), speaks of Mandelstam's translations from Barbier, and specifically of "la Curée," in connection with what she calls his "attempts to come to terms with his epoch." She describes those attempts as "fruitless," and provides the following explanation:

Infinitely more was demanded from those who were capitulating. Besides, Mandelstam was carrying on a dialogue with the Revolution, not with the rising "new order," not with that special kind of "world of Empire" [Mandelstam's "*mir deržavnyj*" in one of his poems —*G. S.*] in which all of a sudden we found ourselves. For O.M.'s explanations there was no addressee in our reality. The chorus of true adherents of the new religion and the new state used, in its ritual observances, the language of the Revolution, but it had no use for a new *raznočinec*[6] with his doubts and tossings about. To the true adherents and to the "Fellow Travellers" everything was clear as it was. "The whole question is who will get the pie," said V.I. [Vsevolod Ivanov]. [...] "With us it cannot be otherwise," "You must understand where you're living," "What can you expect!"—this was heard on all sides, while Mandelstam continued to associate everybody with the fourth estate: "Shall I, indeed, betray to shameless slander . . . the wondrous oath of allegiance to the fourth estate ? . . . " Or perhaps, frightened by the debauch of the true adherents, he proclaimed in those verses his loyalty to that which they had betrayed already ? After all, it was not an accident that he chose to translate Barbier's poem "la Curée": "Et tous comme ouvriers que l'on met à la tâche, / Fouillent ses flancs à plein museau, / Et de l'ongle et des dents sans relâche / Travaillent, car chacun en veut le morceau; / Car il faut au chenil que chacun d'eux revienne / Avec un os demi rongé / Et que, trouvant au seuil son orgueilleuse chienne, / Jalouse et le poil allongé, / Il lui montre sa gueule encor rouge, et qui grogne, / Son os dans les dents arrêté, / Et lui crie, en jetant son quartier de charogne: / Voici ma part de royauté."[7]

There are in this passage, as translated by Mandelstam, two words which Barbier did not use. One of them is *muženēk*, the contemptuously affectionate diminutive of *muž* (husband). The other is *sem'janin*, "the family man." The proud and jealous bitch is awaiting her *muženēk* and expecting him to show her, as behooves a good family man, his share of *la curée*. In translating Mme Mandelstam's quotation into English, Max Hayward used the expression "good mate" for *muženēk* and left the word *sem'janin* untranslated. But it was

---

[5] The complete information about the original magazine publications will be found in the commentary to the Soviet edition.

[6] In his English version Max Hayward translated this word, somewhat freely, as "an upstart intellectual."

[7] See *Vospominanija*, p. 184. I quote this passage in my own translation and give the Barbier quotation in the original French. Cp. *Hope Against Hope*, pp. 176-177.

with reference to that particular word that Mme Mandelstam went on to say: "Barbier's poem was translated in 1923, and in 1933 the theme of the 'family man' cropped up again in the poem about the apartment..." By this she meant the apartment in the Furmanov Lane where the Mandelstams lived before his first arrest (in 1934) and the exile to Cherdyn. The poem begins: "Kvartira tikha kak bumaga..." Mandelstam called this apartment of theirs "moskovskoe zloe žil'ë" ("the evil Muscovite dwelling"), but his widow quotes the lines about "An honest traitor of sorts, his wife's and children's keeper, boiled clean like salt in the purges," and then goes on to say:

> The poem of Barbier was translated in the summer, and in the winter of the same year was published the oath of allegiance to the fourth estate. I believe it was not an accident that it was received so coldly by those on whom the distribution of worldly goods depended.[8]

No mention of Mandelstam's version of "la Curée" is made by the Soviet scholar Yury Danilin in his book on the poets of the July Revolution, though there can be no doubt that it was superior to the earlier ones and combined accuracy with great emotional expressiveness and verbal power. It is true that his book was published at the time when Mandelstam was an "unperson" and his name was not mentionable.[9] Danilin devoted to Barbier a whole chapter, of close on thirty pages. He spoke of the popularity of Barbier in Russia, a popularity that began on the morrow of the publication of his *Iambes* in book form and lasted well into the 1860s. He mentioned the translations of Barbier's poems by his Russian contemporaries who sympathized with the July Revolution (they included Sergey Durov, a member of the Petrashevsky circle to which Dostoevsky also belonged). He quoted two longish passages from "la Curée" in V. Burenin's version. Danilin's view was that Barbier's revolutionary reputation—which he enjoyed in the eyes of the Russian radicals in the 1840s to 1860s, and continued to enjoy with some Soviet literary scholars—had been greatly exaggerated. According to Danilin, it was only because of "la Curée" and "le Lion" that Barbier was given a place in the ranks of revolutionary poets.

Danilin was of the opinion that Russian nineteenth-century translators of Barbier, whether they were of liberal or of radical persuasion, tended at times to "revolutionize" Barbier's meaning, and that some modern Soviet scholars

---

[8] *Ibid.* For the poem about the "evil dwelling" see no. 272 in vol. 1 of the Struve-Filippov edition. This poem, along with many others, is not included in the Soviet one-volume edition.

[9] Mandelstam virtually disappeared from Soviet literature in 1933. He was arrested and banished, first to Cherdyn' in the Northeast and then to Voronezh in Central Russia, in 1934. Released in 1937, he was rearrested and exiled to the Far East where he died in December 1938 (at least, according to the best information at present available) in a Soviet transit camp. For further details of his life see his widow's memoirs and also: Clarence Brown, *Mandelstam* (Cambridge University Press, 1973).

were also guilty of this. Their intentions were of the best, but as a result of this, as well as of the neglect of the "genuine" revolutionary poets of the 1830s, of men like Barthélemy, Viennet, and some others, the fallacy about the revolutionary character of all of Barbier's poetry continued to live on. Danilin, however, had no doubts about "la Curée" (he called it "Dobyča") being a true revolutionary poem, "a torch brandished by an unknown poet," as Alexandre Dumas had said of it. Barbier's disillusionment with the revolution began later, toward the end of 1830. It found its expression in some of the poems about the revolution written in 1831, such as "l'Emeute," "la Popularité," "Quatre-Vingt Treize," and some others. (It is worth noting that all three poems here named by Danilin were chosen for translation by Mandelstam.)[10] Danilin's view is not shared by some later Soviet students of Barbier, such as S. Velikovsky who, in 1957, in an article in the *Vestnik* of the Moscow University criticized Danilin for his "unfairly sharp assessment of Barbier's ideological evolution." In his paper, though it is much shorter than Danilin's chapter, Velikovsky managed to say more worthwhile, even if not very original, things about Barbier as a poet, about his renovation of the satire as a poetic genre.[11]

Be that as it may, "la Curée" remains a poem in which Barbier succeeded in combining his sympathy with the revolution, and the enthusiasm that the three "glorious days" aroused in him, with a passionate invective against "tous

---

[10] Ju. Danilin, *Poèty Ijul'skoj revoljucii*. (Moscow: GIKhL, 1935). The chapter on Barbier, entitled "Satira Ijul'skoj revoljucii 1830-1831 g.: Barb'e," covers pp. 67-94. There is no mention of Mandelstam's translation in the same Danilin's chapter on literature of the July Revolution in vol. 2 of *Istorija francuzskoj literatury: 1789-1970*, ed. I. Anisimov et al. (Moscow, 1956). Barbier's work is discussed here on pp. 192-194 and 209. "La Curée" is quoted as "Dobyča," but in V. Burenin's translation.

[11] See S. Velikovskij, "Khudožestvennoe svoeobrazie 'Jambov' O. Barb'e (K voprosu o stanovlenii graždanskoj poèzii francuzskogo romantizma)" in *Vestnik Moskovskogo Universiteta*, 1957, no. 1, pp. 160-178. See also the chapter on Barbier, entitled "Graždanskaja poèzija na putjakh romantizma (Ogjust Barb'e)," in the same author's book *Poèty francuzskikh revoljucij 1789-1848* (Moscow, 1963), pp. 145-180. In this later study which is not identical with the earlier article, Velikovsky no longer refers to "la Curée" as "Dobyča," but uses the title given to the poem by two nineteenth-century translators, Benediktov and Burenin, viz. "Sobačij pir" (under the same title the poem was apparently translated by Pavel Antokolsky from whose version Velikovsky quotes). It is mentioned, however, that the poem is sometimes called "Razdel dobyči." There is still no mention of Mandelstam's version, despite the poet's official "rehabilitation" by that time (it took place in 1956). Nor is there, for that matter, any mention of Mandelstam's translations from Barbier in the article about the latter in vol. 1 of the *Kratkaja Literaturnaja Ènciklopedija* which appeared in 1962. I have been unable to consult M. P. Alekseev's study of Barbier's reception in Russia, to be found in his introduction and commentary to a volume of translations from Barbier (Odessa, 1922). This volume was, however, published before the appearance of Mandelstam's versions in print. A volume of selected poems of Barbier, edited by Professor E. Etkind, appeared in Moscow in 1953 before the "rehabilitation" and did not contain any of Mandelstam's translations, as far as I know. See, however, below, n. 20, for another anthology edited by Etkind.

ces beaux fils aux tricolores flammes, / Au beau linge, au frac élégant, / Ces hommes en corset, ces visages de femmes, / Héros du boulevard de Gand," who were squatting behind the curtains, sweating from fear (or, literally, "sweating out fear"), trembling and closing their ears. The image of Freedom (Liberté, with a capital "L"), who has the "allures d'une fille," is full of erotic connotations: she is described as "une forte femme aux puissantes mamelles, / A la voix rauque, aux durs appas" and as "la vierge fougueuse, enfant de la Bastille," "qui ne prend ses amours que dans la populace, / Qui ne prête son large flanc / Qu'à des gens forts comme elle, et qui veut qu'on l'embrasse / Avec des bras rouges de sang." This image is followed by another powerful denunciation of Paris which is shown, on the morrow of the revolution, as a filthy sink of iniquity. Then comes the culminating sixth part of the poem from which the whole derives its title: a description, in vigorous images, of the *curée*, of the frantic rush and fight for such things as privileges and material benefits.

The figurative meaning of the word *la curée* is explained in French dictionaries as "Ruée vers les places, les honneurs, un butin, etc." Let us dwell briefly on the title of Barbier's poem and the rendering of it in Russian versions. Both Danilin and Velikovsky refer to it as "Dobyča," which actually means "booty" or "prey" (*butin* or *proie* in French). I could not ascertain whether there was any Russian verse translation under that title, but this rendering certainly leaves something to be desired.[12] In French *la curée* has two primary meanings: (1) *Partie de la bête que l'on donne à la meute*, and (2) *cette distribution même* (as an example of this usage is given the phrase: *Assister à la curée*). There is also the previously mentioned figurative usage. Barbier in his poem used the word in *all* those three meanings. This is impossible either in Russian or in English. French-English dictionaries usually give for *curée* the meaning "quarry" (as a hunting term), adding: "(fig.) booty, scramble, eagerness to seize prey or gain." French-Russian dictionaries give for *curée* either *dobyča* (which, as I have said, retranslated back, would be *butin* or *proie*), or a descriptive phrase corresponding to "*Partie de la bête....*"

The only European language which seems to have an equivalent of *la curée* in the sense of "part of the beast thrown to the pack" is Polish. The Polish word for it is *odprawa*.[13] In my search for a possible Russian equivalent I consulted several prominent linguists. With no result until a young American-

---

[12] See, however, n. 11.
[13] See, e.g., the Polish Academy of Sciences dictionary: *Słownik języka polskiego*, t. v (Warszawa, 1963). In the *Wielki słownik polsko-rosyjski*, compiled by Dymitr Hessen and Ryszard Stypuła (Warszawa-Moskva, 1967), *odprawa* is rendered into Russian as *podačka*, with an explanation in parenthesis: *sobake-posle okhoty* (to the hound after the hunting). While the Russian *podačka* (hand-out) has some implications not to be found in either *odprawa* or *la curée*, its meaning is at the same time narrower than that of *la curée*, and it would certainly not do as a rendering of Barbier's title.

Israeli Slavist, Dr. Omry Ronen, who was then a graduate student at Harvard and a teaching assistant at Yale and is now on the staff of the Hebrew universities in Jerusalem and Tel-Aviv, drew my attention to a word to be found in the dictionaries of Dal', Ushakov, and the Soviet Academy. The word as given in Dal' is *pazanka*, a term of venery, meaning *zajač'ja lapka* (hare's paw). Related to it are the verbs *pazančit'* and *otpazančit'* (to cut the hare's back paws). Ushakov has also a masculine variant (*pazanok*) and the same two verbs which are glossed as "to cut the hunted hare's *pazanki*." The same two variants and the same two verbs are listed in the Academy Dictionary. From the examples adduced there, it follows that the noun is used analogously with *la curée*. The examples are from Leo Tolstoy, Turgenev, Fet, and Driyansky, all of whom hunted a great deal in their lives. Here is an example from a no lesser work than *War and Peace*: "*Djadjuška slez i otpazančil. Potrjakhivaja zajca, čtoby stekala krov', on trevožno ogljadyvalsja.—Na pazanku!—govoril on, kidaja [sobake] otrezannuju lapu s nalipšeju zemlej.*" (The word *sobake* is supplied in brackets by the editors of the dictionary). It is obvious that "Na pazanku!" stands here for "Prends[ta] curée."

Another example, from one of Turgenev's *Sportsman's Sketches*, is perhaps even more clear cut, though the noun is not used in it: "*On otpazančil, vtoročil zajca i rozdal sobakam lapki.*" It appears however, that the words *pazanka*, *pazanok*, *pazančit'*, and *otpazančit'* are used in Russian only with reference to hares and their paws and would not apply to a fox or to a boar (as in Barbier's poem), whereas *la curée* in French and *odprawa* in Polish are more comprehensive terms. Nor does *pazanka* (or *pazanok*) have a figurative meaning (which is also true of the Polish *odprawa*). It could not therefore serve as a translation of Barbier's title, quite irrespective of being incomprehensible today to a great many Russians.

The purpose of this somewhat lengthy lexical digression was, however, to illustrate one of the problems that faced the Russian translators of "la Curée." Both Benediktov and Burenin, the two best-known nineteenth-century translators of the poem, rendered the title as "Sobačij pir," that is, "The Hounds' Banquet" (or "Feast"). This is not bad at all: the hounds "gorging" on the pieces of the beast thrown to them (usually, in the case of larger animals, the intestines and the heart) is one of the aspects of *la curée*. But Mandelstam preferred to stress another aspect of it, implied in Barbier's final scene, an aspect that was more characteristic of the state of things depicted by Barbier and more important from the point of view of the poet himself, namely the fighting over the booty (or, to be more exact, over *la curée*). And so Mandelstam called the poem "Sobač'ja skloka," "The Hounds' Scramble." It is possible that originally he had in mind another, near-synonymous word, *svara*. I suspect that as a result of a typing mistake this might have become *svora* ("pack") in one of the *samizdat* versions of Mme Mandelstam's memoirs, and therefore Max Hayward rendered the title of Barbier's poem as "The Pack of Hounds." I think that Mandelstam knew better than to give *svora* as a translation of "la Curée." The word, however, does actually appear in both Benediktov's and Mandelstam's version. Benediktov has: "*I spuščennykh sobak neistovaja svora / So vsekh rvanulas' sil.*" Mandelstam, in the same passage, uses the word twice: "... i pered svoroj djužej 'Voz 'mi ego!—kričat strelki"; and "Vsja svora, dërgajas' i ërzaja bokami, / Rvanetsja'..." But *svora* here stands for *la meute*. In the original we have: "... la trompe a sonné la curée / A toute la meute des chiens. / Toute la meute alors, comme une vague immense, / Bondit...." In the first of these lines Mandelstam also used the word *skloka*, and used it in a rather strange way which once again emphasized the lack, in Russian, of a proper term for "la curée." Mandelstam wrote: "I skloku trubit rog...."—"And the horn sounds the scramble...." The scramble is, of course, something that spontaneously ensues, but the horn does not *summon* the hounds to it: it sounds *la curée*—the distribution of certain parts of the quarry. Rather, however, than regard this as a lapse on Mandelstam's part, we should see in it an ingenious attempt to get round the absence of an exact equivalent of *la curée* in Russian and introduce at least one of the meanings of that word.

2

When I first read Mme Mandelstam's explanation of her husband's motivation for translating "la Curée," I failed to see a particularly close analogy between Barbier's picture of the "ruée vers les places et les honneurs" and Mandelstam's own position in the early 1920s versus the "capitulants" and the "fellow-travellers." Mme Mandelstam seemed to me to be anticipating her husband's later attitudes or reading back into the early twenties his subsequent growing alienation from the Soviet society which ended by hounding him out and closing all doors to literature for him. But in the second volume of her memoirs, published in 1972, Mme Mandelstam returned to this question, and this time she was both more explicit and more convincing. She wrote that when they settled down in Moscow in 1923 she saw her husband as she had never seen him before: "so concentrated, so stern, so isolated in himself." They were living in the Hertzen House, in what Mandelstam was later to describe as the "pokhabnyj osobnjak," with its "twelve lighted Judas windows."

A shift in his poetry had occurred earlier, she says, in Tiflis, with the poem "Umyvalsja noč'ju na dvore...."[14] In Moscow came the period of oaths

---
[14] See no. 126 in vol. 1 of the Struve-Filippov edition.

taken by the poet: a vow of poverty, not for its own sake but as a spiritual vow, was made in "Žizn' svjatogo Alekseja" ("The Life of St. Alexis") and was complemented in "Aliscans" (two of Mandelstam's adaptations from medieval French poetry).[15] In those two pieces, in their figural composition—says Mme Mandelstam—her husband "expressed himself and his thoughts about our future." Translations from Barbier (or adaptations of his poems, for to some extent they can be considered as such) were not accidental either, she goes on to say: "They represent an attempt to interpret the present by analogy with the past: the tamed mare, the drunkenness and, above all, the partition of the booty by the victors and the bone thrown at the feet of the greedy bitch. . . ." The selection of poems from Barbier seemed to Mme Mandelstam to have been quite deliberate, particularly that of "la Curée": "In it we see the attitude to the popular revolution and the aversion to the victors who avail themselves of the fruits of popular victory. A theme that was topical for us."[16]

Mme Mandelstam omits to mention, however, the fact that Mandelstam himself published an essay on Barbier in the same issue of *Prožektor* as his version of "la Curée." In it he characterized the July Revolution as "the classically ill-starred [*neudačnaja*] revolution." He called it "a cynical abuse of the name of the people," "a little bridge between two monarchies, leading from the semi-feudal restoration to a real bourgeois monarchy, to the king of financiers and of stock exchange dealers." "The wave of European revolutions between 1830 and 1848 (wrote Mandelstam) coincided with the inauguration of the railway era, with the real advent of the steam engine. The city proletariat was convulsed everywhere, as though it felt in its breast a new, unheard-of power of seething steam. Yet this was but an impulse. The movement was ahead."[17]

All this would hardly suggest a parallel with the October Revolution and its impact on Mandelstam himself. On the other hand, Mandelstam pointed out that

the picturesque, the theatrical aspect of the Paris Revolution of 1830 was magnificent and out of keeping with its real achievements. Paris seemed to be copying the 1793 performance of genius. The three days—July 27, 28, and 29th—made a deep impression on the Parisians. Particularly memorable was the powerful tocsin which shook the air in those days, for the Notre Dame cathedral had been occupied by the mutineers. A hurricane, it seemed, had

---

[15] See nos. 462 and 463 in vol. 1 of the same edition.

[16] See *Vtoraja kniga*, p. 134, Cp. also *Hope Abandoned*, p. 115. Mme Mandelstam reproaches the editors of the three-volume American edition for not including Mandelstam's translation of "la Curée." She must have written this before the publication of the revised edition of vol. 2 where it will be found on pp. 465–468. It was not available to us when vol. 1, containing the other poems by Barbier, was being prepared.

[17] Mandelstam's essay on Barbier will be found in vol. 3 of the Struve-Filippov edition. pp. 45–49.

swept over the city: fallen trees, uprooted lampposts, overturned cabs, barricades fashioned by the ancient art of the revolutionary beehive out of all sorts of junk, like the body of a bird's nest: this is what the three-day July storm had left behind.

(There is in this picture drawn by Mandelstam an echo of another poem by Barbier, part of which he also translated, "L'Emeute.")

In Mandelstam's view those three days deserved their poet, and they found him in the person of Barbier. Barbier was not a revolutionary. At the time of the July Revolution he was employed as a clerk in a notary's office. His fellow employees were young writers of romantic disposition, passionate theater-goers, enthusiasts of Victor Hugo, admirers of picturesque medieval antiquities. Barbier shared their tastes, and had it not been for 1830 he would have remained forever a pale and banal romanticist.

Mandelstam points out that Barbier was away from Paris during the glorious July days. He did not see the outbreak of the revolution with his own eyes. He came back to find in the streets the still-hot relics of the fight. But the distribution of power was going on already. "Barbier's poetry was born of the contrast between the majesty of the hurricane that had swept by and the scantiness of the results achieved," wrote Mandelstam. He also mentioned an article by Girardin which had appeared a few days before the publication of "la Curée" and quoted the following passage from it:

Two weeks ago we lived through the days of popular revolt, through moments of bravery and enthusiasm. Now there is a revolt of quite a different kind—a revolt of all the job seekers. They rush to the antechambers with the same zest with which the people had thrown themselves into the battle. From seven in the morning, battalions of dress-coated men speed all over the capital. With every street their numbers grow: on foot, in cabs, in gigs, sweating, panting, with cockades on their hats and tricolor ribbons in their buttonholes, you see all this crowd which advances on the ministerial palaces and besieges the doors of the offices.[19]

Literary enemies accused Barbier of plagiarism, of paraphrasing in his poem Girardin's article. The resemblance at some points is indeed close. But Mandelstam defended the poet. To him, Barbier's skill in drawing poetic inspiration from a newspaper item rather enhanced than decreased the poet's merit. Mandelstam asked: "By what means, by what devices of artistic expressiveness did Barbier produce such a staggering impression on his contemporaries?" His own answer to this question was threefold:

(1) He used the virile iambics (by this Mandelstam meant the use of alternating alexandrines and octosyllabics), as Chénier had done before him—a verse constrained by the meter, with vigorous stresses, adapted to powerful oratorical speech, to the expression of civic hatred and passion.

---

[19] Khardzhiev includes a quotation from Girardin's article in Mandelstam's essay in his commentary to "Sobač'ja skloka."

(2) He did not tie himself by the conventions of literary language, and knew how to use coarse, harsh, and cynical words. This was quite in keeping with the spirit of French Romanticism which was then carrying on a fight for a freshly renewed poetic vocabulary.

(3) He proved to be a master of grand poetic similes, as if meant for the podium.

To this Mandelstam added—and this is very interesting in the light of his own much later, at the height of his poetic maturity, profound interest in, and preoccupation with, the poetry of Dante—that Barbier had learned the efficacy of poetic imagery in the school of Dante of whom he was a keen admirer. And one must not forget, added Mandelstam, that *"The Divine Comedy* was, for its own time, the greatest of political pamphlets." Thus, this early essay on Barbier contains some of the germs of the much later "Razgovor o Dante" ("Talking About Dante").[19]

3

It seems clear to me that it was, on the one hand, the theatrical colorfulness of the July Revolution and, on the other, the effectiveness and expressiveness of Barbier's imagery and of his language (let us recall that Nettement regarded the "cynical daring" of the one and the "brutal energy" of the other as having no match in French poetry), that attracted Mandelstam in "la Curée". His own version of it has something of that "daring" and that "energy," while it keeps, on the whole, very close to the original. It compares well with Benediktov's and Burenin's earlier versions.

Vladimir Benediktov was a skilful versifier, if not a poet by divine right, though modern Russian literary scholarship and criticism have certainly revised the very low appraisal of his poetry that prevailed among his more distinguished contemporaries. But, although he often succeeded in reproducing Barbier's compositional effects and his rather characteristic syntactical structure, he departed from his meter and, instead of the octosyllabics in the even lines—that is, Chénier's French iambs which Mandelstam admired so much—used shorter lines of six syllables. This may account for his lengthening

---

[19] For "Razgovor o Dante" see vol. 2 of the Struve-Filippov edition, pp. 363–413. There was also a separate Soviet edition, edited by A. A. Morozov, with a "Postface" by L. E. Pinsky, a well-known Renaissance scholar (Moscow: "Iskusstvo," 1967). Except for some poems and short prose pieces published in the 1960s in periodicals (mostly provincial), almanachs, and anthologies, this was the only work by Mandelstam to appear in Russia since 1933 when his "Putešestvie v Armeniju" was published in one of the monthlies. There is an English translation of "Razgovor" by Clarence Brown and Robert P. Hughes in *Delos: A Journal on & of Translation*, vol. 6 (1971):65–106, and a Spanish one in *Dante en su centenario* (Madrid: Taurus, 1965), pp. 65–117.

of the poem by twenty-four lines (one hundred and forty-four lines to Barbier's one hundred and twenty: section 3 is twelve lines longer; section 4, eight lines; and section 6, four lines).[20]

Quite apart from this important metrical change there is much in Benediktov's version that looks pale compared to Mandelstam's, even though they often used the same words and the same images (I do not think there can be any doubt that Mandelstam was familiar with Benediktov's translation). Benediktov was sometimes very successful in reproducing Barbier's repetitions of initial words in the lines, whereas Mandelstam sometimes gave up on this. See, for example, "Kogda" in section 1 and "Pariž" in section 5, where Benediktov goes even one better than Barbier.[21] In the famous line about "la grande populace et la sainte canaille," both use the expression "*svjataja svoloč*'," but Mandelstam has "*velikij sbrod*" as against Benediktov's "*čern' velikaja*." More important than the verbal difference is the fact that Benediktov weakens his line by reversing, in both cases, the noun and the adjective and inserting the demonstrative *ta* (that): "*Ta čern' velikaja i svoloč' ta svjataja*," and the line that follows is not only handicapped by its brevity ("k bessmertiju neslas'"), but also lacks Mandelstam's vigor and expressiveness: "V bessmert'e vzlamyvali dver'." This is almost an improvement on Barbier. In general, Benediktov, unlike Mandelstam, often misses Barbier's ruggedness.

I find it also rather significant that, in his essay on Barbier, Mandelstam cited with approval "a whole bunch" of *l'ambes* which came after "la Curée" and which Danilin was to describe later as "antirevolutionary," namely "Quatre-Vingt Treize," "l'Emeute," "la Popularité," and "l'Idole," all of which, as we have seen, Mandelstam also translated, though only one of them —"Quatre-Vingt Treize"—in its entirety (under the title "1793"). It is his only Barbier version in which he departed from the form of the original by changing the alexandrines to five-foot iambics, giving up the rhymes and using feminine endings throughout (Barbier's poem, divided into five six-line stanzas, has the following rhyme scheme: *f, f, m, f, f, m*). Despite these formal changes,

---

[20] It is just possible that Benediktov's translation was done from an earlier version of Barbier's poem. On the other hand, we know that its original version was in regular alexandrines. Benediktov's version is now available, along with a number of translations of Barbier's poems by different hands, in a recent valuable anthology edited by E. Ètkind, *Mastera russkogo stikhotvornogo perevoda* (Leningrad, 1968), vol. 1, pp. 326–329. Volume 2 of the same anthology contains four translations by Mandelstam, including his partial version of Barbier's "l'Emeute" (the other translations are from Petrarch). Burenin, in translating "la Curée," did the opposite of Benediktov: he lengthened some of the even lines to five feet. His version was included in the volume *Byloe: Stikhotvorenija* (St. Petersburg, 1880), pp. 1–4.

[21] Passages from translations by different poets of Barbier's poems discussed in this article, together with their originals, will be found in the Appendix below.

Mandelstam stays quite close to the original. The poem, as many of Barbier's best, is based on a contrast: in this case, between the July Revolution, or at least its aftermath, and the great Jacobin one.[22]

From "l'Emeute" (which he called "Mjatež") Mandelstam chose only the first sixteen lines (for some reason the printed text in *Zvezda* had only fifteen of them and one missing rhyme: line 3 did not rhyme with anything, and this made one suspect that we had to do here with a typographical error).[23] The rest of the poem might have been omitted by Mandelstam for censorship reasons: it described the pillaging of the palace of the archbishop of Paris.

On the other hand, the two other poems from *Iambes* which Mandelstam also mentioned in his essay on Barbier were partially translated by him too. In this respect alone, one would be justified in viewing them as adaptations, and the poet's widow may be right when she implies that he chose from Barbier those poems that especially appealed to him and in which he saw something of either topical or personal significance. These two poems were "la Popularité" and "l'Idole." Both of them he regarded as directed against the revived cult of Napoleon. This was a somewhat strange aberration on the part of Mandelstam: while "l'Idole" is indeed a violent denunciation of Napoleon and of his cult, "la Popularité" was rather aimed at those who tended to deify the people. It reflected Barbier's disillusionment with certain aspects of the aftermath of the revolution.

A propos of Barbier's attitude to Napoleon, Mandelstam wrote in his essay:

In his hatred for Napoleon, Barbier is alone in the entire Romantic school. For Napoleon he reserves the most curious Dantean images. For him, Napoleon is still alive. The poison of the Napoleonic cult, which demoralized the democracy in those days, the poison concocted in the laboratories of the best poets and artists, Barbier regarded as a most dangerous toxin.

From "l'Idole" (usually referred to in Russian as "*Kumir*," while Mandelstam called it, in his essay, "*Istukan*," thus laying stress on the statue of Napoleon that plays an important part in Barbier's poem) Mandelstam at first translated only section 3 which begins: "O Corse à cheveux plats!" It was printed under the title "Kobyla" ("The Mare"; Barbier uses in the poem two

---

[22] Another modern poet who translated "Quatre-Vingt-Treize" into Russian was Benedikt Livshits (1886–1939), who was also a victim of Stalin's purges. Livshits's version retains both the rhyme scheme and the meter of the original. It is perhaps, in some ways, superior to Mandelstam's. See: *U nočnogo okna. Stikhi zarubežnykh poètov v perevode Benedikta Livšica* (Moscow, 1970), pp. 66–67. This little volume has an interesting article on Livshits by Vadim Kozovoy, a memoir of him by Alexander Deutsch (Dejč) and a fragment of Livshits's 1919 article in which he had some rather "sharp" things to say about Mandelstam as a poet (Livshits in those days belonged to the Futurist movement).

[23] This error has not, however, been corrected (or even noted) in the Khardzhiev edition.

different French words for it: *la jument* and *la cavale*).[24] There can be no doubt that in selecting this particular section of forty-eight lines from an overlong and wordy poem, Mandelstam made a good and discriminate choice, probably on purely artistic grounds, and that the anti-Napoleonic sting of Barbier's violent diatribe was thereby made more deadly. A little later, Mandelstam published the translation of the initial section of "l'Idole" (twenty-eight lines). For some reason, it was published without any mention of Barbier's authorship in *Krasnyj Žurnal dlja Vsekh* (1924, no. 5), under the title "Bronza."[25]

From the other poem, "la Popularité," Mandelstam translated only the last twenty-four lines. It was printed under the title "Èto zyb'" ("This Is the Swell"), those being the first two words of Mandelstam's version, corresponding to "C'est la mer!" of the original.

One of the leading Soviet specialists on problems of verse translation, Professor Efim Etkind, in his interesting book *Poetry and Translation*, has drawn a comparison between two translations of the concluding passage of Barbier's "la Popularité"—the one by Mandelstam and the one by Pavel Antokolsky, a contemporary Soviet poet, who has done a great deal of translating from the French and is justly regarded as one of the most competent Soviet translators of verse. Unlike Mandelstam, Antokolsky translated the whole of "la Popularité." Etkind sees affinity between him and Barbier. While seeing the sea, the sands, and the waves in his own way, says Etkind, he takes his cue from Barbier; while keeping close to the original, he writes of the sea during a storm with such elemental and oratorical fury as no other poet could muster. The original, points out Etkind, demands "impetuosity" (*stremitel'nost'*.) There is the grand sweep of the period which covers twenty-four verses, the accumulation of verbs, most of them in the form of present active participles (in Russian they correspond to gerunds: Etkind mentions sixteen of them, but actually there are even eighteen), with some other participles thrown in. There are numerous enjambements which accelerate the rhythm. There are startling metaphors which disrupt the logic of the imagery. In all this, says Etkind, Antokolsky feels quite at home. Having simplified, somewhat "calmed down," the syntactic *élan*, he makes up for it by such an intensification of metaphorical tension that with him Barbier's fury becomes even more unbridled.

Analysing Antokolsky's language more closely, Etkind notes that very often it is more intense, more dynamic than in the original. He also points out that Barbier, with all his impetuosity, preserves the logical articulation of

---

[24] Some of Barbier's contemporaries reproached him for overdoing the denigration of Napoleon: while denouncing the "deification" of the emperor, he was said to have divested him of all human traits.

[25] This is one of the poems not included in the Struve-Filippov edition.

time sequence by the use of "d'abord" and of several "puis," so that the stormy dynamics turns out to be architectonically well organized. Antokolsky dispenses with all this: with him, as is often the case with his own poetry, the elements break loose and destroy the outward harmony, creating havoc. And yet—such is Etkind's conclusion—"no one has succeeded in recreating so powerfully the frantic impetus of Barbier's romantic landscape as did Antokolsky who wrote the way he himself, through the ardent lyrical element of Barbier, sees and understands the element of the sea. . . ."[26]

Turning to Mandelstam's version of the same twenty-four concluding lines of Barbier's poem, Etkind says that Mandelstam's verses "were born of a different vision of the world and of the sea, of a different attitude to the word, to the metaphor." Mandelstam seems to preserve Barbier's images, but within his system of artistic thought they all acquire a peculiarly condensed character, become unexpected, grotesque. Such are the images like "dušistaja vyžimka vod" ("the fragrant extract of the waters"), "v kvadratakh molnijnykh zračkov" ("in the squares of the eye pupils of lightnings"), or "vybeliv sebja do vzbitoj gnevom peny" ("having whitened itself to foam whipped by wrath").[27] Where Barbier writes: "Se redressant géante, et de sa tête immense / Allant frapper les sombres cieux," in Mandelstam's poetic system this image is fantastically transformed: the "enormous head" becomes "the swollen crown [of the head]." In Barbier, the sea rises "from its silent bed" ("de son lit silencieux"), and in Mandelstam all this is compressed into a single line in which the adjective becomes noun: "Razdutym temenem bol'šegolovoj spjački."[28] Etkind sees the separate components of Mandelstam's seemingly obscure intellectual image merge into a grotesquely nightmarish and logically incomprehensible unity, full of furious energy, condensed to the utmost limit.

This wild phantasmagory (he writes) is the result of Mandelstam's attitude to the word which he perceives as an object, and to the sea which he sees, and can only see, thus. The two poets are very different, with different attitudes to the reality and to poetry, and both

---

[26] See E. Ètkind, *Poèzija i perevod* (Moscow-Leningrad, 1963), pp. 101–104.

[27] *Ibid.*, p. 104. It looks as though at least one of Mandelstam's "grotesque" images was due to a misunderstanding of the text. In Barbier's line "Et sous la foudre et ses carreaux . . ." the word *carreaux* has nothing to do with *kvadraty* (squares). Barbier had in mind Jupiter's arrows. Cp. the entry in Robert's *Dictionnaire* . . . "4—Trait de l'arbalète en fer court et pesant, losangé à quatre pans. *Par ext.* Fig. *Les carreaux vengeurs de Jupiter. Les carreaux de la foudre.*" Where Mandelstam got his *zrački* (pupils of the eye) remains a mystery. Antokolsky changed completely Barbier's imagery and replaced the lightning and its arrows by "powderlike sizzling of the spray": could he also have confused *foudre* and *poudre*?

[28] Ètkind, *Poèzija i perevod*, p. 105. It is not quite clear what Etkind means when he speaks of the adjective "becoming" a noun: in Mandelstam, Barbier's "tête immense" became, on the contrary, "bol'šegolovoj,"—that is, a noun and an adjective became a compound adjective.

are affected by their own view, not only of Barbier's verses, but also of nature which lies behind those verses.

And Etkind ends with the following interesting generalization from which one may deduce that to him the two approaches are, in a sense, equally valid:

> However much fidelity, accuracy, proximity to the original we may demand from the poet who is a translator, it is impossible to divest him of his own, unique world-view, of his optics. Impossible—and unnecessary. The problem boils down to this: at what point such a translation ceases to be a translation and becomes "on the motif of," "on the theme of," gets detached from the original, loses the quality of an artistic *portrait*.[29]

Thus formulated, the problem of what is a good *and* faithful translation seems to become rather a matter of subjective evaluation.

4

Certain features of Mandelstam's language in his Barbier translations deserve to be noted.

There are a few neologisms, of differing degree of daring: *sovremen'e, trĕkhcvetka, carjujut* (from *carevat'*)—all in "Sobač'ja skloka"; *morjana*—in "Èto zyb'"; *jas'* (apparently for *jasnost'*, clearness)—in "Kobyla" (in a rather startling juxtaposition with the name of one of the French revolutionary months: *jas' messidora*); *tjaželostupom* (as the instrumental case of a noun)—also in "Kobyla."

There are also several interesting metaphorical expressions, sometimes bordering on oxymorons: *prostovolosyj plač, na kablukakh derzan'ja, v ščetine krikov* (in "Mjatež"); *pod čerstvoju ègidoj, strogàja boka, sražen'ja lob, khrustja ubitymi, nežnyj lug plemen, narodnykh prav zelenyj sonm, osečkoju kolen, vojna cvetet kak more greči* (all in "Kobyla" or "Napoleonovskaja Francija"); *mesti vkus, vysokomernaja bronza* (in "Bronza"); *baraškovoe more* (for *more v baraškakh*), *čajki trupoednye, toščaja bitva* (in "1793").

There is also a curious use, in "Kobyla," of a North-Russian dialecticism *ovid'*, not to be found in any dictionaries of modern Russian, not even in the multivolume Academy Dictionary. The well-known Dal' Dictionary gives its meaning as "horizon" or "reach of the eye" (it is apparently derived from the verb *videt'* (to see). Mandelstam uses it rather strangely, in plural and with epithet "ancient": *po drevnim ovidjam.*

As a matter of curiosity, the use of the word (or name) "Svetlana" at the beginning of "Èto zyb'" may be mentioned. In the original magazine publication this word was not capitalized. The capitalization was introduced in our three-volume edition of Mandelstam's *Works*—on the assumption, presumably, that this was a reference to the heroine of Zhukovsky's wellknown poem. Professor Etkind also capitalized this word, without discussing

---
[29] *Ibid.*

it, when he compared Mandelstam's version with Antokolsky's. It is also capitalized in the recent Soviet one-volume edition in which the texts are said to be based often on Mandelstam's autographs, and several mistakes and omissions in the magazine publications have been corrected. Mr. Khardzhiev, the author of the commentary to that edition, has no doubt that Mandelstam had in mind Zhukovsky's heroine and explains it as "a poetic licence." I am inclined, however, to believe that, despite the epithet *junaja*, the word was rather a kind of a neological formation, suggested, on the one hand, by *morjana* with which it rhymes, and on the other, by the word *svetloj* six lines further.

In the translation of the extracts from "l'Idole" one notes the fairly frequent use of inexact rhymes, not to be found in other pieces from Barbier and not very usual in Mandelstam's poetry at that time. Here are some examples: *ogromnyj:domne, dikarka:garknet, khlëstkij:primorskim, pozvonočnik:cepočkoj, vikhr':krovi, ėgidoj:iga.*

5

Mandelstam's two translations from later Barbier are of the poems called "le Gin" ("Gin") and "les Belles collines d'Irlande" ("Fair Hills of Ireland"). Both are from *Lazare* (1837). In the former, the English title is retained: "Džin." It is the only one of Mandelstam's translations from Barbier in which he did not use one of the canonical Russian meters, substituting for it a kind of *dol'nik*, with lines of varying length and a capricious pattern of accentuation (mostly, however four stresses per line). He adhered, on the other hand, to Barbier's rhyme scheme. The poet's widow has nothing specific to say about this translation, though, as we have seen, she does mention "drunkenness" as one of the themes in Mandelstam's Barbier versions.

"Irlandskie kholmy" (Mandelstam omitted the word "belles" from the title) stands even more apart from the rest of Mandelstam's translations from Barbier in that it is not really a satirical poem at all, though it does voice sympathy with the lot of the Irish people subjugated by the British. Speaking of Barbier's post-*Ïambes* poetry, Mandelstam said in his essay that Barbier "travelled in Italy and England, sang azure grottoes and ancient cemeteries, and left a number of poems inspired by justice and humaneness." He probably chose "The Fair Hills of Ireland" as an example of such poetry. Unlike some of his predecessors (for example, Benediktov and Durov), he was not tempted to translate Barbier's poem about Dante—despite what he wrote about their affinity.

6

Worth noting is the conclusion of Mandelstam's essay on Barbier. Speaking of Barbier's reception in Russia, Mandelstam observed that Lermontov had read him while under arrest and was considerably influenced by him; that he was known and translated in the Petrashevsky circle; that men of the sixties, incapable of appreciating his poetic power, admired him as a satirist;[30] that, characteristically enough, Stasyulevich, the liberal editor of *Vestnik Evropy* and a friend of Turgenev, shocked by the expression "la sainte canaille," had asked the translator to tone it down or replace it by something else; and finally, that Nekrasov had adapted "le Prophète." Whereupon Mandelstam went on to say:

Today's revolutionary poetry, which follows quite a different path, did not succumb to Barbier's classical influence. Echoes of his voice we can hear in Lermontov and even in Tyutchev when he speaks of Napoleon. But what fascinates us in Barbier's poetry is not even his passion, but one almost Pushkinian characteristic: his knack in defining the very essence of a great historical phenomenon in one line, in one pointed phrase.

Mandelstam could not have bestowed a greater praise on Barbier. And therein lies probably the secret of his own attraction to at least some of Barbier's poetry, and of his choice of Barbier's poems for translation at the time when Barbier was a largely forgotten poet.

APPENDIX

Below, the reader will find some examples of translations of Barbier's poems by different hands. They are given with the originals. For "la Curée" we give only the first and the penultimate (fifth) sections. In the case of those poems which Mandelstam translated only partially, "la Popularité" and "l'Idole," we give only the corresponding passages from other translations and from the originals.

Apart from Mandelstam (1891–1938), the following translators are represented in these selections:

(1) Vladimir Grigoryevich *Benediktov* (1807–1873), of whom D. S. Mirsky, in his *History of Russian Literature* (1927), said: "His first book appeared in 1835 and was almost the greatest immediate poetical success of the century. Though hardly a poet, he was not devoid of poetical wit in the seventeenth-century sense of the word. His method consisted in squeezing out of a striking metaphor or simile all it could give. [...] Later on, Benediktov gave up his conceits and developed into a polished versifier of the ordinary type." Some of Benediktov's contemporaries took a much harsher view of his poetry.

---

[30] Etkind, in speaking of the Russian translators of French revolutionary poets (of Barbier and Béranger in particular) in the 1860s, also notes that they were primarily interested in social propaganda and in reaching as wide a readership as possible. He illustrates this with some examples of Kurochkin's deliberate "Russianization" of Béranger's poems. See *Poèzija i perevod*, p. 115.

(2) Viktor Petrovich *Burenin* (1841–1926), a very minor poet but a prolific and not unskilful translator of French and English poetry, who belonged in the 1860s to the progressive camp in Russian literature, but acquired later a sad notoriety as a contributor to the arch-conservative newspaper *Novoe Vremja*, a rabid anti-Semite, and a man who never tired of denouncing and ridiculing all modern trends in poetry. He wrote some rather ingenious and successful parodies under the pseudonym "Count Alexis Zhasminov." His volume of poetry, published in 1880, includes nine poems by Barbier.

(3) Pavel Grigoryevich *Antokolsky* (b. 1896), a contemporary poet, known also for his many translations from French and German, who is living in Moscow. He was a friend of Boris Pasternak and of Marina Tsvetaeva. Some of Antokolsky's translations were included in the volume of Barbier's selected poetry, edited by E. Etkind and published in Moscow in 1953, which was not available to me. A passage from "la Curée" is cited from Velikovsky's book (see above, footnote 11). It shows that, like Mandelstam and unlike Benediktov and Burenin, Antokolsky adhered strictly to Barbier's meter.

(4) Benedikt Konstantinovich *Livshits* (1886–1939), who began publishing verse in 1910. His first book of poems, *Flejta Marsija* (*The Flute of Marsyas*), appeared in 1911. Between 1914 and 1926, he published three more books of verse, and in 1928 collected his poetry in a volume entitled *Krotonskij polden'* (*Crotonian Noon*). Before the revolution, Livshits belonged to the Futurists (see on him: Vladimir Markov. *Russian Futurism: A History*. University of California Press, 1968). In 1933, Livshits published a volume of very interesting memoirs under the title *Polutoraglazyj strelec* (*The One-and-a-Half-Eyed Archer*), and in 1934 an anthology of translations from French poetry—*From the Romantics to the Surrealists*, of which there was an enlarged edition in 1937. As in the case of other victims of Stalin's purges, the entry on Livshits in the Soviet *Short Literary Encyclopedia*, vol. 4, 1967, laconically says of his fate: "Repressed illegally. Rehabilitated posthumously." The brief entry is signed by Pavel Antokolsky.

The texts of Mandelstam's translations in the selection below are given, with the exception of "Èto zyb'," from the Soviet 1973 one-volume edition. The two extracts from "l'Idole" were published in different magazines at different times and under different titles. Section 3 was published under the title "Kobyla" ("The Mare") but Khardziev says that this title was given to it by the editors of the magazine, and he himself publishes it under the title "Napoleonovskaja Francija" ("Napoleon's France"), which I have retained, although it seems to me much less expressive. In his essay on Barbier, Mandelstam refers to it as "Istukan" ("The Idol"). Burenin called it "Idol" (also "The Idol"), and it has been referred to by another synonymous word, "Kumir."

LA CURÉE

I

Oh! lorsqu'un lourd soleil chauffait les grandes dalles
    Des ponts et de nos quais déserts,
Que les cloches hurlaient, que la grêle des balles
    Sifflait et pleuvait par les airs;
Que dans Paris entier, comme la mer qui monte,
    Le Peuple soulevé grondait,
Et qu'au lugubre accent des vieux canons de fonte
    La Marseillaise répondait,
Certe, on ne voyait pas, comme au jour où nous sommes,
    Tant d'uniformes à la fois;
C'était sous des haillons que battaient les coeurs d'homme;
    C'étaient alors de sales doigts
Qui chargeaient les mousquets et renvoyaient la foudre;
    C'était la bouche aux vils jurons
Qui mâchait la cartouche, et qui, noire de poudre,
    Criait aux citoyens: Mourons!
. . . .

V

Mais, ô honte! Paris, si beau dans sa colère,
    Paris, si plein de majesté
Dans ce jour de tempête où le vent populaire
    Déracina la royauté,
Paris, si magnifique avec ses funérailles,
    Ses débris d'hommes, ses tombeaux,
Ses chemins dépavés et ses pans de murailles
    Troués comme de vieux drapeaux;
Paris, cette cité de lauriers toute ceinte,
    Dont le monde entier est jaloux,
Que les peuples émus appellent tous la sainte,
    Et qu'ils ne nomment qu'à genoux,
Paris n'est maintenant qu'une sentine impure,
    Un égout sordide et boueux,
Où mille noirs courants de limon et d'ordure
    Viennent trainer leurs flots honteux;
Un taudis regorgeant de faquins sans courage,
    D'effrontés coureurs de salons,

Qui vont de porte en porte, et d'étage en étage,
  Gueusant quelque bout de galons;
Une halle cynique aux clameurs insolentes,
  Où chacun cherche à déchirer
Un misérable coin de guenilles sanglantes
  Du pouvoir qui vient d'expirer.

Vladimir Benediktov

Собачий пир

Когда взошла заря и страшный день багровый,
  Народный день настал,
Когда гудел набат и крупный дождь свинцовый
  По улицам хлестал,
Когда Париж взревел, когда народ воспрянул
  И малый стал велик,
Когда в ответ на гул старинных пушек грянул
  Свободы звучный клик, —
Конечно, не было там видно ловко сшитых
  Мундиров наших дней, —
Там действовал напор лохмотьями прикрытых,
  Запачканных людей,
Чернь грязною рукой там ружья заряжала,
  И закопченным ртом,
В пороховом дыму, там сволочь восклицала:
  "......... Умрем!"
....
И что же? о позор! Париж, столь благородный
  В кипеньи гневных сил,
Париж, где некогда великий вихрь народный
  Власть львиную сломил,
Париж, который весь гробницами уставлен
  Величий всех времен,
Париж, где камень стен пальбою продырявлен,
  Как рубище знамен,
Париж, отъявленный сын хартий, прокламаций,
  От головы до ног
Обвитый лаврами, апостол в деле наций,
  Народов полубог,
Париж, что некогда как светлый купол храма
  Всемирного блистал,

Стал ныне скопищем нечистоты и срама,
    Помойной ямой стал,
Вертепом подлых душ, мест ищущих в лакеи,
    Паркетных шаркунов,
Просящих нищенски для рабской их ливреи
    Мишурных галунов,
Бродяг, которые рвут Францию на части
    И сквозь щелчки, толчки,
Визжа, зубами рвут издохшей тронной власти
    Кровавые клочки.

                                    1856—57

Viktor Burenin

Собачий пир

Ложился солнца луч по городским громадам
    И плиты улиц тяжким зноем жег,
Под звон колоколов свистели пули градом
    И рвали воздух вдоль и поперек.
Как в море вал кипит, лучам покорный лунным,
    Шумел народ мятежною толпой, —
И пушек голосам зловещим и чугунным
    Песнь Марсельезы вторила порой.
Средь узких улиц здесь и там мелькали
    Мундиры, каски и штыки солдат.
И чернь, под рубищем храня сердца из стали,
    Встречала смерть на грудах баррикад;
Там люди, сжав ружье рукой от крови склизкой,
    Патрон скусивши задымленным ртом,
Что издавать привык лишь крики брани низкой,
    Взывали: граждане, умрем!
....
И что ж? — О, стыд! Париж великий и свободный,
    Париж, столь чудный в гневе роковом
В тот бурный день, когда грозы народной
    Над властью грянул беспощадный гром;
Париж с священными минувшего гробами,
    С великолепием печальных похорон,
Со взрытой мостовой, с пробитыми стенами —
    Подобием изорванных знамен;

Париж, обвитый лаврами свободы,
　　Кому дивится с завистию мир,
Пред кем с почтением склоняются народы,
　　Чье имя чтут, как дорогой кумир, —
Увы, он ныне стал зловонной грязи стоком,
　　Вертепом зла бесстыдного он стал,
Куда все мерзости сливаются потоком,
　　Где катится разврата мутный вал;
Салонных шаркунов он сделался притоном:
　　К пустым чинам и почестям жадна —
Толпа их бегает из двери в дверь с поклоном,
　　Чтоб выпросить обрывок галуна!
Торгуя честию и теша черни страсти,
　　В нем нагло ходит алчности порок,
И каждая рука лохмотьев павшей власти
　　Окровавленный тащит клок!

　　　　　　　　　　　　　　[1860s]

Pavel Antokolsky

　　　　　Собачий пир

Когда тяжелый зной накаливал громады
　　Мостов и площадей пустых,
И завывал набат, и грохот канонады
　　В парижском воздухе не стих;
Когда по городу, как штормовое море,
　　Людская поднялась гряда,
И, красноречию мортир угрюмых вторя,
　　Шла Марсельеза, — о, тогда
Мундиры синие, конечно, не торчали,
　　Какие нынче развелись.
Там под лохмотьями сердца мужчин стучали,
　　Там пальцы грязные впились
В ружейные курки. Прицел был дальнозорок,
　　Когда, патрон перегрызя,
Рот, полный пороха и крепких поговорок,
　　Кричал: "Стоять на смерть, друзья!"
. . . .
Сегодняшний Париж — в промозглых водостоках
　　Смешался с грязью нечистот,

Кипит бурдой страстей, стоустых и стооких, —
　　Волна спадает, вновь растет.
Трущоба грязная, где выходы и входы
　　Салонной шатией кишат,
Где старые шуты, львы прошлогодней моды,
　　Ливрею выклянчить спешат.
Толкучка зазывал, божащихся бесстыдно,
　　Где надо каждому украсть
Лоскут могущества...

Osip Mandelstam

Собачья склока

i

Когда тяжелый зной гранил большие плиты
На гулких набережных здесь,
Набатом вспаханный и пулями изрытый
Изрешечен был воздух весь;
Когда Париж кругом, как море роковое,
Народной яростью серчал
И на покашливанье старых пушек злое
Марсельской песней отвечал,
Там не маячила, как в нашем современьи,
Мундиров золотых орда, —
То было в рубище мужских сердец биенье,
И пальцы грязные тогда
Держали карабин тяжелый и граненый,
А руганью набитый рот
Сквозь зубы черные кричал, жуя патроны:
"Умрем, сограждане! Вперед!"
....

v

Но стыд тебе, Париж, прекрасный и гневливый!
Еще вчера, величья полн,
Ты помнишь ли, Париж, как, мститель справедливый,
Ты выкорчевывал престол?
Торжественный Париж, ты ныне обесчещен,
О город пышных похорон,
Разрытых мостовых, вдоль стен глубоких трещин,

Людских останков и знамен.
Прабабка городов, лавровая столица,
Народами окружена,
Чье имя на устах у всех племен святится,
Затмив другие имена,
Отныне ты, Париж, — презренная клоака,
Ты — свалка гнусных нечистот,
Где маслянистая приправа грязи всякой
Ручьями черными течет.
Ты — сброд бездельников и шалопаев чинных,
И трусов с головы до ног,
Что ходят по домам и в розовых гостиных
Выклянчивают орденок.
Ты — рынок крючников, где мечут подлый жребий —
Кому падет какая часть
Священной кровию напитанных отребий
Того, что раньше было власть.

1923

L'IDOLE

1

Allons, chauffeur, allons, du charbon, de la houille,
    Du fer, du cuivre et de l'étain;
Allons, à large pelle, à grands bras plonge et fouille,
    Nourris le brasier, vieux Vulcain:
Donne force pâture à l'avide fournaise;
    Car pour mettre ses dents en jeu,
Pour tordre et dévorer le métal qui lui pèse,
    Il lui faut le palais en feu.
C'est bien, voici la flamme ardente, folle, immense,
    Implacable et couleur de sang,
Qui tombe de la voûte, et l'assaut qui commence,
    Chaque lingot se prend au flanc;
Et ce ne sont que bonds, rugissements, délire,
    Cuivre sur plomb et plomb sur fer;
Tout s'allonge, se tord, s'embrasse et se déchire
    Comme des damnés en enfer.
Enfin l'oeuvre est finie, enfin la flamme est morte,
    La fournaise fume et s'éteint,

L'airain bouillonne à flots; chauffeur, ouvre la porte
    Et laisse passer le hautain!
O fleuve impétueux! mugis et prends ta course,
    Sors de ta loge, et d'un élan,
D'un seul bond lance-toi comme un flot de la source,
    Comme une flamme du volcan!
La terre ouvre son sein à tes vagues de lave;
    Précipite en bloc ta fureur,
Dans le moule profond, bronze, descends esclave,
    Tu vas remonter empereur.
....

III

O Corse à cheveux plats! que ta France était belle
    Au grand soleil de messidor!
C'était une cavale indomptable et rebelle,
    Sans frein d'acier ni rênes d'or;
Une jument sauvage à la croupe rustique,
    Fumante encor du sang des rois,
Mais fière, et d'un pied fort heurtant le sol antique,
    Libre pour la première fois.
Jamais aucune main n'avait passé sur elle
    Pour la flétrir et l'outrager;
Jamais ses larges flancs n'avaient porté la selle
    Et le harnais de l'étranger;
Tout son poil était vierge, et, belle vagabonde,
    L'oeil haut, la croupe en mouvement,
Sur ses jarrets dressée, elle effrayait le monde
    Du bruit de son hennissement.
Tu parus, et sitôt que tu vis son allure,
    Ses reins si souples et dispos,
Centaure impétueux, tu pris sa chevelure,
    Tu montas botté sur son dos.
Alors, comme elle aimait les rumeurs de la guerre,
    La poudre, les tambours battants,
Pour champ de course, alors, tu lui donnas la terre
    Et des combats pour passe-temps:
Alors, plus de repos, plus de nuits, plus de sommes;
    Toujours l'air, toujours le travail,
Toujours comme du sable écraser des corps d'hommes,
    Toujours du sang jusqu'au poitrail.

Quinze ans son dur sabot, dans sa course rapide,
  Broya les générations;
Quinze ans elle passa, fumante, à toute bride,
  Sur le ventre des nations;
Enfin, lasse d'aller sans finir sa carrière,
  D'aller sans user son chemin,
De pétrir l'univers, et comme une poussière
  De soulever le genre humain;
Les jarrets épuisés, haletante et sans force,
  Près de fléchir à chaque pas,
Elle demanda grâce à son cavalier corse;
  Mais, bourreau, tu n'écoutas pas!
Tu la pressas plus fort de ta cuisse nerveuse;
  Pour étouffer ses cris ardents,
Tu retournas le mors dans sa bouche baveuse,
  De fureur tu brisas ses dents;
Elle se releva: mais un jour de bataille,
  Ne pouvant plus mordre ses freins,
Mourante, elle tomba sur un lit de mitraille
  Et du coup te cassa les reins.

Viktor Burenin

Идол

i

Живей, кузнец, живей, давай сюда угля
  Под слитки тяжкие металла,
Сильней мехами дуй, жаровню раскаля,
  Чтоб пламя ярко запылало.
Брось щедро жаркий корм в отверстый алчно зев
  Палящего огнем горнила,
Чтоб, зубом огненным металл преодолев,
  Его жаровня растопила.
Довольно! Так! реки кипящей полоса
  Все затопляет беспощадно!
Огонь волной, как кровь со свода, полился,
  Схватив металл в объятья жадно.
Раздался вой и треск! чугун свинцом залит.
  Над ними медь струит потоком;
Все обнимается, крутится и визжит,
  Как демоны в аду глубоком!
Но вот огонь, треща слабее и слабей,
  Погас в горниле, дыма полном,

Вскипела медь, открыт затвор печных дверей,
  И льет она подобно волнам.
О жгучая река! кати свой вал, рыча,
  В стремленьи бурном и медяном;
И бросься вдруг прыжком, шумя и клокоча,
  Как дымный пламень над вулканом!
И слейся, слейся в глубь отверстую земли,
  Да совершит искусство чудо,
Чтоб волны медные, что в форму низошли,
  Явились Цезарем оттуда!
....

iii

О хищник! хороша была твоя страна
  При ярком солнце Мессидора!
Как дикий конь узды не ведала она,
  Ей шерсть не бороздила шпора!
Дымилась кровь царей с ее боков крутых,
  И, гриву приподняв на вые,
Она взрывала прах из-под копыт своих,
  Свободная еще впервые!
Еще не провела бичем ничья рука
  По ней позорный след неволи,
И бедра мощные не знали чепрака
  И сбруи пришлеца дотоле!
Шерсть лоснилась у ней, и красотой полна
  Храпела дикая бродяга,
И миру целому казалася страшна
  Ее могучая отвага!
Но ты пришел, твой взор проникнул дикий нрав,
  Ты стал ее ласкать притворно
И, быстрый как центавр, за гриву лошадь взяв,
  К ней на спину вскочил проворно!
Ты знал, что весел ей кровавой битвы гром,
  Стук ядер и сверканье стали,
И с нею облетел полмира ты кругом —
  И вопли битвы не смолкали!
Тогда исчез покой, тогда не стало снов,
  Ночей для отдыха не стало!
И трупы мертвые как прах, шипом подков,
  В крови по грудь, она топтала!

Пятнадцать лет земные племена
    Терпели гнет ее копыта,
И страны чуждые пятнадцать лет она
    Браздила, пеною облита.
И лошадь дикая устала без конца
    Месить вселенную и прахом
Стенящий род людской взвевать с ее лица
    Могучих ног широким взмахом!
Едва дыша, без сил, поникнув головой,
    Усталые понурив взгляды,
В бессилии она дрожала под тобой,
    Но ты, палач, не знал пощады!
Ты шпорой ей провел рубец по животу
    И, разъярен ее храпеньем,
Ты зубы раздробил ей, в опененном рту
    Рванув удила с нетерпеньем!
И, кровью обагрив узду и стремена,
    Ты с ней помчался в поле сечи,
И там во прах скатилася она
    На груды ядер и картечи!

Osip Mandelstam

Бронза

Дай угля, кочегар, дай порошок сыпучий —
Свинца и олова на сплав!

Мешай свинец и медь лопатою могучей,
Старик Вулкан, к огню прибавь!

Ты должен печь кормить, она проголодалась!
Ведь, чтоб ощерилась она,
Чтоб хрустнул на зубах у ней кусок металла —
Она дворцом пылать должна.

И вырвался огонь, растрепанный, огромный:
В нем крови цвет и мести вкус,
Он спрыгнул с купола и заметался в домне —
И сбоку тлеет каждый рсбу.

Все это лишь толчки и бредовые вспышки,
Когда свинец ползет на медь,
Улитки корчатся и плавятся кубышки —
Что грешникам в котле кипеть!

Но кончено. Огонь улегся понемногу,
Дымком курясь, потухла печь,
И бронза в ключ кипит. Дай вареву дорогу,
Высокомерной дай истечь.

О, царственный поток, урча и забавляясь,
Одним прыжком, одним броском
Из ложа своего взыграй наверх как лава,
Как речка, ринься напролом!

И перед лавою земля раскрылась грозной:
Налей в нее свой гневный сплав.
В воронку темную вошла рабыней бронза,
Владыкою из формы встав!

1923

. . . .

Наполеоновская Франция

О корсиканский зверь с прямыми волосами,
Ты помнишь мессидора ясь:
Без бронзовой узды с златыми удилами
Кобылой Франция неслась.
Кобыла дикая трясла мужицким крупом,
Дымилась кровью королей,
По древним овидям топча тяжелоступом
Освобожденный грунт полей.
Ах, к ней еще никто не подходил, зевая,
Чтоб оскорбить иль чтобы смять,
И сбруи чужака она еще не знает,
И на седло не ей пенять.
Всей кожей лоснилась высокая дикарка.
Взгляд прям. Дрожит могучий круп,
И вдруг на целый мир весенним ржаньем гаркнет,
Как тысяча веселых труб!
Явился ты, взглянул на сильных ног затеи
И на крутую стать боков,
Вцепился в гриву ей, кентавр с широкой шеей,
И смял движеньем каблуков.
И зная, что она любила ружей шорох,
Дымок и барабанов дробь,
Ты выпустил ее скакать в земных просторах,
Ей показал сраженья лоб!

Всегда на воздухе, встречая ветер хлесткий,
Всегда в бою, всегда как вихрь,
Хрустя убитыми, как гравием приморским,
По щиколотку в их крови, —
Пятнадцать лет она под черствою эгидой
Топтала нежный луг племен,
Пятнадцать лет топтал битюг по праву ига
Народных прав зеленый сонм.
И наконец, устав по рытвинам, бурьянам
Мотаться крупной головой,
Громить вселенную, вздымая пыль воланом,
И будоражить род людской,
И вся в испарине — до темного румянца —
Как бы осечкою колен,
Споткнулась, — и сдалась на милость корсиканца.
Но ты, палач, без перемен!
Строгая ей бока, ломая позвоночник,
Ты взвил струной свою рабу
И бешеной узды холодною цепочкой
Рванул ей нежную губу;
И в поле, где война цветет, как море гречи,
Стальной огрызок теребя,
Она, как на ковер, упала на картечи,
На ребра положив тебя.

1923

QUATRE-VINGT-TREIZE

1

Un jour que de l'Etat le vaisseau séculaire,
Fatigué trop longtemps du roulis populaire,
Ouvert de toutes parts, à demi démâté,
Sur une mer d'écueils, sous des cieux sans étoiles,
Au vent de la Terreur qui déchirait ses voiles,
S'en allait échouer la jeune Liberté;

Tous les rois de l'Europe, attentifs au naufrage,
Tremblèrent que la masse, en heurtant leur rivage,
Ne mit du même choc les trônes au néant;
Alors, comme forbans qui guettent une proie,

On les vit tous s'abattre, avec des cris de joie,
Sur les flancs dégarnis du colosse flottant.

Mais lui, tout mutilé des coups de la tempête,
Se dressa sur sa quille, et, relevant la tête,
Hérissa ses sabords d'un peuple de héros,
Et rallumant soudain ses foudres désarmées,
Comme un coup de canon lâcha quatorze armées,
Et l'Europe à l'instant rentra dans son repos.

II

Sombre quatre-vingt-treize, épouvantable année,
De lauriers et de sang grande ombre couronnée,
Du fond des temps passés ne te relève pas!
Ne te relève pas pour contempler nos guerres,
Car nous sommes des nains à côté de nos pères,
Et tu rirais vraiment de nos maigres combats.

Oh! nous n'avons plus rien de ton antique flamme.
Plus de force au poignet, plus de vigueur dans l'âme,
Plus d'ardente amitié pour les peuples vaincus;
Et quand parfois au coeur il nous vient une haine,
Nous devenons poussifs, et nous n'avons d'haleine
    Que pour trois jours au plus.

Janvier 1831.

Benedikt Livshits

Девяносто третий год

i

Во дни, когда корабль столетний государства,
Не в силах одолеть слепых зыбей коварство,
Без мачт и парусов, во всю свою длину
В сплошных пробоинах, средь грозного простора,
Готовился пойти под шквалами террора
С новорожденною свободою ко дну,

Вся свора королей, с волн не спуская взгляда,
О том лишь думала, чтоб страшная громада,

Столкнувшись с берегом, не свергла тронов их,
И, шумно радуясь возможности добычи,
Накинулась, в одном объединившись кличе,
На остов, гибнущий среди пучин морских.

Но весь истерзанный неистовством стихии,
Свой корпус выпрямив и не склоняя выи,
Геройским пламенем ощерил он борта,
И на расширенном уже явил плацдарме
Европе мощь своих четырнадцати армий,
Заставив хищников вернуться на места.

ii

О год чудовищный, о девяносто третий
Величественный год! Сокройся в глубь столетий,
Кровавой славою увенчанная тень:
Мы, карлики, отцов бессмертных недостойны,
И ты потехою почел бы наши войны,
Когда бы посмотрел на настоящий день.

Ах, твоего у нас священного нет жара,
Ни мужества в сердцах, ни силы для удара,
Ни дружбы пламенной к поверженным врагам,
А если мы порой и чувствуем желанье
Позлобствовать, у нас лишь на три дня дыханья
    С грехом хватает пополам.

Osip Mandelstam

1793

Когда корабль столетний государства
Устал греметь горохом недовольства,
Открытый всем, как решето дырявый,
В кромешный мрак, в барашковое море —
Террора ветер в парусах раздутых —
Он наудачу вышел за свободой.

И со своих гранитных побережий
Следили жадно короли Европы
За оползаньем медленным империй.
Как будто горбоносые пираты,

Как чайки трупоедные, монархи
Наметили плавучий гроб французов.

А он, худой, гигант с прозрачной кожей,
На удивленье выпрямился килем,
Народ героев нанизал на реи,
Поднес фитиль к давно оглохшим пушкам
И выстрелил четырнадцатью армий —
И в берега свои вошла Европа!

О мрачный год, о девяносто третий,
Большая тень в крови и темных лаврах,
Не поднимайся с сумрачного ложа:
Тебе нельзя глядеть на наши войны,
В семье отцов мы — жалкие пигмеи,
Ты посмеешься нашей тощей битве.

Твое старинное погасло пламя,
Кулак разжался, и душа заглохла, —
Нет к побежденным мужественной ласки,
А если в сердце иногда проснется
Запальчивость — короткое дыханье —
Не более чем на три дня хватает.

1923

LA POPULARITÉ

C'est la mer! c'est la mer! d'abord calme et sereine,
    La mer, aux premiers feux du jour,
Chantant et souriant comme une jeune reine,
    La mer blonde et pleine d'amour;
La mer baisant le sable, et parfumant la rive
    Du baume enivrant de ses flots,
Et berçant sur sa gorge ondoyante et lascive
    Son peuple brun de matelots;
Puis la mer furieuse et tombée en démence,
    Et de son lit silencieux
Se redressant géante, et de sa tête immense
    Allant frapper les sombres cieux;
Puis courant çà et là, hurlante, échevelée,
    Et sous la foudre et ses carreaux
Bondissant, mugissant dans sa plaine salée,
    Comme un combat de cent taureaux,

Puis, le corps tout blanchi d'écume et de colère,
    La bouche torse, l'oeil errant,
Se roulant sur le sable et déchirant la terre
    Avec le râle d'un mourant;
Et, comme la bacchante, enfin lasse de rage,
    N'en pouvant plus et sur le flanc
Retombant dans sa couche, et lançant à la plage
    Des têtes d'hommes et du sang! . . .
Février 1831

Pavel Antokolsky

Известность

Она — морская ширь в сверканьи мирной глади, —
    Едва лишь утро занялось,
Смеется и поет, расчесывая пряди
    Златисто-солнечных волос,
И зацелован весь и опьянен прибрежный
    Туман полуденных песков, —
И убаюканы ее качелью нежной
    Ватаги смуглых моряков;
Но море фурией становится и, воя,
    С постели рвется бредовой, —
И выпрямляется, косматой головою
    Касаясь тучи грозовой;
И мечется в бреду, горланя о добыче,
    В пороховом шипеньи брызг;
И топчется, мыча, бодает с силой бычьей,
    Заляпанная грязью вдрызг;
И в белом бешенстве, вся покрываясь пеной,
    Перекосив голодный рот,
Рвет землю и хрипит, слабея постепенно,
    Пока в отливах не замрет;
И никнет наконец вакханка и теряет
    Приметы страшные свои,
И на сырой песок, ленивая, швыряет
    Людские головы в крови.

Osip Mandelstam

Это зыбь

Это зыбь, это зыбь, — спокойная моряна,
    Вскипающая пред зарей,

Поющая с утра, как юная Светлана,
    Любовь и русый волос свой.
Зыбь, льнущая к пескам, пространства орошая
    Душистой выжимкою вод,
На горле выпуклом разнеженно качая
    Гребцов коричневый народ.
Потом другая зыбь из этой светлой качки
    Выходит для свирепых буч,
Раздутым теменем большеголовой спячки
    Колотит крышу низких туч,
Потом мычащею и скачущей пучиной
    В квадрате молнийных зрачков
Бежит соленою, бугристою долиной
    Размахом тысячи быков.
И, выбелив себя до взбитой гневом пены,
    Блуждает, влажный рот кривит,
Царапает песок береговой арены,
    Как умирающий хрипит.
И, корибанткою, вконец перебесившись,
    Вдавив бедро в намет песков,
Кидает с кровью нам, обратно в ил свалившись,
    Горсть человеческих голов.

www.ingramcontent.com/pod-product-compliance
Lightning Source LLC
Chambersburg PA
CBHW021710230426
43668CB00008B/787